ASTRAL ODYSSEY

ASTRAL ODYSSEY

Exploring Out-of-Body Experiences

Carol Eby

MOTILAL BANARSIDASS PUBLISHERS
PRIVATE LIMITED • DELHI

First Indian Edition : Delhi, 2002
First Published by Samuel Weiser USA, 1996

ISBN: 81-208-1830-x

Also available at:
MOTILAL BANARSIDASS
41 U.A. Bungalow Road, Jawahar Nagar, Delhi 110 007
8 Mahalaxmi Chambers, 22 Bhulabhai Desai Road, Mumbai 400 026
236, 9th Main III Block, Jayanagar, Bangalore 560 011
120 Royapettah High Road, Mylapore, Chennai 600 004
Sanas Plaza, 1302 Baji Rao Road, Pune 411 002
8 Camac Street, Kolkata 700 017
Ashok Rajpath, Patna 800 004
Chowk, Varanasi 221 001

Printed in India
BY JAINENDRA PRAKASH JAIN AT SHRI JAINENDRA PRESS,
A-45 NARAINA, PHASE-I, NEW DELHI 110 028
AND PUBLISHED BY NARENDRA PRAKASH JAIN FOR
MOTILAL BANARSIDASS PUBLISHERS PRIVATE LIMITED,
BUNGALOW ROAD, DELHI 110 007

Table of Contents

To all on the
Spiritual Path

Open your astral eyes and see beyond the world of darkness a world of light, where the divine footsteps of angels lead the way. Bring back the light to replenish the material world, gladden the heart, inspire the intellect, and lift the spirit. Thus partake of Earth, Water, Air, and Fire, and become one with creation.

—Eby

PREFACE

Astral Odyssey: Exploring Out-of-Body Experiences is the first book ever written using its unique comprehensive approach to capture the entire essence of an extraordinary voyage into the vast, uncharted areas of the invisible worlds, where hidden treasures abound from beginning to end. *Astral Odyssey* is a voyage upon which anyone can embark!

> What is the astral world?
> Where is it?
> What is it like?
> Who are its occupants? Are they hostile or friendly?
> Why is it important to go there?
> How did this author, when living a relatively secluded life in a cabin in the woods, learn astral projection?
> How does the astral body fly?
> Is it possible to project into the future on the astral plane?
> How can a person develop the continuity of consciousness necessary to function in the invisible worlds?

There is scientific evidence that perception and existence beyond the limits of the physical body are possible. *Astral Odyssey* is a quest for answers about the true nature of reality. *Astral Odyssey* is a magical journey through alternative states of consciousness of which little is known, in search of a true, complete self.

Although the destination of this strange adventure is an arbitrary location outside the physical body, and the vehicle used to transport awareness to the astral world is the astral body, the various realms encountered along the route comprise much of the fundamental purpose of the voyage. The invisible domains explored as *Astral Odyssey* progresses include a diverse assortment of dream worlds, the mysterious pathways of the hypnagogic and hypnopompic states, and the intriguing enigma of the astral plane. All of these mysterious realms are essential experiences to the development of the continuity of consciousness necessary to reach the ultimate goal of interaction with the higher self and a deeper understanding of self in relation to reality.

Departing from physical reality, *Astral Odyssey* delves into dream worlds, explaining what they are, how to function in them, and how to use them to awaken consciousness to normally inconspicuous emotional difficulties, problem solutions, creative powers, and extrasensory perception.

Astral Odyssey then explores the hypnagogic and hypnopompic states, precarious links bridging the gap between physical reality and the invisible worlds, and discovers a complex network of connections to a multiformity of obscure dimensions. Passageways are found to creative inspiration, mental projection, transition state ESP, dual consciousness, lucid dreams, and out-of-body experiences (OBEs).

Astral Odyssey continues with an expedition to the astral world, presented with detailed, vivid descriptions of sights, sounds, impressions, feelings, and situations, often strange, sometimes humorous, and occasionally frightening. This fantastic realm is resplendent with a wealth of wondrous experiences as well as inexplicable peculiarities.

Astral Odyssey is much more than an expository work taken from years of meticulous notes on dimensions beyond the physical world—it is a handbook of complete instructions, sound advice, practical applications, and well-documented scientific evidence.

For readers who wish to experience the invisible worlds first hand, *Astral Odyssey* offers explicit instructions on how to reach these ephemeral regions, with discussions of potential real or imagined dangers and obstacles and how to avoid them. It is a guidebook for astral travelers, written by an experienced wayfarer of nonphysical reality, explaining in clear, easily understood language, exactly how to master the various states of consciousness that lead to self-induced, fully conscious out-of-body experiences.

To emphasize the explicit instructions provided, *Astral Odyssey* demonstrates, with mental routes, the placement of the invisible worlds in relation to each other and the physical world. The pathways from physical waking consciousness, through the hypnagogic state, and into alternative states of awareness are clearly delineated through the use of the hypothetical models of the dream continuum, the OBE continuum, the four levels of awareness (conscious, subconscious, unconscious, and superconscious), and the higher self.

Besides offering step-by-step instructions and providing guidelines to follow, *Astral Odyssey* shows how invaluable information may be obtained from the invisible worlds and used in the physical world to make life richer, more harmonious, more aesthetic and intellectual, and more meaningful. Claims are supported on an academic level by carefully researched and documented scientific studies. The search into alternative realities reveals a self that is much more than a highly evolved biological form that has developed a brain large enough to question its place in the universe. By focusing on the total self, *Astral Odyssey* is instrumental in releasing the unbelievable potentials that lie within the reach of each person who dares to take the first step over the brink of the material world and into the chasms of nonphysical reality.

Through the discovery of some of the multidimensional facets of the relationship between human existence and the universe, *Astral Odyssey* leads to an appreciation of the true significance of life and our role as creative, rational, emotional, spiritual beings.

ACKNOWLEDGMENTS

Although there is much to learn, much is known about the invisible worlds of dreams, hypnagogia, and the astral plane. I remain grateful to all those throughout the ages whose ideas, experiences, and work contributed to the concepts presented in *Astral Odyssey: Exploring Out-of-Body Experiences.*

Furthermore, I would like to extend special gratitude to my parents for the lessons and values they instilled in me.

I am especially thankful to Judi Bianco for her inspiration, for the hours and material she contributed to this manuscript, for her friendship, and most of all for her spirit which shines brightly for those of us she left behind on the material plane.

For their stories, which add so much to my Astral Odyssey, I thank Patti Chester, Ben Stone, Sue Stone-Douglas, Ross Oates, Jean Higheagle, and Lyla Monello. I am also grateful to Pat Sime, for her efforts in contacting the Doctor, and to Cara Dale, for her special advice from Daniel.

The staff at Rapid City Public Library deserves my deepest appreciation for all their help in gathering research materials. Their dedication and constant improvements in providing service go a long way to make a writer's work possible.

I am also thankful to Richard Draeger for the use of his personal library, which was crucial in the formative stages of this work.

Many thanks to Dr. Benjamin Stone for his generous devotion of time and effort in editing and obtaining materials.

And finally, I extend special recgonition and gratitude to all the helpers from beyond the physical plane who have provided invaluable assistance during my Astral Odyssey and its writing.

List of Abbreviations

EEG: electroencephalogram

EOG: electrooculogram

ESP: extrasensory perception

GSR: galvanic skin response

NDE: near-death experience

NREM: nonREM

OBE: out-of-body experience

REM: rapid eye movement

SEM: slow eye movement

Chapter 1

Discovery of a Hidden Realm

It was late at night. I was crawling across my cabin floor.

Through the darkness I could plainly see the wooden boards beneath me and feel the familiar scratches and nicks in the wood trim where the floor gives way to the hearth. I was headed toward my bedroom door, only a few feet in front of me.

My body ached from exhaustion; I had to force my muscles to move me slowly along. The fatigue was so overwhelming that my only thought was to make it to my bed—it had not even occurred to me to wonder why I was on the floor in the first place!

After I struggled to force my tired, heavy-feeling body in the intended direction, I reached the side of my bed. Suddenly it felt as if a powerful magnetic force jerked me upward from the floor, and the next thing I knew I was waking up in my bed.

I sat up and thought about what had just happened—I had felt certain I had been awake, yet there I was "waking up" in bed. I had been perfectly aware of my actions and surroundings, and had functioned with conscious deliberation in what seemed exactly like my immediate environment rather than a dream world. While I analyzed this strange experience, I was struck with the impact of sudden realization—I had *actually* been out of my body! Was this to be a once-in-a-lifetime experience? I hoped not. Upon discovery of this hidden realm, I wished to learn more—much more!

I had known about astral projection (the phenomenon of exiting the physical body and traveling around in an "astral body") for a long time and believed it existed, but I had thought it was limited to the capabilities of only a few highly developed mystical adepts, occultists, or psychics, and a once-in-a-lifetime experience for a few others.

I first heard about astral projection when I was in my late teens. My Aunt Patti told me about a fascinating adventure she once had.

One day, when she was at home alone, Patti lay down and tried an experiment. She had read about astral projection and was curious to determine if she could experience it. Patti closed her eyes, relaxed, and concentrated on leaving her body. After a while, she just "let go" and felt a part of herself drift upward, away from her physical body. She said she had felt "light as a feather." When she looked down, she saw her physical body, lying unconscious where she had left it. She wished to stay out longer and investigate this unusual realm, but something drew her back into her body.

Patti explained to me that she had successfully induced astral projection, which is completely different from dreaming, ESP, or anything else, and it was the most exhilarating experience she had ever had. She said that during astral projection the soul and consciousness leave the physical body and experience freedom beyond our wildest fantasies.

Patti's adventure left a lasting impression on me that aroused my curiosity and stimulated my imagination. The idea that it is possible to willfully enter another dimension and travel to faraway places intrigued me. I thought about how wonderful it would be if this ability could be developed, and I imagined how much fun it would be to travel to medieval castles in Europe, the sunny beaches of Polynesian islands, or wild African jungles. I fantasized the excitement of exploring the hidden world of the ocean floor, or, for the ultimate adventure, soaring through outer space to visit the blazing red planet of Mars, circumnavigate Saturn with its multicolored rings, and perhaps even go to another galaxy, full of millions of its own shining worlds. At that time I did not realize how plausible it was, but wishful thinking and Patti's story led to my studies of astral projection, and launched my astral odyssey.

When I was in my late 20s, through reading, talking with others, and firsthand experience (to be related later), I began to learn much more about astral projection, now usually referred to as out-of-body-experiences, or just OBEs. (I will use the terms interchangeably throughout this work.) I verified for myself what I had suspected since Patti told me her story; there is much more to existence than just normal waking consciousness in the physical world.

OBEs and Psychopathy

Research in the last half of the 20th century has shown that OBEs are quite common phenomena and unrelated to psychopathy. They have occurred in almost all cultures throughout known history and been the basis for philosophy, religious beliefs, and concepts of life after death. Numerous surveys have been conducted by various researchers since the 1950s,[1] and the results indicate that sometime during their lifetimes approximately 10–20 percent of the adult population will have an OBE, which was defined by D. Scott Rogo, a parapsychology researcher, as any experience in which the subject believes that personal consciousness is located in space outside the physical body.[2] However, some of those who have such an experience may fail to recognize it as an OBE.

In the past, mental health professionals believed OBEs were a symptom of mental illness related to several disorders: autoscopy, dissociation, ego splitting, and a high level of death anxiety.

Autoscopy is the hallucination of an image of a duplicate self outside the actual physical self, perceived from the physical

[1]D. Scott Rogo, "Researching the Out-of-Body Experience: The State of the Art," *Anabiosis—The Journal for Near-Death Studies* 4 (1984): 23–25.

[2]D. Scott Rogo, *Mind Beyond the Body* (New York: Penguin Books, 1978), p. 35.

self. Autoscopy does not even fit the definition of an OBE, because during an OBE the consciousness and senses are located *outside* the physical body, *in* the apparitional form if one is present. If the self is seen, it is the physical self that is perceived from a duplicate, not the other way around. An exception to this is dual consciousness, which will be discussed later. During autoscopy the subject realizes the duplicate self is a hallucination, but during an OBE, if the physical body is viewed, the subject usually believes that it is the actual physical body. Generally, to the person undergoing an OBE the physical body appears lying still, unconscious, but to the person experiencing autoscopy the double appears animated, often mimicking the movements of the physical self. Some psychologists include OBEs with autoscopy, but autoscopy and OBEs are clearly different phenomena and should not be confused.

Dissociation is a general term for a group of behavior disorders in which a person behaves as if certain repressed tendencies, such as guilt, aggression, or anxiety, surface as independent personalities. During OBEs, however, the entire personality remains cohesive; it just seems to leave the physical body and exist in a nonphysical form.

Psychogenic amnesia is a form of dissociation in which affected persons forget who they are and what they have been doing during all or part of their lives. During OBEs the memory functions as in physical consciousness, with subjects knowing exactly who they are and other past information.

Psychogenic fugue, a related dissociation disorder, is a variant of psychogenic amnesia in which the afflicted person changes residence and creates a new identity. An example would be an amnesia patient who travels some distance away from home and develops a new identity to protect the ego. Thousands of persons have experienced OBEs and remained in the same home and kept the same personal identity as before.

A widely publicized dissociation disorder is multiple personality, a condition in which more than one personality is present in the same person, with the personalities alternating outward expression. Each personality displays a unique character, level of intelligence, and abilities, and may or may not be aware of the others. During OBEs the same personality is present out of the body as is present in the body.

Depersonalization, another type of dissociation disorder, is a condition in which a person feels psychologically detached from the body and its surroundings, as if the self and the world were unreal. Both positive and negative emotions are noticeably absent. It does not involve the sensation of being in another body or experiencing reality from a point located outside the body, as an OBE does. Contrary to the experience of depersonalization, people reporting OBEs often describe a heightened sense of reality while exteriorized, with intense feelings, whether of happiness and well-being or panic and dread. During depersonalization many patients complain that the world appears pale and colorless, but many people reporting OBEs are impressed with the unusual brilliance and richness of color they see while exteriorized.

Depersonalization has also been associated with disturbance of body image, in which individuals have a misconception of the size, shape, and weight of their physical bodies or parts of it. Researchers have failed to establish any evidence that OBEs constitute a disturbance of body image.[3]

Among the numerous studies that have been conducted to determine personality or cognitive differences between groups of people who have experienced OBEs and control groups who have not experienced OBEs, no consistent or highly significant deviations have been found in personality traits or mental abilities. (See Irwin 1985, Rogo 1986 and 1984.) One study, however, done in 1982,[4] found direct relationships between people who reported experiencing being out-of-the-body at least one time and the traits of breadth of interest, innovation, stability, risk-taking, and social responsibility, but most of these correla-

---

[3]Harvey J. Irwin, *Flight of Mind: A Psychological Study of the Out-of-Body Experience* (Metuchen, NJ: Scarecrow Press, 1985), pp. 246–247.

[4]D. Scott Rogo, "Researching the Out-of-Body Experience: The State of the Art," 26.

tions were not statistically significant. Another study, published by Harvey Irwin,[5] showed evidence that persons who have experienced OBEs have a higher level of the need for intraception (attention to subjective psychological processes), lower levels of the need for deference (the submission to the wishes of others), and lower levels of the need for achievement, but, as he explains, these findings can only be regarded as areas where further study is necessary.

Dr. Graham Reed called OBEs ego splitting and suggested that they are a stress reaction to a painful situation, such as the loss of a loved one, expressed as an inappropriate tranquillity.[6] Spontaneous OBEs can and often do occur during stressful situations, such as a serious accident or a near-death experience (NDE), to be discussed later, but OBEs also occur during situations in which stress is virtually absent. In fact, people who have learned to self-induce OBEs usually do so from a deliberately relaxed state of mind unrelated to traumatic events.

In 1974 the psychiatrist J. Ehrenwald proposed the theory that OBEs are a defense mechanism against death anxiety, but research attempts have failed to show that people undergoing OBEs have higher levels of death anxiety than people who have not had OBEs. This could be because the OBEs removed the death anxiety before the research was done, if such anxiety actually existed prior to the OBE. No conclusive evidence has either proved or disproved Ehrenwald's hypothesis.[7]

Furthermore, studies have failed to show specific relationships between the occurrence of OBEs and hysteroid responses, neuroticism, psychoticism, or maladjustment.[8]

---

[5]Harvey J. Irwin, "The Psychological Function of Out-of-Body Experiences," *The Journal of Nervous and Mental Disease* 169 (1981): 244–247.

[6]Graham Reed, *The Psychology of Anomalous Experience* (Boston: Houghton-Mifflin, 1974), p. 125.

[7]Rogo, "Researching the Out-of-Body Experience: The State of the Art," 27–28.

[8]Rogo, "Researching the Out-of-Body Experience: The State of the Art," 25–26.

Conscious OBEs and Dreams

After I learned that leaving the body is a fairly common experience within the mentally stable population, one of the next questions I asked myself about OBEs, since I had begun successfully self-inducing them consciously, was how do they differ from ordinary dreams? Conscious OBEs, as opposed to unconscious OBEs, which will be discussed later, have many similarities to dreams, but differ from dreams in important ways.

I have been able to remember many of my dreams since I was a toddler sleeping in a crib; they have ranged from simple images to complex situations involving plot, emotional drama, suspense, characterization, and even special effects. They are almost always in color. I have experienced all five senses in dreams, but literature reports that touch, taste, and smell are rare, with sight the most dominant and hearing second. Like other people's dreams, mine range from realistic and ordinary to fantastic and surreal.

One of the differences that I have observed between dreaming and astral projection is how I critically evaluate the experience while it progresses. In most dreams I lack the critical faculty, but in OBEs I can carefully evaluate each circumstance, just as in physical waking consciousness.

During a typical dream I am convinced that the dream world is veritable physical reality. As the dream events unfold, I accept them as normal physical happenings in the everyday world and have an unquestioning belief in the content no matter how absurd; if I dream of ten-foot-tall rabbits standing around outside a building, I automatically accept them as real. I lose critical judgment and lack self-awareness of my state of mind.

During conscious OBEs, instead of passively accepting the events taking place as physical reality, I question my state of consciousness, my actions, and the images around me. I acknowledge that I am in an alternative state of consciousness and can do things impossible in physical reality. If I see my quilt piled on my porch, I am aware that the quilt is appearing in the wrong place, and that in physical reality, when I went to sleep, it was on my bed, covering my physical body.

In dreams I am usually oblivious to the existence of the physical world, but during OBEs I make a conscious effort to distinguish the OBE from waking reality in the physical world. My OBEs can be so "realistic" that sometimes it is a mystery to me whether I am actually walking along physically, possibly sleepwalking, or exteriorized in astral form, so I look for proof of my conscious condition, such as the ability to float across the room or pass through a wall, to assure myself that I am in my astral body. In dreams I sometimes have amazing abilities, such as flying, as in OBEs, but in dreams I lack the incentive to purposely demonstrate them to ascertain my state of consciousness, except in special situations called lucid dreams, in which I am aware that I am dreaming. Lucid dreams are discussed later.

Dreams can be as realistic as the physical world, too. The difference is that during an OBE I *wonder* which state of consciousness I am in, until I analyze the evidence and form a conclusion, while in ordinary dreams I just accept the drama as physical reality until I awaken and realize it was all a dream.

While an OBE is occurring, my mind is more observant of itself and the state of consciousness it is experiencing, and retains more intellectual abilities than during dreams. While the OBE takes place, I evaluate the situation and make a conscious effort to commit it to memory. I examine with curiosity the images and events, and then analyze what I see, what is happening, and how I react. I compare and contrast the astral plane with the physical plane and the dream environment, noting peculiar similarities and differences. Impressed with the realism of the experience, I test the environment and my abilities, experiment with various hypotheses, form conclusions, and ponder the idiosyncrasies, of which there are many mystifying examples related in the literature, accounts of others, and those taken from my notes.

A major difference between dreams and conscious OBEs concerns the vehicle experienced as containing the self, the dream body compared to the astral body.

While I dream, I believe that the body I am occupying, operating, and perceiving from in the dream is my physical body, and it usually "looks" and "feels" much like the biological form I occupy during waking hours. Sometimes, however, my dream body can fly or breathe under water, but usually I just accept those abilities as physical reality, along with the rest of my dream world, mindless of the impossibility of those feats in a human organism and completely forgetting that I have a real physical body lying in bed asleep.

During an OBE I am convinced that the body I am occupying and functioning in is a subliminal body, either imaginary or nonphysical, but distinct and separated from my physical body, which I realize is lying in bed unconscious while I am out and about in astral form. I observe the phantom body which contains my vital essence, compare it with my organic body, and become aware of the astral form's unique attributes and abilities that are impossible to ascribe to the physical organism.

My dream body varies little, being a fairly accurate representation of my physical body, but my astral body changes extensively, taking on different forms from time to time. It is often a replica of my physical body with the look and feel of solid skin, muscle, and bone, but it is also capable of existing in other shapes and a range of material densities. One time I looked at my astral hand, and it looked like an alien hand, long, thin, and narrow, composed of ghastly pale flesh. Besides appearing solid, my astral body can also be composed of semi-physical material that is airy and weightless, or it can look as if it is made up entirely of light, golden-white.

Another difference between dreams and conscious OBEs is the source of control of the experience. Dream events seem to happen to me and OBE events seem to result more from my deliberate actions.

In a dream it seems as if an exterior source, or a subconscious or unconscious part of my mind, wrote a script and created a set, in which I just passively play my part and go through the actions of the role giving it little, if any, thought. The dream contents can be organized as a well constructed plot, loosely connected relationships, or seemingly unrelated random events. They are usually strikingly different from anything I would create consciously. Although I remain virtually passive in directing dream action, I do react to dream situations and feel love, terror, compassion, and many other emotions, sometimes so intense that I wake up screaming or crying or laughing, but in typical dreams I just submissively go along with whatever action is taking place. During OBEs, however, I have a much greater amount of free will.

Some people occasionally have the ability to direct their dreams, and I have done this a few times. Usually, though, when I start to become aware that I am dreaming and try to direct the action, I wake up. Sometimes, however, I manage to remain in the dream state and change the plot to suit my desires, but then I slip into the new story, which pursues its own course without my control. I also have been able to influence my dreams from a waking state through autosuggestion just before falling asleep, but only to the extent of location or subject matter—the details have been beyond my conscious manipulation.

During OBEs I have much more freedom to direct the action with my conscious mind through the decision-making process; I have the ability to consider available alternatives, choose the one I believe is most appropriate, and follow through with the necessary voluntary motions. If I have set a goal previously, while still in physical reality, when I experience astral consciousness, I usually remember my intentions and deliberately perform the actions conducive to attaining that goal. I am also free to strive for new goals that come to mind while I am out of my body.

Most dream events resemble either a prearranged story or a series of random images and phenomena. Events in the OBE world, on the other hand, seem as if they are subject to laws of probability more like those in physical reality. An appreciable amount of free will is available as I decide from moment to moment what to do. My logical thinking is operable as I rationalize that if I perform a certain action, the probable outcome would be a specific reaction. I choose my conduct according to my beliefs about cause and effect, more as I would in the physical world than a dream world.

However, there are notable exceptions when my free will is ineffective. Sometimes during an OBE it seems as if an external will takes over and controls events contrary to the desires of my conscious mind. For example, as seen in later chapters relating actual OBEs, when I wish to reach a particular destination, an invisible force might pull me back to my body instead, or if I want to fly, my astral body may remain heavy and dense, unable to lift off the ground. These occurrences differ from the passive participation in a dream, because in OBE consciousness I have more ability to try to alter the events according to my desires and attempt to analyze why things are out of control, even though I may fail to change the situation or find the source of the difficulty.

There are some similarities and some differences between the settings encountered in dreams and OBEs. The scenery of both can be vivid or vague, realistic or fanciful. In some dreams the scenery appears just as authentic, even if fanciful, as the scenery during an OBE, which also can be fanciful. In both dreams and OBEs, the world I occupy and the objects in it can manifest, at the time, just as believably as that which is evinced in physical reality. In general, however, dream worlds are more absurd and bizarre than OBE worlds, and OBE worlds conform more exactly with the physical world and the immediate physical surroundings than dream worlds do.

In ordinary dreams I believe that the dream location is actually where I am, and that it is the only world in existence. During astral projection, however, I know that my physical body is actually in bed in the physical world, and that I am functioning in an astral body, located on the astral plane, wherever that happens to be.

The dream setting can consist of an altered form of physical reality with only a few misrepresentations, or a chimerical vision containing preposterous elements and situations. However, from ordinary dream consciousness it is impossible to tell the difference between dream reality and physical reality, because the only reality the dream self comprehends is the dream world.

As mentioned earlier, close resemblance to physical reality is more common in OBEs than in dreams. Often the OBE setting looks like a true familiar place in the physical world, sometimes an exact replication down to the minutest detail, and sometimes a counterfeit copy with distortions and inexplicable quirks of reality, such as the consistent failure of light switches to work in the astral world. The OBE world can also look like an unfamiliar place in the physical world, populated with strangers, or even strange entities.

Many times I have astrally visited places that were unfamiliar at the time of projection, but after one such incident I discovered the same place a short time later in physical reality. This evolved into an unusual, eerie situation.

I was flying over the South Dakota Black Hills in astral form late one night and landed in a large room full of people and bright, colorful devices. I looked around, confused about my location, the function of the room, and the identity of the occupants. In physical life, a couple of weeks later, my friend, Judi, and I decided to investigate a new casino, the Gold Dust, that had just opened in Deadwood. The moment we entered, I was struck with a powerful sense of déjà vu—we walked into the same room I had previously visited in astral form. Later I learned that the Gold Dust opened ten days after my astral visit.

This is an example of an OBE which was precognitive, or a revelation of the future, since it took place before the casino was open. It is also possible for dreams to contain precognitive elements, but when they do, they are usually more distorted and symbolic than OBEs or physical reality.

Besides these differences between dream and OBE environments, there is a distinct difference in the sequential aspects of time and events occuring between these two experiences and physical life.

There is a psychological and experiential continuity between conscious OBEs and physical life that is lacking between dreams and physical life. For example, during OBEs I have a clear recollection of my physical waking life; I know who I am, where I live, how I earn my living, whether I am single or married, that I have no children, what kind of car I drive, etc. During dreams, however, I still remember who I am, but any or all of the other characteristics of my life can be altered, and while the dream progresses, I accept the alterations as fact and forget the way things are in physical reality, or that there even is a physical reality, until I return to "normal" consciousness.

Like the features of my life, time has a separate continuity in dreams—separate from physical time as well as time in other dreams. OBE time is connected with physical time.

In my dreams it can be either night or day, dawn or dusk, even though it may be a different time in the physical world where I am sleeping. Dream time can lapse from one part of a dream to another, just as in a story when the author jumps ahead to a future time. Whatever the time is represented as in the dream, the dreaming consciousness then has an extremely concentrated focus on the dream "present" taking place in the dream. While a dream is going on, it appears as though the time in the dream is the actual time and it is the only time which exists or ever existed.

My dreams usually begin in the middle of some action that seems to be taking place in a location other than in the bed where my physical body is sleeping. I have been aware of the onset of hypnagogic imagery (in the state of consciousness between waking and sleeping), when daily thoughts, worries, and plans gradually change into fanciful illusions that fall together to form a dream, but even then it seems as if I get swept up into some ongoing action and lose contact with physical space and time.

Normally, however, during transition from the waking world to a dream, I lose consciousness for a while, and then I find myself involved in a dream drama that seems to have been in progress indefinitely, with no memory of when it started or how I got there in my dream body, and no sense of continuity with physical time and space. Dream time exists on a uniquely constructed time continuum.

When a dream stops I either begin another one, continue sleeping in a different sleep stage, or just awaken and find my physical self in bed. In any case, it appears as if the time sequence in the dream came to an end, and I reentered the physical time sequence.

During an OBE the time of day or night also can be different from physical time, as in a dream, but perhaps this is because the place that is being perceived is on a different part of the planet or on a different plane of existence altogether. While experiencing an OBE in the middle of the night, however, I may find my astral self in bright sunshine, but at the same time I know I went to bed a couple of hours earlier at midnight, left my body several minutes ago, and traveled swiftly through a dark tunnel to a new location that may be thousands of miles away. I maintain the awareness that my physical body is at a location where it is nighttime while another part of me functions somewhere else, in daylight.

Astral time has a sense of continuity with physical time, through the separation, from the beginning to the end of the OBE, and through the reentry to the physical world. Astral time, then, appears to be composed of the passage of the same ongoing minutes as experienced in physical time, one following another, from one world to the next and back again. Even though there may be brief blackouts, or shifts from one part of day to another as impressions of vast distances are traversed, the same time sequence is continuously experienced in the OBE world as in the physical world.

Instead of suddenly finding myself caught up in some type of ongoing dream action, when I begin an OBE, I am almost always aware of the process of separating from my physical body, by one means or another, in an astral form. Occupying the astral form, I either remain in the immediate vicinity or travel to a new location by various modes, such as walking, drifting, or being pulled swiftly through a tunnel-like structure.

Several times, however, I have gone directly from dream consciousness to OBE consciousness without the intervening experience of separating from my physical body in bed. In most of those instances the dream location was my home, and my dream body suddenly took the form of my astral body. Each time, I realized that I was exteriorized and had all intellectual faculties, including the knowledge that my physical body was in my bed asleep. After the realization, the dream "present" ended, and the time sequence became connected with physical time.

On another occasion, I "awoke" in my astral body away from my home, traveling over the countryside somewhere. I was aware that I was in an altered state of consciousness and that my physical body was at home in bed. After this "awakening," too, the dream time stopped and I experienced the chronology of physical time.

When OBEs end, I often have the sensation of traveling back to my physical body and reentering it without a break in the time sequence from astral time to physical time. I have even watched my astral body reunite with my physical body as ongoing astral minutes became the same as physical minutes.

Memories of OBEs are quite different from memories of dreams. Sometimes clear dreams with intense emotional content can be remembered better than hazy OBEs, but generally, recollection of OBEs is easier. From waking reality, both when awake in physical form and "awake" in astral form, it can be difficult to tell the difference between the OBE world and the physical world, but it is usually easy to distinguish between dream worlds and either the physical or the OBE world. When I awaken from an ordinary dream, I am certain that it was a dream; when I "awaken" from an OBE, I don't know if the experience took place in physical reality or not, but I know it was different from ordinary dreaming.

Even though some of my dreams are vivid and realistic, when I awaken from a dream, I believe that what I experienced during the dream was fantasy, nothing but mental imagery produced by a mysterious part of my mind, although strikingly convincing while it took place.

For example, once I dreamed that I was driving along a narrow, winding road, and my car plunged over a cliff. As it dropped through space, the lurch in my stomach felt real, and when it hit the bottom of the canyon with a loud crash, the ground felt as hard and solid as physical ground, but when I awoke an instant later, with my heart pounding, I felt reassured that it was only a dream.

After waking from an ordinary dream, dream locations leave the impression that they were internal environments fabricated by another part of my self. I feel certain that the dream was an imaginary fantasy that took place in my mind.

Personally, the recollection of dreams is characterized by thinking of them as occurring in a separate reality, which can be realistic but is often absurd, with unique properties distinct from those of the physical world. Dream reality is a reality far removed from physical reality, because it is seemingly composed of a prearranged series of events, in which I passively play my given role, unable to recognize the experience as a dream, and usually neither making the effort nor having the ability to direct the action to my choosing.

Dreams take place in a fantasy world, often with incoherence of parts of the dream or objects in the dream. Dream events can progress along a given course and suddenly switch to new action in a different setting. A sports car can also be a gun, or a person can be both Dotti and Carolynn at the same time.

In remembering dreams I have the impression that I am thinking back to not only a past time, but also to a dimension farther removed from physical reality than the OBE world is. From waking reality, dreams appear as an invention of whimsy and caprice, while OBEs are usually a replication of physical time, events, and places. Memories of entire dreams may be triggered by a wisp of a thought, or the mere hint of an event entering my mind, but then, in a couple of hours, all traces of the dream memory may vanish permanently.

Dreams are forgotten, events from physical life are also forgotten, and probably some OBEs as well, but my memories of

OBEs are more like my memories of what happened yesterday, or even ten years ago, in physical life. When I remember OBEs, the memory is more like memories of past physical reality, because OBEs seem closer to the physical dimension, even though they may contain dreamlike elements. I recall my cognitive abilities operating in a manner more as when I am awake physically.

When I "return" from an OBE, I have the subjective impression that the experience took place in an external reality in which I was present in astral form, a form discernible from either dream or physical form. I ponder over what the OBE was, because I know it was intrinsically different from either a dream or physical reality, although at times OBEs contain elements of both. I have the distinct impression that I was in a wakeful state of consciousness different from ordinary dreaming.

Since, during OBEs, I have at my disposal more intellectual faculties, the ability to act voluntarily, and continuity of space and time with memory of physical life, it appears that the OBE world is in a dimension between dream worlds and the physical world, and in a state of consciousness between sleeping and physical waking. Therefore, remembering OBEs is more like remembering past physical events than like remembering dreams. The memory of OBEs is usually clearer, more intense, more complete, and lasts longer than most dream memories.

The artifice and commonality of ordinary dreams are easily forgotten, whereas OBEs, because of their uniqueness and profundity, make a lasting impression. Memories of OBEs are more like remembering making love for the first time, driving a car for the first time, or where you were when JFK was assassinated. Like other major lifetime events, OBEs become more indelibly etched into our memory banks.

Dream worlds, the OBE environment, and physical reality are all capable of overlapping to some extent when one kind of consciousness shifts to another. As you will see, I have distinguished a dream setting superimposed upon an OBE environment, but I have also experienced the OBE environment superimposed upon my physical location, and on rare occasions I have seen dream images briefly persist in the physical world.

Sometimes when I go from an OBE into a dream, it is similar to going from a normal waking state into a dream. My ability to concentrate gradually deteriorates as stray thoughts and images begin to dominate my attention. The images become more and more distorted and disconnected from my rational thoughts until they ultimately precipitate a dream that I accept as reality while it occurs.

At other times when OBE consciousness changes to dream consciousness, I see the dream images superimposed upon the astral world that I am occupying at the moment. I either just passively step into the dream action, fully aware of what I am doing, or get the two sets of imagery so jumbled that I never fathom where the OBE ended and the dream started.

Passing from a dream to an OBE is similar to passing from a dream to physical wakefulness, only instead of awakening in my physical body, I awaken in my astral body, which can be in the same room as my physical body, in another part of the house, or farther away. When a dream changes into an OBE, there is a spontaneous reconstruction of awareness as the dream melts away and I obtain the same self-directing consciousness that I use in everyday waking experience. My mind gains improved control of my thoughts and actions and the ability to make decisions, such as whether to fly out the window or go back to sleep. I am aware that what I was experiencing a few minutes previously was a dream. Even if I "awaken" in my astral body at a location far away from my physical body, I realize that there was a shift from passive dream awareness to more voluntary action in a more rational world. This situation can easily be confused with lucid dreams, which will be discussed in later sections of this book.

The perception of occasional overlapping among the worlds of dreams, OBEs, and physical reality provides unique opportunities to compare and contrast these different dimensions, and realize that conscious OBEs definitely differ, in many ways, from dreams.

LABORATORY EVIDENCE

These subjective differences between dreams and OBEs are further substantiated by laboratory evidence which indicates that they are separate kinds of phenomena. In his experiments at the University of California, Psychology Professor Charles T. Tart discovered physiological differences between dreams and OBEs by monitoring the electroencephalogram (EEG) of a gifted subject, Miss Z, during several OBEs which she produced at will in a sleep laboratory.[9] When comparing the recordings taken during OBEs with those of normal sleep, Dr. Tart reported a number of differences in the EEG pattern, including a flattening of the alpha waves, a particular tracing caused by electrical impulses emitted by the brain during relaxation. The EEG pattern during OBEs was different from sleeping, dreaming, drowsy, or waking patterns. Rapid eye movements (REMs), normally present during dreaming, were absent. In Tart's opinion, these atypical tracings may have resulted from imagery formed during the transitions between waking and sleeping during the night, or they may have resulted from a dream changing to an OBE.

Dr. Tart also had the opportunity to work with another gifted subject, Robert Monroe, who has written two books of his own about OBEs.[10] However, the variance and peculiarities in Monroe's EEGs made it impossible to draw any definite conclusions, except that he spent a lot of time in the transition states between waking and sleeping. Two OBEs which Monroe did produce seemed to occur during the dream stage of sleep, with REMs and a somewhat slowed alpha rhythm.[11] A later study of

---

[9]Charles T. Tart, "A Psychophysiological Study of Out-of-the-Body Experiences in a Selected Subject," *Journal of the American Society for Psychical Research* 62 (1968): 2–27.

[10]Robert A. Monroe, *Journeys Out of the Body*, 2nd ed. (New York: Anchor Press/Doubleday, 1973); *Far Journeys* (New York: Doubleday, 1985).

[11]Charles T. Tart, "A Second Psychophysiological Study of Out-of-the-Body Experiences in a Gifted Subject," *International Journal of Parapsychology* 9 (1967): 251–258.

the EEG results by Susan Blackmore indicated that the few eye movements exhibited by Monroe were not likely to be REMs typical of a dream state.[12] Perhaps these mixed patterns occurred because during these OBEs, Monroe was at a point on a consciousness continuum where dreams blend with exteriorization.

In 1977, Stuart Twemlow of the Topeka V.A. Medical center conducted similar EEG experiments with Monroe as subject, and during the time which Monroe reported being exteriorized the chart showed a flattened pattern, while galvanic skin response (GSR) showed an unusually deep state of relaxation.[13]

At the American Society for Psychical Research, Janet Mitchell, Ph.D., studied another subject, Ingo Swann, who could induce OBEs from a waking state. Mitchell's results show that during Swann's OBEs his EEGs also produced a flattened pattern with a loss of electrical activity in the brain, especially in the left hemisphere, and a reduction in REMs.[14] Joel Whitton, working in Canada with the OBE adept Alex Tanous, also found a flattening of the EEG record during OBEs.[15]

Blue Harary, another adept who induces OBEs from a waking state, participated in experiments at the Psychical Research Foundation in Durham, North Carolina.[16] Blue's psychophysiological patterns during OBEs were also different from normal sleep and dreaming patterns, with a decrease in REMs. The overall sequence was similar to a state of deep relaxation in the waking state, except that heart rate and respiration increased.

---

[12]S. J. Blackmore, Parapsychology and Out-of-the-Body Experiences (London: Society for Psychical Research, 1978), discussed in Irwin, *Flight of Mind: A Psychological Study of the Out-of-Body Experience*, p. 67.

[13]Stuart W. Twemlow, "Epilogue: Personality File," in Robert A. Monroe, *Journeys Out of the Body*, 2nd ed. (New York: Anchor Press/Doubleday, 1977), pp. 275–280.

[14]Janet Lee Mitchell, *Out-of-Body Experiences: A Handbook* (New York: Ballantine, 1990), p. 11.

[15]Mitchell, *Out-of-Body Experiences: A Handbook*, p. 76.

[16]Rogo, "Researching the Out-of-Body Experience: The State of the Art," 43–44.

A study utilizing nonselected subjects and an experimental OBE induction procedure, done by John Palmer at the University of Virginia, found no correlations between EEGs and OBEs, except the possibility that people with above 30 percent theta waves in their baseline EEG have more vivid and easily induced OBEs.[17] Theta waves are produced by the brain during intense creativity, vivid mental imagery, or altered states of consciousness. Other studies have shown that through biofeedback we can train our brains to produce theta waves, thereby increasing our potential for producing OBEs as well as other psychic experiences.[18]

These EEG studies show consistencies for individual subjects, but a few inconsistencies between subjects, possibly due to the occurrence of different types of OBEs. This could indicate that OBEs take place along a range of consciousness between normal waking and dreaming, without distinct borders to divide one type of awareness from another. The idea of a continuum of OBEs also provides an explanation for the wide variety of subjective differences that occur among personal reports, both among different individuals, and for the same individual at different times.

The flattened patterns of EEG tracings obtained during OBEs are similar to patterns obtained during deep hypnosis, and during fantasizing for people with vivid mental imagery. The results suggest that the subjects were undergoing experiences in consciousness different from either normal waking or normal sleeping, that they were deeply relaxed, and possibly concentrating on something.[19] However, the findings are too inconclusive to indicate a discrete neurophysiological state associated with OBEs. These studies are interesting, but since they are difficult to assess, the only definite conclusion that has been drawn

---

[17] D. Scott Rogo, *Leaving the Body* (New York: Prentice Hall, 1986), p. 14.

[18] Rogo, *Leaving the Body*, p. 14.

[19] Irwin, *Flight of Mind: A Psychological Study of the Out-of-Body Experience*, p. 208.

from them is that OBEs do not occur in the same psychophysiological state as dreams.

To determine if OBEs occur in a distinct physiological state, another interesting research project was undertaken in 1985 by Joe Slate, Ph.D., and funded by the Parapsychological Foundation of New York.[20] Kirlian photography, also called electrophotography or corona-discharge photography, was implemented to take pictures of the auras surrounding the right index fingers of subjects in a normal state of consciousness and compared with pictures taken while they were having experimentally induced OBEs. The OBE induction procedure included relaxation techniques combined with verbal suggestions and mental imagery designed specifically for each subject. All the subjects, when successfully achieving out-of-body states, showed conspicuous changes in the photographs of their index finger auras. The images were consistently rounded and full during normal waking states and separated into two distinct parts during OBEs, a pattern the researchers called the broken-corona effect. They photographed the corona during other altered states of consciousness, such as hypnosis, but obtained the broken-corona effect only during OBEs. This evidence indicates that the out-of-body state is accompanied by distinct psychophysiological changes different from other states of awareness.

* * * * * * *

When I began learning about self-induced conscious OBEs, I discovered that although they are different from dreams in many ways, they are intimately connected with them, so my astral odyssey took me on a tour of dream worlds as I searched for the route to the astral world.

I had read about dreams and studied my own for a long time, but as I learned more about OBEs, I learned that knowl-

[20]Joe H. Slate, *Psychic Phenomena* (Jefferson, NC: McFarland , 1988), p. 105.

edge and awareness of dreams is essential to willfully opening the door to the astral world. Besides leading to both spontaneous and self-induced OBEs, the study and understanding of dreams is necessary to comprehend OBEs relative to other states of consciousness.

While I was learning to deliberately leave my body and to recognize the differences between OBEs and dreams, I studied dreams more intensively through books, papers, periodicals, and introspection. I discovered that there are many different kinds of dreams that appear to exist on a continuum of consciousness, which I call the dream continuum. The dream continuum ranges from a subjective impression of an unconscious state of oblivion to the kind of consciousness we experience when fully awake in the physical world.

The states of consciousness in which OBEs occur appear to be digressions in the normal transitions from waking to sleeping or sleeping to waking, on another consciousness continuum which is related to and interconnected with the dream continuum. As within the dream continuum, within the OBE consciousness continuum there also exists a spectrum of awareness levels, ranging from unconscious to fully awake. The OBE continuum, however, is usually skipped over or left in the subconscious memory.

Through cognitive discipline it is possible to explore the dream continuum, the OBE continuum, and all the in-between states of consciousness. Along these continuums, and in between, lie hidden realms that contain marvelous powers and insights, awaiting discovery and development.

Chapter 2

The Mind Spectrum

Why do we dream? Should such nonsensical journeys into fantasy be taken seriously? What are these nocturnal interludes of mystical drama, with multidimensional ideas concealed in layers of symbolism, that sift through the veil of unconsciousness during sleep, only to elapse into elusive memories when awareness returns to the physical world? Are they real? Are they imaginary?

Are they only illusions processed from "day residue" and repressed and unfulfilled desires? Are they nothing but spontaneous mental reflections of images and events constructed by an overactive imagination for some unknown reason? Or are they glimpses into an alternative reality? Whatever they are, they have been a subject of inquiry and hypothetical formulation since ancient times, as humans have endeavored to uncover the mysteries of the interaction between the waking world we believe is our natural habitat and the dream worlds wherein we dwell during sleep.

Historical Perspective

Throughout history religious leaders, philosophers, and charlatans of diverse cultures have developed belief systems based on dreams. They have envisioned dreams as messages from such sources as the gods, angels, or cosmic consciousness, as well as devils, demons, and fiendish spirits. According to many past and present belief systems, these types of entities communicate with humans through dreams to transmit information about the future, diagnose illnesses and prescribe cures, impart wisdom, or, in the case of evil entities, accomplish some diabolical purpose. Early Egyptians, Greeks, Asians, and Native Americans, to name a few, all tried to interpret dreams and connect them with higher knowledge in an effort to attain healing or guidance in physical life. On the contrary, many religious leaders have defined dreams as evil works. Dreams are still prominent in many modern belief systems.

We can find insight into the development of medieval thought concerning dreams in the writings of Synesius of Cyrene (365–415), philosopher and bishop of Ptolemais. Synesius wrote a treatise, *On Dreams*, in which he attributed to dreams the individuality of the soul, which, according to its nature, could create dream worlds of beauty or horror, depending upon the ego's moral evolution rather than free will. Synesius conceived the dream world as comprised of past, present, and future images, benevolent as well as malicious characters, memories mingled with longings, a realm which could only be interpreted on an individual basis. Also, he expounded that by studying dreams each person could profit greatly through divination. Synesius himself claims to have gained much from dream studies—he even avoided an ambush by hostile magicians because of a warning he received through a dream.[1]

More recent ideas concerning dreams can be found in the work of Sigmund Freud (1856–1939), an Austrian physician and the founder of psychoanalysis, who published *The Interpretation of Dreams* in 1900. Freud wrote that dreams were wish fulfillments in disguise, and distinguished between latent dream-thoughts and manifest dream-content. Latent dream-thoughts were unconscious repressed wishes, desires so offensive to the waking ego that they had to be presented in disguised form to elude resistance and protect the sleep of the dreamer. The disguised form was what Freud called the manifest dream-content.

---

[1]Eliphas Levi, *The History of Magic* (York Beach, ME: Samuel Weiser, 1970), p. 177.

Freud believed that through interpretation of the manifest dream-content a psychoanalyst could discover the basis of psychosis, normally hidden in the unconscious.[2]

Freud's younger contemporary and friend for many years, Carl Jung (1875-1961), a Swiss psychiatrist, had differing ideas about dreams. Jung professed dreams to be mental dramas formed out of ideas from the collective unconscious, an inherited mental realm containing archetypes, or universal symbols, common to all human experience. Jung believed that by interpreting archetypal symbols, we could clarify the underlying causes of psychological functioning.

Sigmund Freud's and Carl Jung's ideas had an impressive impact on 20th century thinking, but Stephen LaBerge of Stanford University Sleep Research Center has taken dreaming beyond mysticism, psychoanalytic theory, and archetypal symbolism, and shown experimentally that people can become fully conscious while dreaming to experience what has become known as lucid dreaming.[3] Since the days of Aristotle, lucid dreams have been a subject of curiosity, but today Stephen LaBerge and others are applying them to research, inner growth, creativity, physical skills, decision making, or using them just for fun.[4]

Sleep Studies

In the 20th century we have learned much about sleep and dreaming through modern research methods and electronic technology. A breakthrough in dream studies occurred in 1955

[2]For more information on Freud's work, see John Rickman, M. D. and Charles Brenner, M. D., eds., *A General Selection from the Works of Sigmund Freud* (Garden City, NY: Doubleday Anchor Books, 1957), pp. 19–20.

[3]Stephen LaBerge, Ph. D. and Howard Rheingold, *Exploring the World of Lucid Dreaming* (New York: Ballantine Books, 1990), pp. 23–24.

[4]Stephen LaBerge, *Lucid Dreaming: The Power of Being Awake and Aware in Your Dreams* (New York: Ballantine Books, 1985), p. 167.

when Eugene Aserinsky, a graduate student at the University of Chicago, and Nathaniel Kleitman, his physiology professor, reported specific eye movements that seemed to occur during dreaming. A later study by William C. Dement and Kleitman confirmed that these eye movements take place during dreams.[5] This occular activity became known as rapid eye movements (REMs) and is used in dream research to determine when a subject is dreaming. The ability to determine when a subject is dreaming opened up countless opportunities to study the dreaming mind.

Dream scientists have categorized sleep as consisting of five electroencephalogram (EEG) stages, with sources differing somewhat in how they are labeled. The first stage, descending stage one, may be accompanied by dreamlike thoughts, images, and sensations. During stages two, three, and four, sleep becomes progressively deeper and REMs are normally absent. Most subjects awakened from a nonREM, or NREM, stage of sleep describe their mentation as "thinking" and distinctive from dreaming. The fifth stage, a modified stage one or ascending stage one, usually just called REM sleep, is the state of consciousness in which dreams form, accompanied by REMs and EEG tracings similar to stage one.

Dreamologists tell us that a normal person has a nightly sleep pattern made up of the five stages of sleep, called the sleep–dream cycle. Each turn of the cycle consists of the five sleep stages. The sleep–dream cycle varies slightly among individuals but remains fairly consistent for each person.

During a typical eight-hour rest, the sleep–dream cycle contains four or five dream periods separated by approximately ninety-minute intervals of non-dream sleep. Normally, after sleep onset, there is a brief period of descending stage one, followed by sixty to ninety minutes of NREM sleep, and then the

---

[5]David Foulkes, "Theories of Dream Formation and Recent Studies of Sleep Consciousness," in *Altered States of Consciousness*, ed. Charles T. Tart (Garden City, NY: Anchor Books/Doubleday, 1972), p. 119.

first REM dreaming period appears, which averages about ten minutes in length. As the sleep–dream cycle progresses, each REM dream period becomes longer, with the final one lasting up to fifty or sixty minutes. As dreams proceed through the nightly sleep–dream cycle, they become more colorful, more vivid, and easier to recall. Altogether dreams account for twenty or thirty percent of sleep time in normal adults.

Sleep is bordered on both ends by two transition states of consciousness; the one between waking and sleeping is called the hypnagogic state and the one between sleeping and waking is called the hypnopompic state. Some researchers insist that dreamlike thoughts, images, and sensations, called "hypnagogic imagery," at sleep onset are indistinguishable from REM dreams. They also point out that dreams occur during short naps, when a person is asleep for less than the sixty to ninety minutes normally required before REM sleep. It appears likely that there are exceptions to the theory that dreams occur only in designated stage five REM periods of the sleep–dream cycle.

Most people recall dreams some of the time, and some people have detailed memory of one or more dreams per night. Although dream research led to the conclusion that everyone dreams, a few persons report that they have never recalled a dream. In a study done by Dement and Kleitman using REMs to determine if a subject was dreaming, eighty percent of the time when subjects were awakened during REM periods, they reported that they had been dreaming prior to the interruption; only seven percent of the awakenings during NREM sleep resulted in reports of dreaming.[6]

Further investigation determined that the longer the subjects slept undisturbed after a REM phase, the fewer dreams were recalled, indicating that dreams swiftly fade from conscious memory if sleep continues unbroken. Therefore, since dreams make up twenty or thirty percent of our sleep time, it looks as

---

[6]Charles Tart, *Altered States of Consciousness*, p. 119.

though a significant proportion of our dream life is lost to conscious memory, but possibly is stored elsewhere.

The Dream Continuum

As we have seen, everyone dreams, but sometimes dreams are easier to recall than at other times. Just as there are individual differences in ability to remember dreams, there are differences in ability to actively participate in dreams using voluntary behavior, or to actually influence the dream environment and its events by willfully changing them. These variations apply among individuals as well as to one individual at different times.

Because there is so much variability in both dream recall and active participation in dream content, we can think of different kinds of dreams as existing on a continuum based upon how much conscious awareness is present, that is, the extent to which the physically awake type of consciousness remembers, observes, or creates the dream. Along this dream continuum distinct boundaries between types of dreams are absent, because one category gradually blends into another, but to facilitate discussion, I will consider various divisions. To understand OBEs relative to waking consciousness, the hypnagogic and hypnopompic states, and dreaming consciousness, and to help reach the state of mind necessary to attain OBEs, it helps to categorize dreams and related levels of awareness along a consciousness continuum, which makes up a portion of the spectrum of interrelated levels of awareness and mental compartments functioning as the mind.

At the distant end of the dream continuum, farthest removed from waking consciousness, is the black void, the realm of unconscious dreams, dreams that are forgotten as soon as they "end" or shortly afterwards. Sometimes I awaken with a total lack of dream memories, feeling I have been virtually nonexistent the entire night. But as dream studies have shown, it is likely that dreams occurred; they just bypassed conscious memory. Unconscious dreams may still influence mental or psychological structure.

Next on the dream continuum are elusive dreams, those dreams only remembered as vague remnants or nonsensical fragments with incoherent content. They are lost vapors of dream fabric that have slipped away and left a hollow feeling of incompleteness.

Elusive dreams become clearer and more cohesive until they fit into the next category, ordinary dreams. With little or no effort, we can recall ordinary dreams as fairly complete dreams. Some are absurd and fantastic, some resemble physical reality, and others are mixed.

In the next category are vivid dreams, strong statements from the mental recesses that contain clear imagery, rich symbolism, and powerful impressions that last for days, months, even years. When I was a small child sleeping in a crib, I had a vivid dream that evoked so much wonder and terror that I remember it to this day.

My crib was positioned alongside a wall, and in that wall, near the foot of my crib, was a window. One night, as I lay there sleeping, I looked up and saw wild animals leaping in through the window, stampeding across the crib, and disappearing into the dark room. Lions, tigers, bears, elephants, zebras, and others bounded in, one after another, at a full gallop. I was afraid I would be trampled to death, there were so many and they were running so fast. Finally, as a giraffe charged in, I couldn't restrain myself any longer. I screamed as loudly as I could and started to cry.

The next thing I knew, my mother was closing the window and the animals magically disappeared in her presence. I was thankful for that and, though still shaken, felt tremendous relief. My mother mentioned something about the draft coming in through the window. I thought she meant giraffe, which to me verified my experience in physical reality. I certainly had just seen a giraffe coming in, and now I believed it was real to her, too. Then she said something about a nightmare, and I thought she was referring to the horse that had jumped across my covers earlier, possibly a special kind of mare that exists in the night. She tried to explain to me that there were no animals in the room, but I failed to understand how she could believe that if she had seen them too. She went back to bed, but I was so shaken by the terror and confused by reality concepts that I stayed awake for a long time.

Whether vivid dreams are terrifying nightmares or visions of ecstasy, they are usually of an intense emotional nature, giving the impression that they contain profound meaning on a psychological or psychical level, or relate to an important aspect of waking life. Perhaps it was the confusion resulting from my animal dream that stimulated a lifelong quest into the nature of dreams, reality, and OBEs.

A comparatively rare and interesting type of dream, the lucid dream, was named by the Dutch physician Frederik van Eeden, who wrote "A Study of Dreams" in 1913.[7] During a lucid dream, the dreamer becomes aware that the experience is a dream as the dreaming mind understands its true condition. The dream continues, and the waking mind gains control. Once in control, the waking mind can direct the dream more in accordance with its wishes than the dreaming mind does. Lucid dreams involve more awareness than vivid dreams, so they are on the near end of the dream continuum, close to waking consciousness.

The earliest lucid dream I can remember occurred at about age 10. By that time, I had long since learned to distinguish dream worlds from the physical world. Throughout my childhood, I had many flying dreams, in which I had the ability to fly through the air using my own power to escape danger or soar above the ground purely for enjoyment.

I had one particular dream which spontaneously became lucid, so I decided to see if I could fly to the moon and have a look around. Taking off was difficult, because I felt heavy and

---

[7]Frederik van Eeden, "A Study of Dreams," in Charles T. Tart, *Altered States of Consciousness*, pp. 147–160. Also see pp. 116–117 for background information.

gravity-bound, but once I got started I soared to the sky, accelerated at a remarkably fast rate, and rushed upward through the blackness. I couldn't wait to see what the earth looked like from the moon. Finally, I stopped moving. I opened my eyes and found myself in bed, disappointed and still wondering what it would be like to be on the moon.

Lucid dreams can be triggered by dreams with intense emotional content, physically impossible events, such as flying or breathing underwater, or recognition of other incongruities. They can also occur spontaneously. The shift in consciousness when a dream becomes lucid is as definite as the change from ordinary dreaming to waking in physical reality. The self suddenly realizes that it is dreaming, and the dream imagery remains intact upon this realization until the dreamer either awakens to physical reality, goes back to "normal" sleep, changes the dream, remains in the lucid dream state and controls it, or goes to the hypnopompic state of consciousness. From a lucid dream the dreamer can also go to the OBE state of consciousness. A concentrated effort is required to maintain mental control at the moment a dream becomes lucid, because consciousness can easily lapse back into a normal dream or awaken to physical reality.

Lucid dreams are much rarer than ordinary dreams, but many individuals spontaneously or voluntarily attain this state of consciousness quite regularly. Various surveys have shown that about three-fourths of respondents reported having had lucid dreams and many had them more than once.[8] It has been found that the ability to self-induce lucid dreams can be learned by most people.[9] Once the lucid dream is attained, mental conditions are favorable to voluntarily self-induce an even more fascinating level of awareness, the OBE.

I have experienced another strange kind of dream, sometimes associated with OBEs, the false awakening. It appears to

---

[8]Susan J. Blackmore, *Beyond the Body: An Investigation of Out-of-the-Body Experiences* (London: Heinemann, 1982), p. 116.
[9]LaBerge, *Lucid Dreaming*, pp. 18–19.

be the opposite of a lucid dream; instead of awaking in a dream, I dream of awaking. During the false awakening I realize that what I experienced just previously was a dream, always in a dream environment that resembles my home, but instead of actually waking, I enter another dream, which I believe, at the time, is a true awakening to physical reality. The new dream unfolds, with content similar to the physical reality located in my home, until I realize that it, too, is a dream, and awaken either to physical reality or another false awakening.

Sometimes an entire series of these dreams takes place, each initiated by dreaming that I awaken from the previous one, convinced that I am awake in physical reality, but actually in a new dream. Each dream in the series has a similar theme and location, and subjectively appears to be a dream rather than an OBE. The sequence contains points of lucidity, from which consciousness lapses back to an area on the dream continuum somewhere between vivid dreams and lucid dreams. At the lucid points I understand what is happening, that I am enmeshed in a false awakening series. Even with these points of lucidity, I occasionally have a difficult time getting out of this peculiar dream phenomenon. I experienced false awakenings before I ever experienced conscious OBEs, but after learning to self-induce OBEs, false awakenings became more frequent.

Similar to false awakenings is another kind of dream, a dream within a dream, in which the dreamer dreams of dreaming. In late November 1992, I had the following dream within a dream.

I dreamed I was lying in my bed, which was different from my physical bed, in my bedroom, which was different from my physical bedroom. In the dream, I was awakening from a dream and briefly remained in the hypnopompic state. (Whether it was an actual hypnopompic state or a dream hypnopompic state, I don't know.) My dream self still could hear music emanating from the dream from which she (the dream self) just awoke, the dream within a dream.

The music was upbeat, beautiful instrumental music, played mostly on brass instruments and synthesizer with a jazz rhythm and new age style. The piece was unfamiliar. It sounded like something I was hearing for the first time. I delighted in its clarity, melodious runs, and rich harmony. The thought that such original, complex, joyful music could just automatically flow out of a dream world thrilled my dream self, and she began laughing.

Then my dream self went back to sleep, into the dream within a dream again. (I have no recollection of what the dream in the dream was about.) My dream self awakened a second time, hearing more of the same musical composition playing from the dream within the dream, and laughing even harder than before, laughing at the wonder of such carefully composed and gorgeous music automatically sounding out from her dream.

As my dream self was listening to the music and laughing, I gradually became aware of entering the hypnopompic state. As my awareness passed through the hypnopompic state, my laughing dream self became my physical self, and I awakened to the physical world, with a clear memory of the music lingering in my mind and happiness filling my heart.

This type of dream is much like a false awakening, but there are some differences. In the dream within a dream, although I dreamed I awakened, as in a false awakening, I also *dreamed* that my dream self went back to sleep and had a dream. In a false awakening I dream that I stay awake, believing that I am actually awake. In false awakenings, the dream environment more closely resembles my actual physical environment, but in the dream within a dream, the dream bedroom was definitely different from my physical bedroom. On the dream continuum, I would place the dream within a dream a step farther away from waking consciousness than the false awakening, somewhere between vivid dreams and false awakenings.

Closely related to false awakenings and dreams within dreams are post-dream dreams. They start out even closer to waking consciousness on the dream continuum, because post-dream dreams are preceded by a partial or complete awakening to the physical world, but then they lapse back into a deeper area. The awakening is slow, with a prolonged hypnopompic state, from which the dreamer drifts back to sleep, reentering the previous dream, which continues from where it left off. The brief awakening before a post-dream dream could be considered a combination of the hypnopompic and hypnagogic state, a level of consciousness from which elements of lucidity are easily introduced into the post-dream dream. These dreams are especially conducive to OBEs and may occur in any REM period of the sleep–dream cycle.

The final segment of the dream continuum is also, in a different sense from false awakenings, opposite from a lucid dream; instead of physical waking consciousness entering the dream, the dream enters physical waking consciousness. The dream world actually overlaps the physical waking world for a brief period. At least three kinds of dreams exist in this strange part of the dream continuum—incubus or succubus attacks, night terrors, and persistent dream images.

Incubus attacks (victims being attacked by male entities) and succubus attacks (victims being attacked by female entities) usually take place during the first one or two REM phases of the sleep–dream cycle, and the dream environment is most likely the actual location of the physical body. These ghoulish attacks are made up of horrifying scenes of being choked, strangled, smothered, or crushed. They are often accompanied by semiwakefulness, which enhances realism, and a feeling of paralysis, which intensifies fear.

Although I have never experienced them, a close friend of mine encountered incubus attacks frequently when she was a young woman. Judi experienced what appeared to her, at the time, to be malicious assaults in bed, when her consciousness was between sleeping and waking.

Lying in bed, on the verge of waking, she would feel powerful hands grip her throat, or the sensation of having something like a pillow pushed against her face. As she attempted to ward off the brutal assault with defensive motions, she would discover, to her further alarm, that her muscles were paralyzed. Her entire body would be in a catatonic state, ostensibly awake, but unable to make the necessary movements to either protect herself or escape. Lying helpless, enduring threatening sensations, she would believe someone was there, trying to traumatize or even kill her. Several panicky seconds would elapse before the paralysis subsided. Movement quickly dispeled the menacing assailant.

Judi noticed that her incubus attacks occurred during periods of extreme stress in her life. Although the exact cause of incubus and succubus attacks is speculative, Western mystery tradition has some interesting beliefs concerning these terrifying phenomena.

An incubus or succubus is defined as an evil entity that attacks and rapes sleeping persons. According to esoteric literature, incubi and succubi are the astral bodies of deceased persons whose Earth lives were low, brutal, and selfish, driven by lust, alcoholism, gluttony, and avarice.

After physical death, while residing on the seventh, or lowest, subdivision of the astral plane, and facilitated by the illusory, nonmaterial, timeless qualities of that environment, incubi and succubi become proficient at the art of delusion and use their powers to attack sensitive persons. These astral entities seek victims who are inclined to similar vices and attempt to draw them to fatal influences that could lead to their destruction. If, however, the incubi and succubi fail to find like-minded sensitives to use to gratify their loathsome appetites, their unfulfilled desires will eventually burn out and they will progress to higher planes.[10]

Whether or not this belief is accurate, incubus or succubus attacks are realistic and terrifying. The victim feels the crushing body weight of the attacker, or overpowering hands closing off breathing by smothering or strangulation until convinced that death is imminent.

Dream researchers believe incubus or succubus attacks have a physiological basis, a malfunctioning of the awakening

---

[10]C. W. Leadbeater, *The Astral Plane* (Wheaton, IL: Theosophical Publishing House, 1977), pp. 75–77.

process during which the natural inhibition of the motor nervous system during REM sleep is prolonged after mental arousal and produces sleep paralysis. In their book *Conquering Bad Dreams & Nightmares* Barry Krakow, M.D., and Joseph Neidhardt, M.D., relate that sleep paralysis occurs in large numbers of healthy people, more often during periods of stress.[11] Sleep researchers are still searching for an adequate explanation for incubus or succubus attacks.

Night terrors, which may or may not be defined as dreams, are another aberration of peaceful slumber. They most often frighten children, but can also appear in adults. A sufferer of night terrors abruptly awakens, often screaming and totally disoriented, from deep NREM sleep, stage three or four of the sleep–dream cycle.

Rather than being composed of images or plot, as in REM dreams, the major content of night terrors consists of raw emotion—severe anxiety, intense dread, or pure terror, often accompanied by panic, dilated pupils, profuse sweating, heart palpitations, and hyperventilation. According to some, frightening hypnopompic hallucinations, feelings of entrapment, threat, suffocation, or choking, fear of death, falling sensations, or time and space distortions may be present, adding special effects to the terrifying experience. One surprising characteristic of night terrors is that often as soon as they are over, the sufferer has no recollection of the experience!

If night terrors are chronic, the condition is currently referred to as sleep terror disorder. The cause presently remains a mystery, but hypotheses include malfunctioning of the autonomous nervous system, arousal disorders, emotional disturbance, and dream content.

I have experienced night terrors consisting of pure emotion both as a child and as an adult, during periods of extreme stress or trauma in my life. A close friend of mine, Ben, had recurring

---

[11]Barry Krakow, and Joseph Neidhardt, *Conquering Bad Dreams and Nightmares* (New York: Berkley Books, 1992), p. 259.

experiences that resembled night terrors accompanied by hypnopompic hallucinations, when he was a child.

Between ages 5 and 10, Ben would "dream" that he was awake but unable to move because his blanket was made out of thousands of spiders woven together. He would lie there and look down at their little red eyes staring back at him. He was certain that if he moved, the spiders would attack him "en masse," and leave only his skeleton in bed for his mother to find in the morning when she came in to awaken him.

Other, slightly less horrifying types of realistic images can manifest beyond the dream world into the waking world. Several times I have awakened from vivid dreams with dream visions and sensations existing briefly in physical reality.

For example, once I dreamed that one of my best friends, Susan, and I were walking down a narrow, well-lighted hallway with a door at the end. Susan was walking in front of me, and as she opened the door, a bat flew out and swooped toward her head. I yelled for her to watch out; she ducked, and the bat flew into my face. I awakened brushing it away, feeling its leathery wings and tiny claws thrash against my skin and pull my hair before it flapped away under my covers and disappeared.

Dreamologists call such experiences persistent dream images or hypnopompic hallucinations. They are sometimes accompanied by sleep paralysis, which, as in incubus attacks, entails a temporary inability to move despite concentrated efforts.

Another type of persistent dream image occurs in verbal form, as if the "audible" content of a dream slightly outlasts the "visual." Occasionally, upon awakening, words are running through my mind, either in the form of a short phrase, which can be repetitive, or in a form similar to a story or lecture. They "sound" exactly like my own thoughts, being presented in the same manner that I imagine my own voice or recall the voice of someone else. Although the words flow effortlessly through my mind, just as during waking consciousness when I am thinking about something, the content seems foreign to my knowledge. The verbalizations can continue for a few seconds if I pay attention to them, but as soon as I move, or a physical noise disturbs me, or I focus on the outside world, they stop.

At the time the words form, they are clear and intelligible, but memory of their meaning usually vanishes instantly when I direct my attention away. If I concentrate, however, I can retain the last sentence or clause long enough to write it down or contemplate it during the day. Dream scientists refer to this type of phenomena as "spontaneously appearing qualitatively unusual thought processes and verbal constructions" and usually refer to them in the context of hypnagogic imagery rather than hypnopompic imagery.[12]

Another unusual type of dream, defined by Dr. Charles Tart,[13] is the high dream, so called because in these dreams the dream self "ingests" psychedelic drugs and experiences the effects of those substances just as vividly as if in physical reality the person actually takes mind altering chemicals and enters a "high" state of mind. These dream "highs" have a remarkable resemblance to actual drug-induced altered states produced in waking consciousness. Sometimes, after the dream, the effects linger in waking reality for a few minutes.

In the same category as high dreams we could include dreams in which the dream self consumes alcohol, with the dream body and mind becoming intoxicated. (One good thing about these dreams is that there is no hangover.)

It is interesting how the dream source can reproduce such convincing altered states of consciousness on the mental condition of the dream self, so similar to those produced in physical reality, without the actual ingestion of chemicals or alcohol. I would place high dreams and intoxication dreams on the dream continuum somewhere between vivid dreams and persistent dream images.

---

[12]Daniel L. Schacter, "The Hypnagogic State: A Critical Review of the Literature," *Psychological Bulletin* 83 (1976): 453.

[13]Tart, *Altered States of Consciousness*, pp. 171–176.

Closely related to high dreams and persistent dream images are orgasmic dreams in which the dream self has a sexual encounter with a dream lover, and the physical self wakes up in the middle of an orgasm as powerful and fulfilling as one in waking life with a physical partner.

From any of the segments of the dream continuum can be found a branch leading to another special kind of dream, a dream about having an OBE. Dreams of OBEs may become lucid, revert back to an ordinary dream, or lead to an actual conscious OBE, where they connect with another consciousness continuum, the OBE continuum.

Similar to OBE dreams are death dreams, which can also branch off from various points along the dream continuum. In death dreams, the dream self dies from some explicit cause and experiences being out of the dream representation of the physical body, and in a dream representation of an astral body. One of my friends had a remarkable example of a death dream.

One sweltering August day, she was trying to do some yard work, but the temperature soared several degrees over a hundred and finally drove her into her cooler home. Drained of energy, she lay down upon the sofa. It was about 5:00 P.M. when she turned on the television to listen to the news.

While a news story reported that people were dying of heat stroke in Europe, my friend dozed off, missing the number of people who had died and the country where the heat wave was taking place.

She dreamed she was walking along the road in front of her house. She could see her son sitting on the stoop and a dark complexioned man standing beside a two-tone blue convertible. The man was tall and thin, and looked as though he was on the verge of emaciation. His hair was greased straight back from the forehead, and he was wearing blue jeans, a yellow pullover shirt, and tennis shoes. The car was an older model Ford that looked as if it had seen better days.

My friend walked toward her son and the tall, lean man. The tremendous heat became overwhelming. She felt her strength wane, and became weaker and weaker, until she began to stagger. As she collapsed on the dusty road, her last "conscious" thought was that she only had a little farther to go if, somehow, she could just keep moving.

In the dream, the next thing my friend was aware of was that she was hovering above the dream representation of her incapacitated body, looking down at it as it lay upon the road. She saw her son and the stranger run toward her unconscious form below. From her floating astral form, she tried to tell them not to hurry because it was too late, but evidently her words were inaudible, for she saw the man lift her body into his arms and remark to her son that she was suffering from heat stroke and they would have to take her to the hospital.

My friend watched the scene below and called out repeatedly. Her son cried while the man carried her unconscious form to the car. They ignored her astral body and failed to hear her as she futilely attempted to get their attention.

Her frantic attempts to call out must have been what awakened her, because she was struggling about on the sofa when she returned to physical reality. She had been asleep for only about 20 minutes. As she pondered her dream, she thought that if death was that easy—just passing from one form to another—she'd quit worrying about it.

These different kinds of dreams range from unconscious dreams at one extreme to dream images persistiang in the waking world at the other extreme, and they show how different states of consciousness can be organized along a continuum based on the amount of waking consciousness present. As I have outlined it, the dream continuum can be modified to include all possible types of dreams and illustrates the existence of different levels of awareness relative to each other.

Integrating the Mind Spectrum

The dream continuum, the different kinds of dreams, and related stages of mental functioning can be used as a model to interpret the complex interactions among the different levels of awareness that make up our psychological processes—the interplay of the conscious, subconscious, and unconscious. Most importantly, in the present context, the dream continuum and the levels between waking and sleeping contain openings with pathways to alternative states of consciousness, what we could call the superconscious, levels of awareness where extrasensory perception (ESP) and OBEs take place.

By learning to function consciously along the dream continuum, it is possible to integrate the conscious, subconscious, unconscious, and superconscious to explore these paths to alternative levels of reality. The four terms, conscious, subconscious, unconscious, and superconscious, refer to the following meanings throughout this book.

The conscious part of the mind includes mental activity that we are aware of—immediate perceptions from the senses and activated mental processes such as memory, emotion, imagery, reasoning, creativity, decision making, learning, and thought. Conscious observation of the external physical world includes discerning publically verifiable qualitative and quantitative information, categorical knowledge and rules of society, and events near and far, first hand or otherwise. Conscious observation of the internal world includes comprehending information from the senses (hunger, pain, body position), deductive reasoning, logical induction, inference, problem solving, reflection on past experience, and emotion. All of these external and internal concepts, intangible as well as tangible, make up cognitive reality. The conscious mind has the ability to selectively direct attention to any of the particular processes that allow us to perceive and experience cognitive reality and to deliberately choose and execute actions according to conditions and goals.

Through the use of these abilities, the conscious mind has three important functions: monitoring, interpreting, and controlling. It is responsible for monitoring the internal and external environments, interpreting the conditions perceived, and controlling behavior in response to stability or change. Through the formation of language, the conscious permits communication as it carries out these three main functions in association with others.[14]

The subconscious consists of cognitive information that both the unconscious and conscious have access to, but of which we are intermittently aware. The conscious operates selectively in monitoring the environment, only registering as much information as it can manage directly; therefore many perceptions that go unnoticed by the conscious are retained in the subconscious. Information that the conscious perceives directly is stored in the subconscious as well, in the form of memory. As ongoing thoughts and events take place, each requires attention in its turn, with new activities constantly pushing old ones aside, creating a stream of consciousness that flows into the subconscious.

Learned responses are also stored in the subconscious, making it unnecessary for the conscious mind to deliberate on such automatic actions as walking, avoiding sudden danger, or riding a bicycle.

Conscious and subconscious contents include external and internal information from four sources—the senses, intellectual concepts, feelings, and inspiration, dividing our cognizance into four levels, physical (earth), mental (air), emotional (water), and spiritual (fire).

The conscious and subconscious contain cognitive information; a different kind of knowledge resides in the unconscious. Unconscious mental processes and contents are blocked from direct conscious access. Rather than experiencing them directly through introspection, we can learn about them only through inference or indirect methods.[15]

---

[14]J. F. Kihlstrom, "Conscious, Subconscious, Unconscious: A Cognitive Perspective," *The Unconscious Reconsidered*, Kenneth S. Bowers and Donald Meichenbaum, eds. (New York: Wiley & Sons, 1984), pp. 150–151.

[15]J. F. Kihlstrom, "Conscious, Subconscious, Unconscious: A Cognitive Perspective," p. 156.

The unconscious contains the neurophysiological processes that keep the physical body alive and healthy under ideal conditions, or those that cause disease and death through psychosomatic illnesses under adverse conditons. The unconscious creates, maintains, and controls the brain, nervous system, and nerve impulses, and mediates between the organic mental apparatus and mental activity. It operates through electric impulses and chains of biochemical reactions that take place automatically, outside our volition. Along complex systems comprised of billions of neurons (nerve cells), organic and inorganic substances, and a vast array of supporting cells, the unconscious actively regulates cognition through the subconscious and conscious parts of our minds by converting thoughts into electrochemical reactions. The unconscious mind codes thoughts, messages, and responses in biophysiological pathways which scientists are just beginning to understand.

The unconscious also contains deeply embedded responses to events—mental processings of emotional reactions which influence beliefs and attitudes, affect the physical body, impact behavior, and form self-image. Repressed anger, unresolved trauma, and forgotten fears lurk in the unconscious, beneath our awareness, where they interact with the subconscious and conscious to create functional disturbances in the psychological system. The physical expression of unconscious conflicts can cause psychosomatic disorders. Love, harmony, and strength also form unconscious mental pathways resulting in tendencies toward health, balance, productivity, and creativity. Indirect methods used to reveal unconscious mental contents include word associations, hypnosis, and study of dreams.

The term superconscious is used to refer to the part of the mind involved in ESP, which includes telepathy, clairvoyance, clairaudience, precognition, retrocognition, and psychometry. Telepathy is the transfer of thoughts, feelings, or images directly from the mind of one person to another without using physical means. Clairvoyance is the observation of objects or events concealed from or outside the normal range of the ordinary physical senses. Clairaudience is the supernormal hearing of sounds or verbalizations. Precognition is the present perception of future events and retrocognition similarly pertains to past events. Psychometry is the paranormal perception of an object's history or psychic vibrations through touch.

Together, the conscious, subconscious, unconscious, and superconscious animate the lump of organic matter we call the brain. Could the mind spectrum have more?

The Higher Self

From the earliest ages of cultural development throughout human experience, different societies have believed that individuals consist of more than a physical body with a brain and a functioning mind. Most belief systems envision a spiritual part—a subliminal, nonphysical soul that survives physical death and is the vehicle which contains the true self. While avoiding excess anthropomorphism, we could think of this spiritual part as a higher self which oversees the conscious, subconscious, unconscious, and superconscious levels of mental activity. The higher self would function as an aggregate level of consciousness, aware of the contents of these four mental layers and perhaps others which are outside the experiential abilities of our organic brains at our present stage of physical, intellectual, emotional, and spiritual evolution.

If we can accept the existence of a higher self as a cohesive element uniting the different types of consciousness, perhaps we can imagine it also forming a connection between personal physical reality as experienced through those levels of consciousness and higher planes of reality of which we are normally oblivious.

The higher planes of reality could be composed of matter and energy systems beyond our material space and time dimensions. If so, the higher planes would be undetectible by our physical bodies' senses or technological instruments designed from physical matter to measure aspects of the physical world.

Perhaps such systems of matter and energy are the realm of knowledge, wisdom, and ability transcending that of physical reality; there may be higher energy systems made up of principles presently known, those yet to be learned, and others incomprehensible at our current stage of development.

If the higher self is in contact with such higher planes of existence, and if the conscious mind could form a more substantial link with the higher self, perhaps we could accelerate our evolution toward health, knowledge, peace, and wisdom. Communication with a higher self in contact with planes of reality beyond our normal conscious perception could explain experiences such as psychic healing, divine inspiration, ESP, and OBEs. Through a connection with invisible worlds on higher planes of reality, the higher self could have access to hidden resources of wisdom and knowledge to apply to underdeveloped potentials.

"Thoughts are things," is an ancient mystical belief, and implies that thoughts exist as a type of material or form of energy. Albert Einstein proved that nothing is created and nothing is destroyed. Matter is converted into new forms of matter or energy, and energy is converted into new forms of energy or matter. Since thoughts are electrochemical energy forms, it seems plausible that every thought that was ever formed must still exist somewhere in a form of energy or matter.

Knowledge could also exist as thoughts in energy forms on higher planes of reality. Perhaps the higher self has access to knowledge energy forms and other energy forms as well, such as health, love, and wisdom. Such a higher self, being an aggregate consciousness of the self and being in touch with higher planes of reality, could act as an inner counselor of tremendous power. A higher self with such power could lead the individual along pathways to the highest and deepest levels of awareness by penetrating the extremes of both the outer and inner worlds. Such far-reaching awareness would stimulate personal growth beyond preconceived limits to new dimensions of understanding self, the universe of which it is a part, and the relationship between self and the universe.

Hopefully, the concept of a mental spectrum consisting of the hypnagogic and hypnopompic states, the dream continuum, the OBE continuum, the four levels of consciousness, and a higher self will help in understanding suggestions, given throughout the remainder of this book, that attempt to extend awareness to invisible worlds around us. Extended awareness of the invisible worlds includes actual visitation in a nonmaterial body. A journey through our own mental recesses, into and out of ourselves, should improve psychological balance, increase creativity, reveal hidden powers of ESP, and prepare the way to experience the astral plane with full waking consciousness.

Chapter 3

Journey to the Center of the Self

Sometime around 3.5 billion years ago, primitive, living cells began forming on Earth and started the slow process of evolution that led to the species present today. From this process emerged the human brain, which believes itself to be the ultimate biological structure. It consists of more than 100 billion neurons!

A significant proportion of those neurons are more active during REM sleep, or dreaming, than during wakefulness.[1] Furthermore, out of a normal life span of 74 years, about six years and nine months are spent dreaming. Other animals dream, too. Cats, dogs, monkeys, and other mammals have REM stages of sleep and are assumed to be dreaming during that time. The chances are remote that anatomy and physiology would evolve to enable so much time spent dreaming unless it serves a vital function, because in evolutionary terms, only the efficient survive. We can therefore logically assume that dreaming must be necessary.

Dream deprivation experiments offer further evidence that dreaming is necessary. After being awakened from all REM sleep for several consecutive nights, a significant number of human research subjects suffered impairment of mental ability and deterioration of emotional stability. They became irritable and anxious and had difficulty concentrating. During the nights following dream deprivation, these subjects spent an inordinate

[1]J. Allan Hobson, *The Dreaming Brain* (New York: Basic Books, 1988), pp. 157–202.

amount of time in REM sleep, as though they were making up for the loss. Then they resumed normal sleep patterns, mental ability, and emotional stability. Those who did not suffer mental and emotional degeneration had shifted dreaming to NREM stages of sleep.[2]

As the mind drifts into the hypnagogic state, slumbers through the first four stages of sleep, and then bursts into a REM phase, the brain undergoes an energy trade-off; the activity of some of the neurons is inhibited while other neurons become excited, creating a shift in the electrical impulses of the brain. When we awaken, the electrical activity of the brain shifts back to the waking set of neurons. It is reasonable to assume that as different states of awareness are experienced on different parts of the dream continuum, different combinations of neurons switch on and off.

With concentration and practice, we can learn to observe subjectively, through introspection, the functional changes of the neurological shifts and gain some insight into the purpose of the biological machinery resulting from 3.5 billion years of evolution. If we look inward, deep into the center of ourselves, into the inner workings of our minds during waking, sleeping, and the transition states between, we can discover some truly amazing abilities of that three-pound mass of cells making up the human brain.

Dreams are a reflection of the forces behind the neurological shifts. Whether dreams are whimsical fragments or vivid psychological thrillers, the thoughts, images, and actions composing them had to be conceptualized.

When I focus on dreams, I wonder what intelligence formed the concepts they represent. Could such detailed and complex creations originate from an external source, as introspection suggests, or are they emitted by a part of my mind from which I normally remain separate?

---

[2]Harry Fiss, "An Empirical Foundation for a Self Psychology of Dreaming," in *Cognition and Dream Research*, Robert E. Haskell, Ph.D., ed., a special issue of *The Journal of Mind and Behavior* 7, nos. 2 and 3 (1986).

What is the dream source?

Whatever it is, wherever it is, out in a collective unconscious or deep within my being, I consider the "author" of my dreams to be a remote part of my psyche, an inner genius of the great beyond that creates imaginative psychological dramas for the purpose of integrating the conscious, subconscious, unconscious, and superconscious levels of my mind, an inner genius that organizes different kinds of information gathered by different levels of awareness, an inner genius that I refer to as my higher self. Everybody has one.

If we learn to function consciously along the dream continuum, and in the hypnagogic and hypnopompic states, and if we study the results of others who have explored the mystical worlds contained therein, we may begin to expose some of the secrets of the depths of awareness which we usually ignore. Within those depths of awareness we can discover at least three functions of dreams—self-understanding, problem solving or creative inspiration, and psychic understanding.

By providing a communication channel between the conscious mind and the higher self, dreams can furnish astonishing insight into the unconscious psychological forces within; they can become a source of inspiration for increased creativity and solutions to practical problems; and they can reveal hidden aspects of the past, present, and future through the operation of ESP. Exploration of the dream continuum can deepen understanding of oneself to promote psychological balance and result in reduced anxiety, more energy, increased optimism, and greater motivation. Through practical application of creative and problem solving information received from dreams, physical life can become more rewarding on an aesthetic level and more successful on a vocational level. Psychic dreams can relay information from the superconscious—messages that cultivate our skills of telepathy, clairvoyance, clairaudience, retrocognition, and precognition. Expanding awareness along the dream continuum also opens the mental pathways to OBEs.

To integrate dreaming consciousness with waking consciousness, it is necessary to retain more dream memories in waking as well as to involve more awareness while dreaming. Learning to function consciously along the dream continuum involves remembering dreams, interpreting dreams, inducing dreams, and controlling dreams. While these four skills are being developed, it is possible to venture (or stumble) farther into less known realms of awareness and explore other, normally invisible, worlds around us, worlds referred to in esoteric literature as the astral plane.

To expand awareness along the dream continuum, it is necessary to work from both ends of the sleep–dream cycle, to utilize both the hypnagogic state and the hypnopompic state. By starting from the waking state and maintaining awareness as far as possible into the hypnagogic state, the unique characteristics of this state can be used to strengthen awareness in the deeper stages of sleep, to induce dreams, and to control dreams. The hypnopompic state, with its own special properties, can be used to go back into the dream world with increased awareness or bring aspects of the dream world into the waking world. Beyond the hypnopompic state, it is important to make a concentrated effort to remember dreams upon waking, understand their meanings, and relate them to daily life. In so doing, awareness is increased at all levels of consciousness, and all levels of consciousness are integrated to work together. This creates mental synergy.

To benefit more from the higher self, the conscious mind can make an effort to develop two-way communication with it by embarking upon a journey to the inner self, by following pathways through different levels of awareness to the dreaming mind. The conscious mind can develop and maintain this connection by learning to function along the dream continuum—to interact with the dreaming mind through dream recall, interpretation, induction, and intervention.

Dream Recall

Remembering dreams is the first step, essential to conscious functioning along the dream continuum. It is necessary to bring more unconscious dreams to conscious memory and put more dream fragments together to form complete episodes.

One method used in learning to remember dreams is autosuggestion—when you are lying in bed just before going to sleep, tell yourself you will remember your dreams upon awakening. Repeat the intention to remember your dreams over and over as you pass into the hypnagogic state, which is a state of consciousness more susceptible to suggestion than ordinary waking consciousness.[3] Try to hold the thought of remembering your dreams for as long as possible while you pass from waking to sleeping. Then, after you have slept, when you start to awaken, hold still. Dream researchers have found that subjects who learned to emerge from sleep to waking while remaining in the same position significantly increased their dream recall.[4] Try to wake up slowly, turn your thoughts away from waking reality, and search inward for the dream world from which you just emerged. You may prolong the hypnopompic state, increasing awareness of fading dream images, or even go back into a dream with partial or total waking consciousness.

After waking, as dream memories blend with waking consciousness, hold the images in your mind, reexperience the emotions, and follow the clues backward and forward from the first fragments you recall. Concentrate on the pieces as they come together until you comprehend all of the dream content that comes into awareness. Then think back to the previous day's events to see if you can make a connection. Associating dream events with physical events establishes the dream material more firmly in the waking mind. As soon as you think you have a secure grasp upon your dream memories, write them down in a notebook kept beside the bed, or record them by whatever means is available, because if you wait until later, there is a good chance that the dream memories will vanish. They are elusive.

---

[3]Daniel L. Schacter, "The Hypnagogic State: A Critical Review of the Literature," *Psychological Bulletin* 83 (1976): 468.
[4]Hobson, *The Dreaming Brain*, p. 142.

Sometimes it is more effective to write down any dream fragments, visions, thoughts, or feelings immediately upon recall, no matter how insignificant they seem at the time. Then just relax, and hold the incident in mind. Usually, associated dream parts will soon filter through to consciousness. As soon as new dream segments enter consciousness, write them down, also. It is all right if the material is out of sequence; you can always rearrange it later. Eventually you should have an entire dream episode.

If an alarm clock or activity from the physical world interferes with your awakening time, just use autosuggestion while drifting into sleep to tell yourself to wake up half an hour earlier. I have succeeded at this regularly, but it still surprises me when I wake up, look at the clock, and see the hands on the exact minute that I told myself to awaken.

After practicing autosuggestion and either of these recall methods for two or three weeks, you will probably have enough dream material to keep you writing well into the morning, if the time is available. It is amazing how well autosuggestion works!

If it fails, however, there are some other methods you can use to help stimulate dream memories. For example, practice using your memory to recall daily events. Every so often during the day and before going to sleep at night, try to recall what you did earlier that day, or earlier that week, until your mind becomes accustomed to using its memory. Then, when you wake up in the morning, try to remember what went on in your consciousness while you were asleep. Memory is like many other skills—the more you use it, the better it works. This applies to memories in dream life as well as in physical life, with transference of ability from one to the other.

Persistence with these methods should stimulate remembrance of more and more dream material until eventually several dreams a night can be recalled on a regular basis. While strengthening dream recall, keep writing down dream fragments and dreams; writing dreams down substantiates them in physical reality and seems to form a more tangible bridge between waking consciousness and other levels of the mind. This connection creates easier access to the higher self and makes it possible to function with increased awareness along the dream continuum and associated spectrums of consciousness.

Eventually you will probably have more dream material than time to write it down if, as most people, you have other responsibilities. This is a definite sign that you have accomplished your goal of improving dream recall. Now, instead of trying to write down all of your dreams, choose a few which capture your interest and write detailed accounts, keeping them organized in a dream journal. As communication with the higher self improves, your conscious mind will know which dreams contain the most important messages, and these are the ones upon which you should concentrate.

Dream Interpretation

The second major skill to be mastered in learning to increase awareness along the dream continuum is dream interpretation. Dream interpretation can be learned as dream recall becomes proficient, because the best way to begin learning dream interpretation is the same as the best way to learn dream recall—by writing dreams down.

Somehow the actual process of writing dreams down can automatically trigger the waking mind to perceive the insights available from the dream world. Through the act of writing dreams down, sometimes their meaning crystalizes the instant the words mark the paper, sometimes it takes longer.

Telling a dream to someone else can have the same result. Through the verbalization of a dream, meanings can automatically take form as the dream becomes a part of physical life and the waking mind associates the dream elements to daily concerns. The listener can also provide instructive input. The important thing is that once a dream is expressed in some form, it becomes a part of your waking life and a means to reach the higher self. You should also write down verbalized dreams so you have a record of them.

Even dream material that appears silly or trivial should be written down while you are learning to interpret your dreams. Often a dream that appears meaningless or confusing upon awakening will reveal surprising insight after it is written down, set aside for a while, and reread from a fresh perspective. A diagnostic meaning or solution to a problem may then become clear, as if the higher self succeeded in transmitting useful information from the subconscious, unconscious, or superconscious to the conscious mind. Sometimes the conscious mind seems to require time to assimilate the dream symbolism and convert it into terms it can understand. The amount of time required could be a minute or two, a few hours, or many years.

It is gratifying when dream meanings arise on their own, but often dream interpretation requires extensive thought. Dream books are filled with a wide variety of approaches to dream interpretation and different methods may work for different people. Each person's higher self may have unique symbols and message formats for reaching the conscious mind. These symbols and concepts could originate in either the conscious mind or the higher self. There are three different kinds of symbols—acquired, personal, and archetypal.

To obtain an acquired symbol, for example, a person may read a popular book on dream interpretation and learn that a car may be a symbol for the self. If the conscious mind accepts this symbolism, the higher self may produce dreams using different types of motor vehicles to represent different aspects of the self, such as a sports car to represent the irresponsible self, a truck to represent the working self, or a motorcycle to represent the rebellious self.

Besides acquired symbols, the higher self may use personal symbols which already have specific meanings for the individual. People, animals, objects, or events that have gained significance in past situations become symbolic of particular patterns of emotion and behavior unique to each person. An example of a personal symbol may be a grandparent's home symbolizing a return to traditional values.

The higher self will also use archetypal symbolism to represent ideas that have a basis in universal, inherited thought. This includes general cultural and traditional values and taboos, such as life and death, love and hate, good and evil, friends and enemies, or hopes and fears. An example of an archetypal symbol would be the theme of death to represent transformation.

Any particular symbol could fit into one or more of these categories. To develop an instinct for dream symbols, it is helpful to read some of the dream interpretation books that are available, a few of which are listed in the bibliography. But remember, although many of the symbols written about may apply, each individual has a unique, personal system of dream symbolism.

It is easy to learn the meaning of many of the symbols your higher self uses in dreams. When you read through your dreams, watch for objects and situations that recur, and write them down in a list to keep track of them. Pick one that seems to have a special significance or attraction, relax while quietly holding this image in mind, and listen to the inner thoughts, ideas, associations, and feelings that spontaneously arise to consciousness. Write them down. Soon the meaning of that symbol will become clear. When it does, write the definition of that particular symbol in a personal dream dictionary. Do this for other objects, persons, animals, places, themes, and actions that appear in your dreams until you have a collection of uncoded symbols with which your higher self and conscious mind can communicate. Keep in mind that some symbols can have more than one meaning and the meanings can change over time.

If you find a symbol that puzzles you, watch for it as it recurs in dreams. Every time it appears, write the dream in your dream book with a brief account of the events, feelings, and concerns in your waking life during the few days prior to the dream, and then see if eventually you can make an association between the two.

Do not worry about getting the meanings of your dream symbols right or wrong. Be confident that if the symbol has meaning for you, it will be right. Even if your conscious mind comes up with a meaning different than the higher self intended in that particular dream, as long as the interpretation of the symbol has significance to you, the higher self may then incorporate it into future dreams with the definition you gave it.

As this project continues, knowledge of your dream symbols accumulates at an increasing rate, as one association triggers several more, and each of the new ones stimulates even more, until eventually, you have a whole system of symbols to translate the language of dreams.

As dream interpretation improves, a stronger connection is formed between the conscious mind and the higher self, and the conscious mind will become more alert along the dream continuum, more familiar with invisible worlds.

Rosalind Cartwright, a dream researcher, has learned from sleep laboratory work that a person's group of dreams occurring throughout a sleep–dream cycle constitutes a complete coherent statement, with each dream containing a singular meaning, but all of the dreams together forming a broader intellectual concept. The separate dreams explore different aspects of a situation, usually with the immediate present reflected in dreams in the early phases of the sleep–dream cycle, relationships to similar situations in the past found in midcycle dreams, and the present and future oriented ideas represented in the later stages of the sleep–dream cycle.[5]

The patterns of related and contrasting dream themes and much dream material from the early REM periods may be lost unless all dreams in a sleep–dream cycle are captured immediately. The entire series of dreams occuring during a sleep–dream cycle is much more useful in dream interpretaion than just the last one or two, because the group as a whole represents interrelated aspects of a particular situation.

To retain the complete series of a night's dreams, it is helpful to use autosuggestion to wake up after each REM phase dur-

---

[5]Rosalind Dymond Cartwright, *Night Life: Explorations in Dreaming* (Upper Saddle River, NJ: Prentice Hall, 1977), p. 129.

ing a sleep–dream cycle. As you enter the hypnagogic state before going to sleep, mentally repeat the intention to wake up and remember each dream as soon as it is finished. When you wake up and your conscious mind grasps a dream, write it down immediately to actualize it in physical reality, or at least jot a few key words to provide a trigger to remember the entire dream later. Then use autosuggestion again to prepare the conscious mind to receive the next dream statement in the cycle. Upon completion of the sleep–dream cycle, after writing down all the dreams in as much detail as possible, a common theme should be discernible.

Sleep lab experiments have demonstrated that during sleep it is possible for subjects to realize when their dreams are taking place—that we have the ability to keep part of our consciousness alert enough to observe when we are dreaming and respond.[6] Therefore, with concentration and practice, it should be possible to use autosuggestion to intercept all the dreams of a sleep–dream cycle before they fade away.

As you become more adept at dream interpretation, you will be intrigued to discover that dreams are made up of complex symbolism with many different levels of meaning. An examination of dream content will reveal surprising insights into situations.

Self-understanding dreams can help us achieve deeper understanding of confusing emotions, social fulfillment, and goal attainment. Self-awareness is the first step to solving all personal problems and improving social interaction. Dream interpretation can greatly enhance self-awareness by indicating, directly or symbolically, aspects of our personalities perceived by the higher self, but missed by our consciousness. Dreams can expose unrecognized causes of emotional and interpersonal conflicts and provide solutions to the problems that arise from those conflicts. Only when we become aware of destructive tendencies in ourselves and others can we begin to modify behavior into more constructive habits.

---

[6]Cartwright, *Night Life: Explorations in Dreaming*, p. 35.

One of the reasons dreams can be difficult to interpret is because they often show negative personality traits, attitudes, and behavior through unique, sometimes humorous psychodramas that display possibly painful knowledge of ourselves and those around us. If the conscious mind wants to avoid information it is too immature to accept, it will use psychological defense mechanisms to block out truth that hurts. It may be difficult to confront that pain, but trust the higher self. Remember, it understands all the mental layers and will work to integrate them into a healthy, happy, well-functioning whole. The conscious determination to tolerate the pain and grow from it will prepare the conscious, subconscious, unconscious, and superconscious to combine their efforts to acknowledge the higher self's power to heal emotional wounds.

Dreams also show us our favorable attributes, which can be used in positive ways.

In dream research, study after study has shown that dream content is related to the dreamer's emotional concerns—that dreams provide direct access to the emotional themes underlying waking life. Dreams reflect past and present situations and future hopes and concerns with associated feelings, and paying attention to dreams is a useful way to get in touch with the inner self.

Dream interpretation allows the higher self to expose to conscious awareness concealed motives, obscure needs and goals, inner conflicts which need to be resolved, incomplete personal relationships that seek closure, and repressed feelings and impulses which find a safe intrapsychic outlet through dreams. Our higher selves create acquired, personal, and archetypal symbols to represent these psychological conditions and express them repeatedly in recurring dreams or dream themes in an attempt to resolve the inner conflict and transform energy wasted on emotional discomfort into psychic power that can flow more freely and be available for constructive enterprises.

When you read through your dreams, watch for themes concerning trauma, childhood experiences, interpersonal relationships, and spirituality. You may discover some habitual behavior patterns, innate attitudes, or outmoded beliefs that can cause blocks in your physical life and repeated failures in goal attainment. Once psychological balance is attained, problem solving dreams, creative inspiration dreams, and spiritual dreams become more frequent. As you become more proficient at interpreting dreams and identifying the symbolism, you will build a better rapport with the unconscious levels of your mind and experience more of the higher consciousness types of dreams on the continuum.

If we pay attention to our dreams and learn to understand their symbolism, we can see outstanding examples in which the higher self provides practical solutions to creative projects or technical problems through goal oriented or problem solving dreams. The dream content is related to the solution of a problem or the attainment of a goal, either directly or indirectly, and often in symbolic form. Upon waking from a problem solving dream, the conscious mind experiences a flash of insight—the dream may only symbolically solve the problem, but when the correct associations are made, the answer is clear. Dreams can be a dynamic source of insight into intellectual and practical problems, or valuable inspiration for creative pursuits. Dream history is full of famous examples of important discoveries, inventions, or creative works that resulted from dream messages.

A dream provided the solution to a difficult problem in organic chemistry: the German chemist Friedrich August Kekule von Stradonitz (1829–1896) was bewildered by the chemical structure of the benzene molecule until he had a dream about a snake biting its tail. Upon waking he realized what the snake meant—rather than consisting of a chain of carbon atoms, as previously discovered organic compounds, the benzene molecule exists as a ring of carbon atoms. Stradonitz' idea proved to be correct, and the understanding of carbon rings opened up a whole new division of organic chemistry, the aromatic compounds. Modern organic chemists still distinguish between "open chain" and "ring" molecular structure.

The German-born American pharmacologist and physiologist Otto Loewe (1873–1961) found the answer to a frog heart experiment in a dream. He isolated the chemical acetylcholine from the vagus nerve of one frog and used it to control the heartbeat of another frog. Loew used the results from his classic frog experiment to formulate a theory of chemical transmission of nerve impulses, and shared with Sir Henry Hallett Dale the 1936 Nobel Prize in physiology and medicine for the discovery.[7] Ironically, modern dream researchers have learned to induce and inhibit acetylcholine responses experimentally to control REM sleep and dreaming so they can study the biochemical processes that take place in the brain during different states of consciousness.[8]

Some other scientific problems allegedly solved by dreams include Albert Einstein's (1879–1955) Theory of Relativity, which was symbolized by a sled ride, and Dmitri Ivanovitch Mendeleev's (1834–1907) Periodic Table of Elements, which was represented in a dream by the structure of chamber music.[9]

Technological insight has also been revealed through dreams in surprising ways. Elias Howe (1819–1867), American inventor of the sewing machine, had a nightmare in which cannibals were boiling him alive, and to keep him in the pot they jabbed him with spears which had holes in the pointed ends. Upon waking and thinking about the holes in the sharp ends, he solved the problem he had been struggling with, how to design the sewing machine needle.[10]

Excellent artistic creations, also, are credited to dreams. Two English writers gained inspiration from the dream world; Samuel Taylor Coleridge (1772–1834) claimed he received the lines of the poem "Kubla Khan" in a dream, and Arthur Christopher Benson (1862–1925) said he dreamed the whole poem "The Phoenix." The Scottish writer Robert Louis Stevenson (1850–1894) reported that his dreams were responsible for many

---

[7]Hobson, *The Dreaming Brain*, p. 117.

[8]Hobson, *The Dreaming Brain*, p. 119.

[9]Jeremy Taylor, *Dream Work* (Ramsey, NJ: Paulist Press, 1983), p. 7.

[10]Robert L. Van de Castle, *Our Dreaming Mind* (New York: Ballantine Books, 1994), p. 37.

of his story plots, including *Doctor Jekyll and Mister Hyde.* The Italian composer Giuseppe Tartini (1692–1770) described a dream he had of the devil playing a violin, from which he awoke to write down the music that became the *Devil's Trill Sonata.*[11]

Apparently, problem solving and goal oriented dreams are fairly common; according to a study done in 1892 by Charles M. Child, one-third of his sample of 186 students reported that they had solved problems during sleep.[12] This would be a worthwhile subject for current investigation using modern research methods.

Dreams can provide indirect solutions to problems; the surface content of a problem solving or goal oriented dream may be forgotten as soon as the flash of insight occurs upon waking. I had a problem solving dream which revealed the theme and organization of this book, but upon waking and receiving the sudden inspiration, I forgot the dream; all that remained in my conscious mind was the knowledge of how to arrange the material with which I had been struggling and a connection with a vague dream fragment.

Another type of creative inspiration dream is more direct. One of my hobbies is oil painting, and on numerous occasions I have had dreams in which visions of beautiful, original paintings flashed before my "eyes." Unless I sketched them soon after waking, they evaporated from my conscious memory. I have also received songs, poetry, and fashion designs from dreams. For me, all that is necessary is to keep an open mind and pay attention.

All of the examples show that dreams can provide a dramatic and dynamic synthesis of subconscious, symbolic ideas and conscious information that facilitates creativity in practical and artistic endeavors.

Besides increasing self-awareness and assisting problem solving and creativity, dream interpretation can demonstrate ESP. In several studies of ESP cases in the United States, Ger-

---

[11]William C. Dement, *Some Must Watch While Some Must Sleep* (San Francisco: San Francisco Book Company, 1976), pp. 96–99.

[12]Dement, *Some Must Watch While Some Must Sleep*, p. 99.

many, Great Britain, and India, researchers found that up to two-thirds of ESP experiences occurred in dreams.[13]

If you write down and study your dreams carefully and correlate them with a brief diary of physical life, you may be surprised to discover that many of them are psychic, or show evidence of ESP. Psychic dreams are usually of three kinds: precognitive, clairvoyant, and telepathic, but clairaudient and retrocognitive dreams could also occur. Psychic dreams are probably activated by our natural psychic ability, or ESP, which functions, or can be focused upon more easily, when our attention to daily concerns is held in abeyance, such as when we are deeply relaxed, in the hypnagogic or hypnopompic states, or asleep.

Dream researchers believe that spontaneous precognitive dreams occur more frequently than either spontaneous clairvoyant or telepathic dreams.[14] Although many psychic dreams are precognitive, the dream representation of future events may be so disguised or clouded with symbolism that they seem to be ordinary dreams until studied later. I have read my personal accounts of dreams that I have written down over the past twenty years and have been amazed at how many had precognitive implications. (Some of those dreams I hope never come true!) Precognitive dreams may portray events of the future hours, days, or years before they occur in physical time.

Occasionally, instead of using a lot of symbols, precognitive dreams show exactly what will happen in the future. In 1986, I wrote down a dream that I was teaching algebra and apprehensive about whether I could remember math well enough to teach it. At the time of the dream, in physical reality, I consciously had no intensions to teach math or anything else, but circumstances led to a career change and my acceptance, in 1990, of a position as a college algebra instructor. The apprehension motivated me to prepare more thoroughly for the assignment.

---

[13]Montague Ullman, Stanley Krippner, and Allen Vaughan, *Dream Telepathy* (New York: Macmillan, 1973), p. 24.

[14]Ullman, et al, *Dream Telepathy*, p. 204.

If we carefully analyze previous dreams, we can see in them predictions of events that occured later, diagnosis of the causes, and corrective action that could have been taken to prepare for, solve, or avoid problems or benefit from opportunities yet to come. Unfortunately, there is no known way that I am aware of to positively identify a dream as precognitive until after the event takes place in physical reality. Even then, we cannot be sure if it was a real prophetic illumination or only a coincidence.

There are, however, possible clues to indicate that a dream may be precognitive, or psychic in some other way. Psychic dreams often appear clearer and more realistic than ordinary dreams, with less symbolism. Sometimes psychic dreams are accompanied with or followed by certain feelings, such as heightened feelings of significance or conviction, which may indicate that the dream is psychic. Special visual, audial, or other sensory effects may be present in psychic dreams and absent from ordinary dreams, such as unusual lighting, strange sounds, or bodily feelings and sensations.

One night I had a dream about a dear friend whom I had not seen or talked to for about a year. The dream was lighted by a diffuse, blue light, as if I was looking through a camera lens with a blue filter. The light was serene and of extraordinary beauty. Within a day or two, my friend called me and we got together; our relationship acquired a new depth of love and understanding that neither of us had experienced before. The blue light may have been a clue that the dream was precognitive.

Even though precognitive dreams may seem to be of limited value in seeing the future at the time they occur, by looking back upon them after the external events they foresaw have taken place, the conscious mind can become convinced that the higher self has the ability of precognition. Assured of this ability, the conscious mind becomes more open to the possibility of precognition, and by removing blocks of preconceived limitations, allows the higher self to become more proficient at communicating precognition.

In clairvoyant dreams, the superconscious level of the mind accesses remote or concealed exterior information concerning present events and situations either related or unrelated to our lives.

At Athens State College in Alabama, a research project indicated that it is possible for subjects to dream clairvoyantly to perceive the contents of cards sealed in envelopes and placed either on a nightstand or under the pillow. The correct responses were far above those expected by chance alone and improved over repeated trials.[15]

Telepathic dreams are dreams in which direct mind to mind communication takes place, with the dream self being either the receiver or the sender. Sleep laboratory studies of dream telepathy have indicated that people who believe in the possibility of ESP, are relaxed in a lab atmosphere, and have good dream recall are likely to be successful in receiving a telepathic dream sent by an experimentor. In one study, fifty six out of eighty such subjects reported dreams that corresponded with randomly picked target pictures that were used for subject matter to be telepathically sent.[16] Furthermore, dream telepathy experiments have shown a higher incidence of success than similar experiments with subjects who were awake.[17]

Telepathic dreams could function as a means of communication between friends and loved ones when the subject matter on the sender's mind is too painful or embarrassing for a candid discussion in waking life. The dreaming self has a greater detachment from the problems of a close friend or loved one and through sleep is more open to telepathic messages given out by others. Information transmitted through telepathic dreams could help disclose major concerns and problems encountered by those near us. The loved one's higher self may be sending messages concerning obvious problems such as fears, frustra-

---

[15]Joe Slate, *Psychic Phenomena* (Jefferson, NC: McFarland, 1988), p. 89.
[16]Ullman, et al, *Dream Telepathy*, p. 206.
[17]*Dream Telepathy*, p. 206.

tions, and anxieties, or problems that are not apparent to the waking consciousness, such as intolerance, low self-esteem, or addictive behavior. The dreamer may also send out telepathic information for similar reasons.

One night I dreamed that one of my close friends, an attractive young woman, was driving her van along a hilly, curvy coastal road. She deliberately drove the van off the road and caused it to roll down an embankment. As the dust settled and the overturned van rocked to a halt, I shuddered, unable to bear the thought of her being injured or killed. Then she emerged from the van uninjured, looked at me, and smiled.

Upon awakening, I thought the van symbolized her life situation, a family woman with a husband and two small sons, and the road symbolized her life path, in which her marriage had ups and downs and changes of directions. I was not surprised when a few weeks later she phoned and told me she had left her husband and was getting divorced. This dream could have had precognitive as well as telepathic implications, but, due to the nature of that particular situation; I understand why my friend was reluctant to discuss her divorce plans until the appropriate time.

As with precognitive dreams, there is no way that I am aware of to immediately varify a clairvoyant dream or a telepathic dream without comparing the dream content with actual physical events. This is the psychic dream paradox.

As you explore dream interpretation, you will find numerous examples of self-understanding dreams, creative and problem solving dreams, and psychic dreams. Unraveling the complicated networks of information presented in dreams reveal a higher self of far superior wisdom, intelligence, creativity, and psychic power than we ever imagined possible within ourselves.

Dream Induction

When you have become adept at dream recall and interpretation, instead of passively waiting to receive the valuable messages they contain, try dream induction, or controlling the subject matter of your dreams before they occur.

Two early investigators in this area of dream study were the French scientist Alfred Maury (1817–1892) and his colleague, the self-educated Marquis Marie Jean Leon Harvey de Saint-Denis. Both Maury and Saint-Denis used hypnagogic imagery to induce dreams. In fact, it was Maury who, in 1848, coined the term "hypnagogic" based upon the Greek words, *hypno*, meaning sleep, and *agagos*, meaning induce.[18] Maury studied the effects of pre-sleep stimuli on hypnagogic imagery and dreams. Saint-Denis studied the linkage between an emotional feeling and a person or idea. He practiced holding that emotion in consciousness while going to sleep and during sleep to induce dreams.[19] The importance of both Maury's and Saint-Denis' work lies in the use of the self as experimental subject and the connection between hypnagogic imagery and dream incubation.

Dream investigators have found that contemplation of a topic, problem, or goal before going to sleep can precipitate a dream about the subject matter, the solution to the problem, or fresh ideas about how to attain the goal.[20] The hypnagogic state, characterized by disconnected and spontaneous thoughts, images, sounds, and feelings, is a state of consciousness in which the mind is particularly receptive to suggestions either presented by the self or an outside source. Researchers have shown that the subject matter of dreams can be influenced by suggestions presented during the hypnagogic state.[21]

---

[18]Schacter, "The Hypnagogic State: A Critical Review of the Literature": 454.
[19]*The Dreaming Brain*, pp. 32–36.
[20]For more information on this, see Ann Faraday, *The Dream Game*; Patricia Garfield, *Creative Dreaming*; William C. Dement, *Some Must Watch While Some Must Sleep*; Rosalind Dymond Cartwright, *Night Life: Explorations in Dreaming*; Gayle Delaney, *Living Your Dreams*; Joe H. Slate, *Psychic Phenomena*; Alex Tanous and Timothy Gray, *Dreams, Symbols, and Psychic Power*; and Patricia Maybruck, *Romantic Dreams*.
[21]Slate, *Psychic Phenomena*, p. 88.

To induce a dream, begin from waking consciousness by deciding what kind of a dream you want to experience. You could consider a self-understanding dream, a creative or problem solving dream, or even a psychic dream, but to start out, it is probably best to try something simple, such as dreaming about a specific object, person, animal, or place, or perhaps one activity, such as driving or swimming.

Before going to sleep, decide what you want to appear in your dream and write it in your dream book in the space for your next dream. As you enter the hypnagogic state, hold that item or experience in your thoughts and tell yourself you will dream about it. Remind yourself that you will remember the dream upon awakening. Concentrate upon the desired dream fragment as you become drowsy. When thoughts wander, turn them back to the intended subject. Keep bringing your mental focus upon the desired dream every time pictures form in your mind and crowd out your thoughts. Try to change these spontaneous hypnagogic images into the selected item. When you wake up, remember your dream and write it in your dream book below the statement you wrote before going to sleep.

The two entries might match. If so, go on to something more complicated next time. If the entries differ, however, just set them aside for awhile and later review them. Consider the item you wrote down before sleeping and see what associations come to mind. Then consider the subject matter of the dream and related associations. Try to find a connection between the waking statement, the dream content, and any of the related associations. If you discover a relationship, make a note of it after the record of the dream. Whether or not you make a connection, repeat the experiment with any modifications you feel are necessary the next time you go to sleep. If you keep trying, eventually you should succeed at dream induction.

When you have mastered the induction of simple dream elements, you are ready to try something more difficult, such as the solution to a problem or insight into a personal matter. Continue to write your dream induction goals in your dream book.

Begin more complicated dream induction from the waking state by telling your higher self that you are open to communication through your dreams. Declare to yourself that you will remember and understand messages presented in the form of dreams to your conscious mind. Assure yourself of all the benefits you will gain from messages you receive from your higher self. Reinforce these ideas during waking hours as well as just before you drift off to sleep.

Since it has been shown that it may be possible to induce psychic dreams through hypnagogic suggestion, dream induction could be used to help offset the psychic dream paradox by psychic dream induction. To induce a psychic dream, as you are going through the process of autosuggestion, include the instruction that you will recognize your precognitive, clairvoyant, or telepathic dream elements. After you wake up, as you are recording your dreams, write down any peculiar imagery or feelings you may have experienced during or immediately following the dream. Later, when comparing the induced psychic dreams to physical events, be particularly alert to visions, sounds, or feelings associated with the ones confirmed as psychic. These clues can be used to help distinguish other psychic dreams from ordinary dreams.

Another way dream induction could be beneficial is through mood determination. In a study at the University of Texas at Austin, David Cohen and Charles Cox found that after pre-sleep stress, dreams were less pleasant, more exciting, dealt less with the present, were more symbolic, and contained more water imagery, which clinical practitioners recognize as a sign of depression.[22] These findings agree with the results of other research on stress and dream content. Psychologists believe that the functions of dreaming are information processing (incorporating negative and positive information in a healthy way), creativity, and

---

[22]David B. Cohen and Charles Cox, "Neuroticism in the Sleep Laboratory: Implications for Representational and Adaptive Properties of Dreaming," *Journal of Abnormal Psychology* 84 (1975): 102.

problem solving.[23] In some conditions, however, such as stress overload or repressed trauma, it appears possible that the psychological functions of dreaming occasionally break down.

According to Joe H. Slate, of Athens State College in Alabama, just as the suggestibility of the hypnagogic state influences dreams, the hypnopompic state influences thoughts and feelings after awakening. During the hypnopompic state the mind is receptive to dream elements that can affect emotional disposition and behavior after sleep.[24] During a stress overload or for some other reason, if dreaming fails to constructively process negative information and feelings, the mood of a dream could have a major impact on the contents of thoughts and types of feelings present in the hypnopompic state that is reached after a dream has ended. Through this influence, dream content can determine feelings and attitudes experienced during waking.

Nightmares haunted by fiendish characters, or marked by evil, frightening themes, or set in melancholy moods could result in feelings of anxiety or depression in the hypnopompic state, which can influence the emotional character of the day following the dream. If the detrimental mood lingers until the hypnagogic state before the next night's sleep, more bad dreams may result. Dreams that are joyful or harmonious can also affect emotional disposition in waking and sleeping, and result in inner peace and optimism.

Because of the suggestability interaction between dreaming, the hypnagogic and hypnopompic states, and waking, self-perpetuating cycles can operate to create long-term influences on emotional patterns. Since our psychological state affects our

---

[23]Readers should go to Rosalind Dymond Cartwright, *Night Life: Explorations in Dreaming* and "Affect and Dream Work from an Information Processing Point of View"; James L. Fosshage, "The Psychological Function of Dreams: A Revised Psychoanalytic Perspective"; and Henry Fiss, "An Empirial Foundation for a Self Psychology of Dreaming" for greater detail on this subject.

[24]*Psychic Phenomena*, p. 88.

dreams and our dreams, in turn, affect our psychological state, negative emotions, if improperly processed, can instigate a powerful downward spiral of psychological distress. It is reasonable to break a destructive dream cycle, and with practice, it may be possible to alleviate psychological disturbances such as anxiety, depression, or irritability with dream induction.[25]

Dream induction through hypnagogic suggestion can be used to interrupt that cycle by stimulating pleasant dreams. After a nightmare, when the hypnopompic state is reached, the suggestibility of this state can be used to go back into the dream and change the ending to a happy one. These two methods can help promote a healthy, relaxed, cheerful, optimistic, tolerant attitude toward life, and make it easier to confront the underlying problems that caused the negativity in the first place. If the underlying causes are unknown, dream induction may be useful in delineating them.

In research to find ways to reduce nightmares, Barry Krakow, M.D., and Joseph Neidhardt, M.D., found evidence suggesting that chronic nightmares cause anxiety and depression in waking life. They conducted two studies to determine the effects of treatment methods to decrease the frequency of nightmares. Krakow and Neidhardt evaluated the subjects' anxiety and depression levels both before and after the treatment They found that after successful reduction in nightmare frequency, the symptoms of anxiety and depression decreased dramatically, even though the subjects received no additional psychotherapy to treat the anxiety and depression. After several months, Krackow and Neidhardt administered more psychological tests and found that the subjects still showed significant improvement.[26]

Since it is possible for dream induction to influence mood, it may be worthwhile to try a similar approach to improve other

---

[25] *Psychic Phenomena*, p. 89.

[26] Barry Krakow, and Joseph Neidhardt, *Conquering Bad Dreams and Nightmares* (New York: Berkley Books, 1992), pp. 179–180.

areas, such as weight control, concentration, motivation, self-esteem, self-confidence, or elimination of addictive behaviors. The possibilities seem endless.

Dream Intervention

The final step in learning to function consciously along the dream continuum is dream intervention, or controlling your dreams while they take place. Dream intervention is possible through the special state of consciousness called lucid dreams. As we saw in Chapter 2, a lucid dream is a dream in which the dreamer becomes aware that what is occurring is a dream. Once a dream becomes lucid, it is often possible for the dreamer to voluntarily control the dream contents.

Lucid dreams are a strange limbo disrupting our definitions of waking and sleeping, because the subject feels awake and is capable of responding to the outside world, but psychologically and physiologically is dreaming in REM sleep. To actually attain waking consciousness in the dream world is to enter a mysterious dimension of our lives, unimaginable to those who have never had a lucid dream. Lucid dreams are the mental state in which we truly confront the hidden aspects of our deeper selves and widen our conscious experience by a leap of awareness. By combining the waking self with the dream self, we actualize a new concept of self as a creative being.

To stimulate lucid dreams, try autosuggestion techniques similar to those used for dream induction. During waking hours, right before going to sleep, and in the hypnagogic state, tell yourself that you will become aware during a dream, and that you will maintain awareness of whatever state of consciousness you are experiencing. Repeat autosuggestions such as these for as long as you can while you pass through the hypnagogic state. If necessary, experiment with different hypnagogic messages until you find one that works.

Try to develop the habit of looking for clues characteristic of dream worlds, such as inconsistencies of events, time, or objects. Concentrate on attaining conscious awareness while dreaming by looking for recurring irregularities in your dream world, such as having a conversation with someone who has physically died, or other physically impossible activities. Use these incongruities to remind yourself that you are dreaming. In both daily consciousness and the hypnagogic state, remind yourself of what your particular dream irregularities are. Tell yourself that you will recognize them when they occur, critically evaluate them, and become aware that you are dreaming.

One of the easiest times to stimulate a lucid dream is during the hypnopompic state immediately after an ordinary dream. Try to stay relaxed and detached from the outside world, think about the dream you just had, and reenter it, this time with waking consciousness intact.

Develop the habit of regularly analyzing your conscious state. During waking hours, while relaxing, napping, or in the hypnagogic and hypnopompic states, continually ask yourself if you are dreaming. Try to remember to ask yourself if you are dreaming while you are in a dream.

To stimulate lucid dreams, try to integrate all states of consciousness. Besides attempting to place waking consciousness in the dream world, try to place dream consciousness in the waking world by drawing or creating dream elements in symbolic form and placing them in your physical environment, visiting a physical location that appears in dreams, or acting out a dream drama. (Be careful, though, if you have nosey neighbors or household members who may think you are a little odd.)

Many recently written books are available about lucid dreams and contain a wide variety of methods that have proven useful in reaching this peculiar state of consciousness.[27]

Lucid dreaming has been a popular subject for research in the late 20th century, and several important findings have become evident. It has been suggested that lucid dreaming is help-

---

[27]For books on lucid dreaming, see Stephen LaBerge, *Lucid Dreaming: The Power of Being Awake and Aware in Your Dreams*; Jayne Gackenback and Stephen LaBerge, eds., *Conscious Mind, Sleeping Brain: Perspectives on Lucid*

ful in healing, spiritual growth, diminishing stress, and in improving psychological well-being, creativity, decision making, and performance. Lucid dreams can also be a source of wish fulfillment or fun.

Once you have mastered lucid dreaming, you have successfully increased awareness along the dream continuum through dream recall, dream interpretation, dream induction, and dream intervention.

* * * * * * *

The dream world may be one of our most valuable and most neglected psychological resources. All of these examples of different kinds of dream messages and dream applications show how dreams provide an effective link to transform the energies from the internal world of feelings and subliminal knowledge to the outer world of personal relationships and material forms. Through this transformation, we attain greater psychological balance and deeper understanding of physical, mental, emotional, and spiritual life.

It is possible that through prejudiced attitudes toward dreams and early training to dismiss dreams as meaningless flights of fancy, we have allowed many of our best opportunities to slip away. Dreams are one of the most powerful mental forces we have. Dream recall, interpretation, induction, and intervention, and eventually voluntary, self-induced OBEs, help us learn to manipulate our level of conscious awareness and discover the hidden potentials that lie buried within each of us. The release of new potentials allows us to expand the limitations and expectations we set for ourselves, which leads to greater insight and fuller development.

The ability to function along a wider range of consciousness allows us to perceive more of the knowledge, wisdom, and

---

Dreaming; Jayne Gackenback and Jane Bosveld, *Control Your Dreams*; and Keith Harary and Pamela Weintraub, *Have an Out-of-Body Experience in 30 Days: The Free Flight Program.*

spiritual truth contained in the universe. Only a few individuals in western societies deliberately use journeys through consciousness to interact with the knowledge and wisdom of the higher self to provide psychological balance, emotional outlets, healing, inspiration, creative insight, clues to individual and collective social problems, and ESP. Increasing awareness along the dream continuum results in a cultivation of abilities of concentration, observation, memory, logic, and will power. As these skills are applied to the dream continuum, they become stronger and more effective in physical waking reality.

The connection between dream awareness and OBEs has long been evident in esoteric tradition, and researchers are beginning to find confirming data. Recent studies have shown significant positive correlations between vivid dreams, dream recall, dream analysis, lucid dreams, and OBEs.[28]

It was when I began to explore the dream world that some strange phenomena began to take place, as if the acts of dream recall, interpretation, induction, and intervention automatically set in motion the unfolding of previously unexplored levels of consciousness. First I began remembering more dreams and more detailed dream content, then their meanings became clearer, and soon I found I could willfully influence the content. Suddenly I experienced my first conscious OBE, in which I "woke up" in my astral body, crawling across my cabin floor. In the next phase, I developed the ability to extend the hypnagogic and hypnopompic states, experienced lucid dreams more often, and learned to use those peculiar states of consciousness to voluntarily leave my body. As my personal astral odyssey progressed, I explored these uncharted regions of the mind and soon discovered they are interrelated in surprising ways and form a network of pathways, intersections, and dead ends, like a labyrinth of consciousness.

---

[28]Susan J. Blackmore, *Beyond the Body* (London: Heinemann, 1982), p. 116.

Chapter 4

The Labyrinth of Consciousness

What is the universe (one verse)? One part of a song? A unitary division of a poem? Do other verses exist? Does our definition of the universe include the totality of physical objects, excluding nonmaterial reality, or does it pertain to both?

We habitually comprehend our existence as physical life taking place in a universe comprised of three-dimensional structures of matter and space, supplied with energy in various forms, advancing through a one-way time sequence. Is this all there is?

By following seldomly used mental pathways, we can reach neglected corners of our minds, where different realities converge and form junctions with windows and doorways that open to alternative worlds. These alternative worlds provide us with with new perceptions, concepts, and experiences, in which the material structure, physical laws, and time progression of our normally perceived universe break down. The hypnagogic and hypnopompic states are two such crossroads of reality, and navigation through them may carry us forth on an odyssey to invisible worlds. With practice, waking consciousness can participate in these two enigmatic transition states that we all pass through every time we go to sleep or wake up.

Exploration of the Hypnagogic and Hypnopompic States

Studies have examined EEG information combined with the measurement of eye movements by electrooculogram, or EOG.

They have shown that during the hypnagogic state it is possible for the waking consciousness to remain intact and maintain undistorted thought patterns, contact with the external world, and the knowledge that visual images that appear, called hypnagogic hallucinations, are imaginary.[1] Researchers of hypnagogic phenomena have found that most persons experience it if they are aware that it exists and pay attention to it.[2]

Many people may hesitate to talk about their hypnagogic and hypnopompic imagery out of fear of association with mental pathology, but research has failed to find a relationship between the occurrence of transition state phenomena and mental or physical disorders. On the contrary, results indicate that those who consciously experience hypnagogic phenomena generally feel a sense of well-being and have well-balanced personalities.[3] Studies of the hypnopompic state yield similar conclusions.[4]

In chapter 3 we saw that the hypnagogic and hypnopompic states are levels of awareness in which heightened suggestibility occurs, and we learned how they can influence other states of consciousness. In this chapter we will see that these intermediate levels of awareness present some other intriguing possibilities.

Studied more thoroughly than the hypnopompic state, the hypnagogic state has been found to be accompanied by distinct physiological characteristics—relaxation, a decreased frequency and lower amplitude of EEG tracings showing theta wave production, the occurrence of SEMs (slow eye movements), slowing of pulse and respiration, and possibly less activity of the frontalis, which is the muscle in the forehead. These physiological changes are accompanied by psychological changes includ-

---

[1] Charles T. Tart, ed., *Altered States of Consciousness* (Garden City, NY: Anchor Books/Doubleday, 1972), p. 88.

[2] Andreas Mavromatis, *Hypnagogia* (London: Routledge & Kegan Paul, 1987), p. 5.

[3] Mavromatis, *Hypnagogia*, p. 7.

[4] Mavromatis, *Hypnagogia*, p. 8.

ing withdrawal, ego abandonment, "regression" of thought processes to more "primitive" organization, and strange visions, sounds, and sensations.

Most people conform fairly closely to the five stages of the sleep–dream cycle, but the hypnagogic state is much more variable in appearance and duration of imagery, sensations, and EEG stages. Although the appearance and duration are random, there is a somewhat discernible order to the types of phenomena that appear. They often start out as brief flashes of color or light followed by geometric forms or faces. Then dreamlike hallucinations and thought processes appear and become more and more distorted and complex up to a definite point, at which they revert back to rationality. This marks the entry to the deeper stages of the sleep–dream cycle.

The progression of visual imagery is paralleled psychologically by the knowledge that the phenomena are imaginary, followed by the inability to distinguish them from physical reality, and finally the conviction that they are the only reality. As these psychological changes take place, physical body image perception regresses. During the initial images, the hypnagogic state is accompanied by complete awareness of being inside the physical form occupying the actual physical location. As the imagery progresses, sensory perceptions of actual physical external and internal bodily sensations decrease, until the dreamlike episodes prevail and existence is perceived from a dream body, with obliteration of awareness of the physical form lying in bed.

Some people are not even aware of the existence of the hypnagogic interval, while others are alert to extended periods of complex and fantastic mental phenomena. The more we pay attention to hypnagogic imagery, the more frequently it appears and the longer it lasts. More time in the hypnagogic state allows greater familiarization with internal worlds, and provides an opportunity to increase control over our mental state and improve concentration as we focus awareness upon and manipulate the mental imagery. Ordinarily, there will be periods of time, several nights or weeks, when hypnagogic phenomena is abundant, long-lasting, and vivid, while at other times, months may go by without so much as a noticeable glimmer.

It is important to distinguish between two types of mental imagery; one type, caused by the imagination, seems to originate and take place inside the brain, behind and above the eyes, and the other type, hypnagogic imagery, seems to manifest through the inside of the eyelids. Mental pictures caused by the imagination are more deliberate than hypnagogic imagery, which seems to appear by its own volition from outside the mind.

To see what happens in the hypnagogic state, I have monitored my mental activity during sleep onset. To do this, it is necessary to keep the physically awake type of consciousness alert just enough to subjectively observe the changes in mentation as the mind goes to sleep. Even though the act of observation might change the quality of the states of consciousness the mind passes through, it is an interesting experiment.

To observe the shifts in consciousness, I relax in a comfortable position, close my eyes, forget worldly concerns, watch my mental screen inside my eyelids, and listen to my inner dialogue. I keep an alert, but passive attitude, cease to be analytical or judgmental, and openly accept whatever phenomena occur.

After watching blackness for a brief period, sometimes only a few seconds, at a certain conscious level between wakefulness and sleep, I begin to lose control of my thoughts and have difficulty directing the subject matter upon which to focus mentation. Fugitive thoughts and images appear, seemingly from outside my mind and with a free will of their own, and dominate my attention as it slips away from the physical world. Gradually my mind's analytical and critical abilities diminish and it passively accepts the imagery it is experiencing.

With just enough concentration, however, I can hold onto comprehension of what is happening and pay attention to the stray thoughts and images without causing them to go away. For example, an amorphous, swirling gray cloud may appear on my inner visual screen, and then disintegrate into intense hues of fuchsia, electric blue, lime green, or other colors. They may all appear as bouncing, quivering blobs and shape themselves into an intricate pattern of tiny diamonds, triangles, circles, and squares, all neatly fitted together to form an elaborate design, which then dissipates and leaves black emptiness. Out of the depths of the blackness tiny gold spinning shimmering disks may issue forth, which then dart and glide about the dark background and fade away to be replaced by more colorful blobs. The forms are vivid, the hues intense, and the textures smooth with a slight luster. Brilliant flashes of light may intermittently appear and extinguish the darkness or other images present.

My mind may wander back to practical matters concerning daily life, when my stream of consciousness is abruptly broken by a vision, which may be bizarre and composed of disconnected elements, such as a cracked egg spilling out nuts and bolts and tiny gears. Or my own thoughts may be interrupted by an unrelated inner dialogue that seems to come from an outside source. Suddenly I may feel my arm or leg jerk, or feel as if my entire body dropped a foot or so, causing all of my muscles to contract at once.

The intrusive visual material seems to originate from outside my consciousness, beyond my control, but, if I manage to stay alert, I discover that I can manipulate the colored forms with only a little effort. For example, if I see a blue square looming up at me on my mental screen, I can change it to red, just by "thinking" it red, or I can convert it to a yellow triangle, instead. If I remain detached and listen to the dialogue, while it occurs, it seems meaningful and intelligent, pertaining to some aspect of my being. But if I think about them, the words begin to slip away. If I make a concentrated effort to retain them, and succeed, they seem nonsensical and inconsistent. It seems as if my conscious mind is incapable of processing that information. The involuntary spasms and twitches, called myoclonic jerking, are often the last thing I remember as I plunge into the unconscious stages of sleep before ordinary REM dreams appear, but sometimes this muscle activity arouses me back to semi- or complete wakefulness.

After a brief awakening, if I continue to monitor my mental processes, my attention to daily matters eventually lapses and the renegade thoughts soon return and dominate rational thinking. I intensify my concentration on observing, but while focusing attention upon a progression of colorful abstract forms, my awareness momentarily blanks out. When it returns, I find myself caught up in more complex and prolonged imagery. The abstract forms may become a flock of cartoon birds that flutter around me in a cartoon world, or I may find myself in a strange room decorated with unfamiliar carpets, drapes, and furniture, sometimes with people who seem to have more of a right to be there than I. I could suddenly be surrounded by a landscape, such as a sunny hillside with wildflowers swaying in the breeze, or, without knowledge of a destination, be driving, walking, or floating in some other dreamlike location. Overall, I become less an observer of the mental phenomena and more a participant in the action taking place. I enter the scenes, lose contact with physical reality, and continue a normal sleep cycle.

As psychologists have found, the hypnagogic state is commonly accompanied by spontaneous mental phenomena in the form of visual (sight), auditory (sound), and kinesthetic (movement) perceptions. Olfactory (smell), gustatory (taste), tactile (touch), thermal (temperature), and somesthetic (body shape and size) sensations may also appear. I have noticed that after a period of weeks or months when hypnagogic imagery has been absent, or at the beginning of the hypnagogic state, the images can be vague and dull, but later they become vivid and bright. It may take several weeks of practice to see distinct visions.

Researchers of hypnagogic mentation characterize it as spontaneous, intrusive, unusual, symbolic, fleeting, autonomous, variable, vivid, novel, lifelike, animated, unrelated to personal experience, disconnected, bizarre, fantastic, original, colorful, and changeable.[5] The visions are often distinct with fine detail, sharp delineation, and intense color; even the grays can be in-

---

[5]Daniel L. Schacter, "The Hypnagogic State: A Critical Review of the Literature," *Psychological Bulletin* 83 (1976): 453–475.

tense. The images constantly move about on the mental screen, change shape, and transform into different objects. Images may disappear and be replaced by new, totally unrelated ones. If a passive state of mind is retained, their appearance and variability seem autonomous, and they seem to originate from an external source. Numerous researchers have also found that as visions progress during sleep onset, they usually follow the sequential pattern of development from simple light flashes to geometric shapes, to various objects, and then to longer dreamlike fragments.[6] At any stage of this process, the forms may appear abstract or bizarre.

The visual images may be accompanied by sounds of rushing, buzzing, humming, or more organized audial material, such as speech or music.

At the beginning of the hypnagogic state, the imagination dwells on personal concerns or drifts in fantasy. After it descends deeper into the hypnagogic state, thoughts become increasingly uncontrolled and consist more and more of analogical reasoning, symbolic ideas, and metaphorical representations.[7] For example, I recently saw a hypnagogic image of a fashionable piece of jewelry, a gemstone ring, and the words "ring true" formed in my mind. Eventually these images and thoughts deteriorate to more abstract associations. Verbalizations may appear in which vague concepts form as grammatically correct sentence constructions that lack logical or coherent meaning between the subject, verb, and other parts of speech, such as one I noted, "No shine has placed it." Nonsensical words, made up of meaningless combinations of vowels, may appear either within these sentences or disjointed.

As the hypnagogic state deepens, orientation in space and time become confused, the here and now of physical existence become lost. Without a grasp of space and time, the self, too, becomes lost, and ego boundaries dissolve. External and internal

---

[6]Schacter, "The Hypnagogic State," 60.

[7]Mavromatis, *Hypnagogia*, pp. 64–65 and 160–185.

reality become one; subjective and objective reality become one. The imagery is no longer contained in the self; the self is contained in the imagery.

Deep in the hypnagogic state, with awareness still functioning, synesthesia may occur, in which imaginary sensory impressions may seem to enter through multiple modes. For example, colors may appear as sound, or visions as feelings. As contact with the physical world decreases, the body may experience kinesthetic hallucinations, which include sensations of falling, drifting, spinning, or vibrating, or somesthetic hallucinations, such as impressions of growing smaller, larger, or disappearance of body parts or the entire body.

Some researchers attribute the bright flashes and geometric colors of the hypnagogic state to what they call entoptic phenomena, or entoptic lights, which are caused by phosphenes, intraocular fluid, and self-light of the retinas of the eyes. Electrical stimulation of phosphenes in the eyes produces ideoretinal light in the form of visions, designs, and light patterns that closely resemble hypnagogic imagery.[8] Could this luminous dust be such stuff as dreams are made of?

Although studied less frequently, the hypnopompic state, too, can feature visual, audial, and other sensory-like material, usually in the form of persistent dream images of various types, but also other hallucinatory phenomena. Actual spoken or imaginary verbalizations may form spontaneously as poetry or prose, and imaginary music may sound from within. Hypnopompic material can be rich in creative ideas, problem solutions, or warnings in the form of psychic messages

Both the hypnagogic and hypnopompic states require further research before we have an adequate understanding of the potential of our mental abilities lying dormant, just beneath the surface of awareness.

---

[8]Schacter, "The Hypnagogic State," 460.

Passage to Invisible Realms

Besides being spectacular arenas of surrealistic fantasies and anomalous sensations, the hypnagogic and hypnopompic states are gateways to invisible worlds, realms where diverse adventures in internal and external conscious experiences are waiting to unfold. When waking consciousness remains active in the hypnagogic and hypnopompic states, it is possible to venture through these gateways to alternative states of consciousness such as creative inspiration, mental projection, extrasensory perception, dual consciousness, lucid dreams, or OBEs, besides the normal sleep–dream cycle and associated segments of the dream continuum. Before voluntarily passing through these gateways, however, it is necessary to learn to maintain the delicate mental balance between waking and sleeping.

One method to stay alert and prolong the hypnagogic state is suggested by Sylvan Muldoon, one of the 20th century's foremost OBE adepts.[9] Lie back in bed (or another comfortable place) and hold your forearm up, balanced on your elbow. Every time you pass beyond the hypnagogic state, your arm will fall and wake you enough to remind you to commit to memory any thoughts, feelings, visions, or ideas you may experience in the hypnagogic state. This has proven many times to be a successful method.

More recently developed methods to prolong the hypnagogic state utilize biofeedback training that results in increased alpha and theta brain wave production and increased hypnagogic imagery. Other experimental devices include a special finger ring with a tilt detector that chimes when the raised forearm begins to fall, and a repeat alarm clock set to ring every five minutes so that the subject tries to remain alert enough to repeatedly depress the bar to prevent the clock from sounding.[10]

---

[9]Sylvan J. Muldoon and Hereward Carrington, *The Projection of the Astral Body* (York Beach, ME: Samuel Weiser, 1977), p. 163.
[10]Schacter, "The Hypnagogic State," 458–459.

To become aware in the hypnopompic state, learn to wake up slowly by using autosuggestion before you go to sleep. As soon as waking consciousness stirs, push daily concerns aside, relax, and drift back towards sleep while observing mental experience. It is difficult to control the mental state enough to prevent returning to sleep or awakening completely, but once you accomplish it, you will know it and it will seem easy, until the next time you try.

When you are alert in these semi-wakeful drowsy states, you will discover that sometimes you can choose to enter alternative states of consciousness or they may appear spontaneously. Either way, the radiance of consciousness will illuminate corners of the mind previously obscured by shadows of neglect, and light the way to invisible worlds beyond.

Creative Inspiration

Creative inspiration is one alternative possible from the hypnagogic and hypnopompic states. Many of the scientific or technical problem solutions and creative works discussed in chapter 3 may have emanated from transition state awareness rather than REM dreams. Confusion surrounds the terminology in the literature on dreams and hypnagogic imagery; some authors consider them the same and others differentiate between the two. Since many of the creative insights discussed throughout dream literature occurred before scientists knew about REMs and sleep stages, writers and researchers simply referred to the state of consciousness in which they occurred as dreams.

To use the transition states for creative inspiration or problem solving, go into the hypnagogic state expressing to the higher self the work to be done or the problem to be solved. Make the autosuggestion quietly, in a relaxed and subdued manner; sustain a passive, receptive attitude. Go to sleep. When waking consciousness begins to stir, look for the answer in the hypnopompic state. Be sure to have a pen and notebook or a tape recorder within reach.

Mental Projection

During the hypnagogic or hypnopompic state, it may be possible to project consciousness away from the physical body into another place or object. Mental projection differs somewhat from OBEs in that consciousness seems to occupy a point in space or in an object rather than an astral replication of the physical body. Mental projection may be a form of astral projection in which the astral body assumes the form of a point in space, a point inside an object, or even becomes an entire object.

Mental projection is one of the many types of projection my friend, Judi, experienced. Here is an example of how it occurred for her one day in the late 1960s.

It was a typical early spring day for South Dakota. The weather was fairly warm, only a slight breeze occasionally stirred, and brief snow flurries intermittently blotted out bright sunshine. The snowflakes were large and drifted slowly through the air. They melted almost immediately upon striking a surface and left slushy puddles on the ground.

Judi had gone shopping for a couple of hours, and it was early afternoon when she arrived home. Among her purchases was a book by Alan Watts. Because of the beautiful weather, she decided against going immediately into the house; instead, she sat in the car and watched the snow fall.

While she sat there, she picked up the book and glanced through it. She reached a section where Watts expressed the idea that we should flow with our feelings rather than fight them. This passage caught her interest and she read a couple of paragraphs.

The concept intrigued her, because she had practiced it quite often while experiencing physical pain. Having an unusual sensitivity to drugs, Judi's body reacted acutely when she used pain relievers, and sometimes became early dysfunctional. She even avoided the use of common drugs, such as aspirin or Novocaine injections. She had assumed that she just naturally had a high pain tolerance, but as she studied Watts' idea of flowing with feelings, she wondered if, because of her avoidance of pain medications, she had developed a unique approach to physical pain.

Judi's thoughts led her farther, and she considered that since the concept had been used successfully with pain, it would be interesting to try it in other areas of life. She sat and let her mind puzzle over the possibilities. She gazed at the snowflakes floating toward the ground. After a few moments she wondered what it would be like to flow with the feeling of being a snowflake.

In an instant she was drifting high above the car, slowly falling downward, surrounded by other snowflakes descending lazily through the air. She was carried along on gentle air currents. She swayed from side to side, and sometimes floated upward, and then drifted further down.

The journey seemed to last a long time, but it must have taken only a few moments. The sunlight shined all about her, and sparkled on her and all the other snowflakes more vividly than Judi had ever seen, as they all fell gracefully through the air. She felt more enjoyment than she had ever experienced by just watching it snow. She was absorbed by a feeling of total peace and contentment.

She looked down—suddenly she was only a couple of inches above the ground! Panic struck because she knew that once she hit the ground she would melt and be gone. Immediately, she was sitting in the car with no memory of separating from or reentering her body, only new insight into the fleeting existence of a glittering configuration of ice crystals.

Transition State ESP

Another interesting pathway branching off the hypnagogic and hypnopompic states leads to the superconscious. Transition state awareness produces mental conditions that allow the functioning of our natural ESP abilities—precognition, retrocognition, telepathy, clairvoyance, and clairaudience, discussed previously in connection with dreams. Literature on the paranormal, scientific investigation, and case studies all provide evidence that ESP is associated with the hypnagogic and hypnopompic states. For me and others that I have talked to or read about, all that is necessary is to relax, forget mundane concerns, remain partially awake, keep a passive, receptive attitude, and pay attention. (This sounds a lot easier than it is.) Once consciousness is well into the hypnagogic state, after the phantasmagoria of inner space has begun, a complete, realistic scene or message may suddenly intervene.

For example, on the night of August 28, 1990, I was lying in bed watching hypnagogic flashes burst into color, and brilliant blobs form different shapes of various hues. Suddenly a disastrous scene spontaneously appeared. It was on my mental screen, behind my closed eyelids, fully detailed and completely intact. I had the impression that one part of my self stood on the edge of the scene watching, as if physically present in the new dimension, while another part of my self lay in bed watching mentally, but the self in the picture was invisible to the self in bed as the vision proceeded.

In the scene, the night sky exploded into flames. Against the orange glow was silhouetted a huge airplane, skidding along the ground, moving from the left to the right of my "visual field." A large piece of the plane, perhaps the right wing, partially broke off and formed a black, somewhat trapezoidal shape in front of the rest of the wreckage. Flaming chunks of debris flew away from the center, which was an intensely burning inferno.

My heart cried out, "No, no!" as I thought about the possibility of victims dying inside the blazing crash that very moment while I watched helplessly, unable to rescue them or ease their suffering. Dismayed, I wished myself away from this terrible scene and instantaneously returned to full waking consciousness, shocked at the realism and tragedy portrayed. I lay awake, tense, for a long time, reluctant to go back into the hypnagogic state.

The next morning when I turned on the television to watch the news, I was struck with amazement—the very same scene I had witnessed in my vision the night before played across my television screen. All the details were the same—the crashing plane moving from the left to the right of my screen, the fire, the detached piece that appeared to be a broken wing.

The newscast continued. A U.S. Air Force transport plane crashed and burned at Ramstein Air Base in West Germany at 12:30 A.M. as it was carrying equipment to the war in the Persian Gulf. Ten people were confirmed dead, five were hospitalized, and two were missing. The plane was a C-5 cargo plane, the largest type of transport plane in the U.S. fleet.

It is difficult to classify this instance as either precognition, retrocognition, clairvoyance, or telepathy. If the plane crashed at 12:30 A.M., August 29, West German time, in Western South Dakota it would have been late afternoon on August 28, at least six hours before I went to bed. Therefore, I visualized the event six or more hours after it happened, but I was unaware of the actual plane crash at the time. If the term clairvoyance is applied to the paranormal seeing of events a few hours after they take place, this could be classified as clairvoyance, but a more appropriate term might be retrocognition. It could also have been clairvoyance of the news broadcast being shown at the time I saw the hypnagogic vision, precognition of my seeing the news broadcast, or telepathy from someone who saw either the accident or the broadcast. ESP defies classification.

In a pilot study conducted by Daniel L. Schacter and Edward F. Kelly, the researchers found a positive correlation between hypnagogic hallucinations and ESP. The subjects, using biofeedback equipment, voluntarily entered the hypnagogic state. In another part of the building an experimenter, acting as sender, concentrated on a randomly selected slide, while the subject reported the contents of hypnagogic imagery. Upon statistical analysis of "direct hits," the study showed some significant results indicating the transmission of target material, while the hypnagogic imagery of one subject showed "striking" resemblance to the slide used.[11]

---

[11]Daniel L. Schacter and Edward F. Kelly, "ESP in the Twilight Zone," *The Journal of Parapsychology* 39 (1975): 27–28.

Schacter and Kelly's study presents experimental evidence in favor of the premise that ESP functions in the hypnagogic state. This research indicates that information can be sent telepathically from one person in waking consciousness to another in the hypnagogic state. Only speculation can attempt to explain why a vision of an air disaster, with no known sender, should appear to someone without a direct conscious involvement with any of the people or events concerned.

In literature on dreams, experiences similar to this are often referred to as psychic dreams. Again, this could reflect inconsistencies regarding the use of terms associated with dreams and hypnagogic or hypnopompic images. Most of the psychic dreams we read about could have taken place in the hypnagogic state, REM sleep, the hypnopompic state, or some other state. Unless the subject is in a sleep lab and hooked up to recording equipment, we can only speculate.

In the literature on paranormal phenomena, experiences such as my vision of the cargo plane crash are often included within the same classification as astral travel or OBEs. Some other terms used to refer to OBEs and similar experiences include ESP projection, traveling clairvoyance, psychic telescope, and remote viewing, but the usage is often confusing as to whether these terms are meant to be synonymous with astral projection and OBEs or pertain to clairvoyance or some other type of ESP.

Based on personal experience, I feel that what I call astral projection or an OBE is different from my transition state ESP of the airplane accident. Right before I visualized the crash, I was aware of lying in bed, in the hypnagogic state, paying attention to my mental imagery. The crash scene spontaneously appeared on my mental screen behind closed eyelids, while I still felt I was lying in bed, in my physical body. An instant later, however, my "inner self" briefly merged with the crash scene, aware that another, now distant part of my being, was lying in bed. The "inner self" that entered the vision did so instantaneously, more as mental focusing than actually leaving the physical body, although there was the slight sensation of being exteriorized. Upon wishing to be away from the exploding wreckage, the part of my self that entered the vision *mentally* remerged with the self that was lying in bed, and the vision disappeared.

The type of experience in which I witnessed the vision of the airplane crash may be a form of OBE, but to differentiate it from what I usually experience during OBEs, I refer to it as transition state ESP.

The subjective experience is different when I have a "normal" OBE, one of the other consciousness states possible from the hypnagogic and hypnopompic states. In the initial phases of a normal OBE, I often have definite images and sensations of separating from my physical body in a subliminal body and traveling to a distant location. If I look, I can actually see my astral form move out of its physical confinement, and I can feel the motion of this quasi-material phantom departing as if I am inside it. Sometimes, though, I just get out of bed, leaving my physical form behind, and walk away in my astral body, or I may float out, roll out, or fall out, failing to notice the separation process, but aware of the departure from the physical body's location and the journey to a new place.

Most of the time, during a normal OBE, once separated and away from the physical form, my entire consciousness is in the astral double, and I see, touch, and hear the "world" only from the astral double's location, using only its senses. Usually during the OBE the mental impression is more one of knowledge that my physical body is in bed somewhere else, rather than one of the experience of being in that physical body while I am projected. One exception is during an intriguing state referred to as dual consciousness.

Dual Consciousness

Usually when my senses and consciousness "leave" the physical body and use the "astral double" as a vehicle to observe and interact on the "astral plane," I assume that my physical body is unconscious, because in case studies of OBEs, the exteriorized subject often looks at the physical form and observes it as unconscious, and during my OBEs I usually lack cognizance from the physical form's viewpoint. Sometimes, however, particularly if the astral double is near the physical form, I may experience dual consciousness, or the sensation of experiencing consciousness in both bodies at the same time. This can occur in several ways.

During one type of dual consciousness, the senses of the physical body and those of the astral body appear to operate simultaneously, with information coming through both sets of senses at once and entering one mind. The impression is of one mind being in two places at the same time.

For example, during one incidence of dual consciousness my physical body was in bed, lying on its back, and my astral body was floating a few inches above it, lying on its back. My physical eyes saw the back of my astral form at the same time my astral eyes saw the ceiling. My physical eyes may have been open or closed—I don't know. It is difficult to describe this condition in which one mind interprets input from two bodies, with consciousness existing in two places at the same time, but this is what many astral projectors claim has taken place during their OBEs, and I have experienced this confusing phenomenon several times.

During another type of dual consciousness, it seems as though the mind is located in only one place, the physical body's location, instead of two, but perceiving two places at once. This can occur upon reentering the physical form after an instantaneous return from an astral journey. An instantaneous return is one in which there is no sensation of movement from the astral location back to the physical location; one instant the astral body is in the astral environment, and the next it is reuniting with the physical body. While the astral form is blending with its physical form, it is possible to see both the astral environment which was occupied in the previous split second and the physical environment surrounding the body. The two dimensions remain briefly superimposed before the astral world fades away and the physical world dominates consciousness.

One time when I experienced this type of dual consciousness, I was astrally standing in my living room, looking at a misplaced dressing table that, in physical reality, was actually in my bedroom. Suddenly, instead of standing, feeling the floor beneath my feet, I felt the mattress supporting my reclining body, but I could still see the dressing table in the living room. The instantaneous return allowed me simultaneously to receive two sets of stimuli—one, the mattress sensed by my physical form, and two, the misplaced dressing table sensed by my astral form. As I watched, the living room faded away and the bedroom surrounding the dressing table came into focus. I found myself back in my physical body, wide awake, trying to determine exactly when it was that my physical eyes had opened.

During the type of dual consciousness experienced upon the rejoining of the astral and physical bodies, subjectively it appears as if consciousness is in one place, the physical body's location, while it temporarily perceives two worlds, the astral and the physical.

The only way to fully comprehend dual consciousness is to experience it.

There are several plausible explanations for dual consciousness. According to classical astral projection theory, a silver-colored cord connects the projected double to the physical body, and no matter how far away the astral form travels, the silver cord remains intact, stretching until it is as thin as a fine thread.

The alleged purpose of the silver cord is to keep the organic form alive through this vital connection with the spiritual essence contained in the astral body while it is projected elsewhere. Communication between the astral body and the physical body takes place through the silver cord. If, during an astral journey, the connection is ever severed, supposedly the physical body dies. Under normal circumstances, the astral and physical forms remain linked until the final separation at death.

It is feasible that sometimes there could be a momentary crossover of information passing along the cord between the two bodies. Messages could get mixed up or filter from one set of sensory equipment to another. Hypothetically, sights, sounds, and sensations detected by the astral form could travel along the cord to the physical brain, giving the impression of dual consciousness, or the perceptions from the physical viewpoint could travel through the cord to the projected mind.

Perhaps such crossovers are intended—they could have a purpose. Some projectors have claimed to retain consciousness in both bodies, being able to perform ordinary activities in the physical body while the astral body is out on a journey far away.[12] During this type of projection, the projector can describe, through the physical body, what the astral body is seeing or experiencing. Maybe such projectors have learned to coordinate the two sensory systems and the connection between them for this intended function.

Another plausible explanation for dual consciousness could be that the organic brain is automatically conditioned to process information from the mind, which can be thought of as the mental energy that keeps the brain active. When the mind is only partially in the brain, with another part in the astral form, and perceives information away from the brain, the brain may habitually transmit it from its own viewpoint, thereby giving its owner the impression of dual consciousness.

Another conjecture is that dual consciousness is an illusion. During the transfer from one form to the other, when separation or reunion is incomplete, or when the astral double is near the physical body, it is plausible that consciousness has difficulty remaining in only one of the forms. Perhaps it flips back and forth between the physical body and the astral body so quickly that it only appears to be in two places at one time.

Hypnagogic and hypnopompic hallucinations, inspirational insight, mental projection, transition state ESP, OBEs,

---

[12]For more information on dual consciousness, please see Eileen Garrett, *My Life as a Search for the Meaning of Mediumship*; Ingo Swann, *To Kiss the Earth Good-bye*; Emanuel Swedenborg, *The Spiritual Diary*; Alex Tanous and Timothy Gray, *Dreams, Symbols, and Psychic Power*; and Stewart Edward White, *The Betty Book.*

and dual consciousness all present problems with definitions and classification. Parapsychological research from as far back as the 19th century has found evidence that the hypnagogic state is receptive to the functioning of ESP,[13] but there seems to be a complex array of mental phenomena reachable from the little used byways of consciousness during both drowsy states between waking and sleeping. Mental projection, transition state ESP, and OBEs have many characteristics in common, but also exhibit many differences. Psychic dreams and transition state ESP may or may not be the same thing, and nobody knows for sure if there is a difference between hypnagogic imagery and ordinary REM dreams. Few scientists have even attempted to explain dual consciousness. Further research is necessary to determine where clairvoyance ends and astral or mental projection begins, where reality gives way to dreams, or what, if anything, separates a dream from hypnagogic and hypnopompic hallucinations. Our brains will have to invent a more highly evolved language before they can comprehend the concepts of their own capabilities.

LUCID DREAMS

To further complicate matters, the hypnagogic and hypnopompic states both provide gateways that open to another strange dimension of awareness, lucid dreams, which researchers have only recently begun to study in depth. Lucid dreams appear to have practical applications ranging from improving mental and physical health to enhancing skills used in job performance and recreation. A lucid dream can also progress directly or indirectly into an OBE. As shown by a number of studies cited by Harvey J. Irwin, a statistically significant positive relationship exists between the occurrence of lucid dreams and OBEs, implying that persons with a tendency to have lucid dreams are more likely to

[13]Schacter, "The Hypnagogic State," 469.

have OBEs than those who do not.[14] Esoteric sources have long purported a connection between lucid dreams and OBEs.[15]

Lucid dreams can be attained from several states of consciousness: the hypnagogic state, an ordinary dream, or the hypnopompic state. An OBE can also revert to a mental state with dreamlike elements and resemble a lucid dream. False awakenings, dreams within dreams, and some of the other more unusual types of dreams can reach points of lucidity.

To attain a lucid dream from the hypnagogic state, monitor your consciousness while remaining awake for as long as possible. You may see your hypnagogic imagery form a dream and encompass part of your awareness while another part observes. Experiments in which the subject continuously speaks into a tape recorder while drifting deeper and deeper into the hypnagogic state have been successful in inducing awareness of the formation of dreamlike images into dreams.[16] Whether or not these are "real" dreams, identical to REM dreams, is controversial, because, as mentioned previously, it has not been determined if hypnagogic images are the same as dream images. Furthermore, the act of verbalization may qualitatively alter the hypnagogic state to a different, undefined state of consciousness. Another way to induce lucid dreams from the hypnagogic state is through autosuggestion, as described in chapter 3.

Ordinary dreams are another state of consciousness from which lucid dreams may be obtained. Ordinary dreams can spontaneously become lucid, or they can be changed into lucid dreams by watching for and recognizing incongruities of dream content.

The hypnopompic state also provides an opportunity to enter a lucid dream. When shifting consciousness from an ordi-

---

[14]H. J. Irwin, *Flight of Mind: A Psychological Study of the Out-of-Body Experience* (Metuchen, NJ: Scarecrow Press, 1985), p. 204.

[15]I found the following books helpful in this subject: Oliver Fox, *Astral Projection: A Record of Out-of-the-Body Experiences*; Sylvan Muldoon and Hereward Carrington, *The Projection of the Astral Body*; and Ophiel, *The Art and Practice of Astral Projection*.

[16]Tart, *Altered States of Consciousness*, p. 105.

nary REM dream to physical reality, awaken as slowly as possible. At the instant awareness approaches physical reality, relax and try to go back into the previous dream, and prolong it with the knowledge that it is a dream.

Obtaining lucid dreams from all three of these states of consciousness requires practice and concentration to keep them intact. While a lucid dream continues, it is possible to observe it to enrich conscious experience, control it to satisfy a goal, or use it to experience astral projection.

Like the hypnagogic and hypnopompic states, lucid dreams are a mental gateway to the astral plane. From lucid dreams it is fairly easy to have an OBE, either by leaving the dream environment and directly entering the OBE environment, or going from the lucid dream to the hypnopompic state and then the OBE environment. Either way can occur spontaneously or, with practice, intentionally. Directly or indirectly, spontaneously or intentionally, when an ordinary REM dream becomes lucid and turns into an OBE, self-awareness experiences a definite shift, similar to the shift from ordinary dreaming to physical awakening.

In my experience, when a lucid dream evolves directly into an OBE, I have the impression that at the moment I suddenly realize I am dreaming, I just step from the dream environment into the astral environment. On most occasions when this happens, the dream environment appears as the inside of my home, with my dream body located in a position corresponding to within twenty feet or so from my physical body. These OBEs initiate from the dream body's location.

At times when a lucid dream evolves indirectly into an OBE, after the dream becomes lucid the dream environment vanishes, and I become aware in my physical body, in the hypnopompic state, often with my body vibrating and sometimes with buzzing or rushing noises in my head. From this state it is possible to leave my physical body, often conscious of the separation, and wander about on the "astral plane" in an astral form.

OBEs

Although there are others, the preceding sections indicate three states of consciousness from which OBEs are possible: the hypnagogic state, lucid dreams, and the hypnopompic state.

Even without a lucid dream, the hypnopompic state is conducive to an OBE. It is necessary to simultaneously prolong the waking process and prevent falling back to sleep. If the attempt to remain in the hypnopompic state is successful, various methods to leave the body might result in an OBE. Similarly, induction of OBEs is possible by prolonging and maintaining awareness during the hypnagogic state.

OBEs are also possible from a waking state. It is rare for an OBE to just spontaneously occur under ordinary waking circumstances, but here is what happened to a special friend of mine, Sue.

Sue and Bob have been extremely close friends for 25 years—close enough to feel as though they are "soul mates." In 1976 Sue was living in Colorado Springs, while Bob lived in West Burlington, Iowa. Even though a strong bond existed between them, they had been out of touch with each other for a year, with no visits, phone calls, or letters.

Bob had just moved back to West Burlington from Jacksonville, Florida, and was living with a woman and her daughter, when he telephoned Sue. Sounding obviously upset, he said, "I've gotta talk to you," then suddenly, "Sorry, gotta go. I'll call you back," and he abruptly hung up. From the troubled sound of Bob's voice, Sue intuitively believed something was seriously wrong. She waited all night for his call, but the phone was silent.

The next day, Sue was even more worried; it was late morning and she was still waiting for Bob's call. She decided to take a walk in a nearby park.

It was a cold, crisp day. Sue sat on a swing, wrapped her arms around the chains, and clasped her hands in front of her chest. Stationary, just sitting quietly on the old wooden swing seat, she looked at the playground surrounded by trees. She thought about Bob, and decided to use the power of positive thinking. She concentrated as hard as she could on the hope that he would call her soon.

After a few minutes, Sue thought she was dreaming. All of a sudden she was in a place where she had never been before, the pharmacy where Bob worked. There was Bob, in his white blazer, standing behind the counter. Sue made particular note of his blue necktie and brass nameplate, and she was aware of another employee, female, working nearby.

While Bob was working, he looked straight at Sue and said, "I'll call you between 5:00 and 5:30." An instant later, Sue was back in the swing—up in the air in forward motion, with her feet off the ground! She was so startled she almost fell off the swing!

Sue went home and sat by the phone. Between 4:00 and 4:30 (Mountain Standard Time), the phone rang. It was Bob. (He was in Central Standard Time, where it was between 5:00 and 5:30.)

Bob said he knew she had been worried and apologized for the way he had dropped the previous phone conversation. Then he mentioned that while he had been at work, he had said out loud, "I'll call you between 5:00 and 5:30." The other pharmacist, a female, who had been working with him asked, "Why?" Bob, unaware that he had spoken out loud, asked, "Why what?" Puzzled, the female pharmacist asked, "Why are you going to call me between 5:00 and 5:30?" "What!?" Bob replied.

When Sue heard this, she realized that she actually had been to the pharmacy—in astral form. When she told Bob about her experience, he confirmed that he had been wearing a blue necktie and brass nameplate. As she later remarked, while telling me about her astral journey, "It scared the hell out of me; I thought I had fallen asleep!"

Although Sue and Bob still talk about their strange experience with mysterious astral forces, Sue has never attempted out-of-body travel again.

Waking state OBEs occur more often upon a sudden jolt or impending danger, such as an accident that could cause serious injury. For example, a young woman recently told me she had left her body when she was involved in a car wreck. An instant before the impact, she ejected out of her physical body in astral form to a point above the crash. Although her companion, who had also been in the crash, had remarked to her later about the impressive noise of the smashing metal and shattering glass, she had heard nothing. An instant after the accident, she returned to her physical form inside the mangled vehicle, and, miraculously, both she and her companion walked away without injury.

Some people are less fortunate and leave their bodies after serious injury or illness, or during surgery, in what has become known as near-death experiences, or NDEs. My good friend, Ross, died two years before I met him.

It happened in Dallas, Texas, on the night of August 17, 1990. With his friend, Cindy, Ross was leaving a restaurant when he was attacked and severely beaten with a tire iron by a couple of drug-crazed maniacs. When the paramedics arrived, they phoned ahead to the Methodist Hospital Trauma Unit and told them to have a body bag ready, this guy was dead. A paramedic told the assistants to put Ross on the gurney and take him to the basement of Methodist Hospital Trauma Unit, where they perform autopsies for criminal investigations.

While Ross' body was lying in the Emergency Medical Service unit, in front of the restaurant, Ross saw everything as if from a point above, at about the level of the roof of the restaurant. He saw Cindy, who was a nurse, tending to his wounds—the skin of his forehead was flopped over his face, his teeth had all been kicked out, plastic from a false tooth was imbedded in his upper lip. He saw all of this! He watched it all, just as though he had been standing on the roof of the restaurant.

Then somewhere, he doesn't know when and he doesn't know why, "It was as though suddenly the 'film burned,' as when the film in a motion picture camera stops turning and the light burns a white hole in the image. The whiteness was empty;

there were no bodies, there were no people, there was nothing, only a whiteness whiter than anything I had ever seen."

The whiteness grew until it encompassed everything. Inside the whiteness Ross found peace that he cannot explain now and did not understand then. Everything that he can think of representing peace and love happened during those few moments while he existed in the whiteness.

The next thing Ross knew, someone was saying, "We've gotta stitch his head." He hated that moment—the time when he went from that bliss back to experience the pain that he was suffering. He would rather have died and stayed on that other plane. All of a sudden he heard someone saying, "This poor bastard, he's not gonna make it." Then he heard, "Well, there are enough vital signs, let's go ahead and stitch him up, and then Dr. Moody wants him to go upstairs into the hyperbaric chamber." Ross thought, "Being over there in that white satisfaction was a hell of a lot better than being here."

The assailants who beat him up were arrested and charged with murder.

The doctor who was normally in charge of the Methodist Hospital Trauma Unit was at a social function when they brought Ross in. Fortunately, by some quirk of fate, his replacement happened to be a neurosurgeon. The neurosurgeon, Dr. James Moody, immediately gave orders to have Ross taken to the third floor to a hyperbaric chamber, which was to be utilized to the absolute maximum pressure. Ross was also administered a new drug to reduce inflammation and swelling of the brain stem. The doctor who came in to assist Dr. Moody said he never would have considered this treatment, he would have just ordered the body bag.

If the regular doctor had been on duty that night, Ross definitely would have gone into the body bag. Because a neurosurgeon was present and took action, even though the outlook was grim, Ross is physically alive and walking today. Many of us are certainly happy about that!

The murder charges against the attackers were reduced to aggravated assault.

Examples of some other circumstances from which OBEs can occur would be under anesthesia and during childbirth or coma. Trance, meditation, hypnosis, and various drug-induced states may also be included. Some of these could be psychologically and physiologically the same as the hypnagogic and hypnopompic states.

Whether OBEs emanate from the hypnagogic state, a lucid dream, the hypnopompic state, or some other mental state, many different types of OBEs are possible. OBEs appear to exist along an OBE continuum, a range of conscious awareness similar to the dream continuum—unconscious OBEs are at one end of the continuum, while OBEs mixed with dream elements are in the middle, and fully conscious OBEs are at the other end.

At the extreme nearest waking consciouness are fully conscious OBEs in which the projector, with complete mental faculties, enters an astral world. It could be a world resembling the physical world, free of distortion, or a higher world in which superconsciousness is possible. At this end of the OBE continuum, I have had OBE's that were so realistic that I thought I was actually functioning physically, in the physical world, until such paranormal phenomena as floating or passing through a wall convinced me otherwise.

In the intermediate range, close to the fully conscious extreme, are OBEs in which the astral world is similar to physical reality, with minor distortions. Farther down the continuum are OBEs which contain a mixture of the astral world and a dream world. Beyond that, the OBE world contains more and more distortions until it turns into a dream environment similar to physical reality, which, even farther down the continuum, then becomes more and more bizarre as it approaches absurdity.

Along the OBE continuum may be places where it connects to the different dreams along the dream continuum. From fully conscious OBEs, I have passed into the intermediate range and seen dream worlds become superimposed upon the astral world. When I stepped into them, as I crossed the line from an OBE environment into a dream environment, I experienced a definite shift in consciousness, as definite as the change in awareness from full wakefulness to sleeping dream awareness. At other times when I have been at junctions between these two continuums, I have become so confused I never could determine if the experience was a dream or an OBE.

Along the branches connecting the OBE continuum to the dream continuum, but closer to the dream continuum, may be dreams of having an OBE. I started having these dreams occasionally after I actually began having conscious OBEs. Dreams of OBEs usually contain moments of lucidity, and may or may not develop into actual OBEs.

It could be that some OBEs are so far removed from waking consciousness that only vague memories of them remain, and are incorporated into dreams. It is also possible that some projection-like experiences may be only dreams with dream imagery of OBEs for subject matter.

At the farthest extreme of the OBE continuum are unconscious OBEs, of which the projector has no conscious memory or awareness of being out of the body. OBEs could be further qualified as spontaneous or induced, and induced OBEs could be broken down into self-induced and induced by an outside agency, such as an experimental procedure or a drug.

So, unconscious OBEs can be either spontaneous or induced. According to some beliefs, spontaneous unconscious OBEs are a normal, regular occurrence. Many sources claim that everyone projects out of the physical body in astral form during sleep, but is rarely aware of it. Although it seems plausible, I have never read or heard of this being confirmed scientifically.

The literature on astral projection contains examples of both induced and spontaneous unconscious OBEs in which another person in physical waking consciousness sees the person appear in astral form. The projector leaves the physical body and travels, in astral form, to another location, where a friend or acquaintance, or perhaps a stranger, senses the apparitional presence. Spontaneous unconscious OBEs occur if the projector unintentionally appears to the other person and is unaware of doing so; self-induced unconscious OBEs occur if the projector intends to appear to the other person and succeeds in doing so, but is unaware of it.

I have had two unconscious OBEs that I am aware of, but since I do not keep notes about all the times I have attempted a conscious OBE and failed, I am not sure if either of these two instances was spontaneous or self-induced. I could have been trying to project and succeeded in doing so, but for some reason failed to retain conscious memory of it.

In 1990 I self-induced several OBEs in an attempt to reach my friend Judi's house in astral form, as an experiment to see if we could experience a mutual projection. Between my house and the house Judi lived in at that time is a cement plant, where I had been previously employed as a chemist. Another close friend, Jean, was still employed in the same lab, and often worked graveyard shift from 10:30 P.M. to 6:30 A.M. On a few occasions, when I passed over the plant in astral form on my way to Judi's, I was inadvertently drawn into the lab. I was only mildly annoyed by this, rather than overly concerned, because in case studies, I had read of other projectors who were swept away by astral currents of unknown origin (they always came back, as far as we know), and I had experienced such phenomena many times before.

Jean is an exceptionally intelligent, trustworthy, and responsible person whom I have been lucky to have as a friend for many years. After I told Jean about these experiences, she became interested and said she would watch for me and keep notes of what she saw while she worked graveyard shift. I told Jean I would try to appear to her, since she would be awake and might be capable of observing me in astral form. Although we succeeded twice, I have no clear conscious memories of seeing Jean during my astral visits to the lab, and the dates of my notes about such visits differ from Jean's notes.

On two different nights, Jean detected my astral form while she was working at the cement plant. On July 21, 1990, at 11:56 P.M., Jean was in the lab, running a chemical analysis, when she felt my presence. She said either I stood where she was standing or she stood where I was standing, she did not know which, but she stepped aside. We talked and Jean asked if I was on my way to Judi's, to which I replied, "yes." Jean wished me a "sunshiny trip," and as I left, I asked Jean not to say anything or mention my visit to M., who we thought would have difficulty understanding events such as OBEs, and might form prejudiced opinions against anyone who kept an open mind in these matters.

I failed to remember my astral visit with Jean in the lab that night, but I did have one of those strange dream experiences that I described as a dream within a dream in chapter 2; however, the contents I remember were unrelated to the cement plant or Jean.

I kept trying to project to the cement plant while Jean was working graveyard shifts, and she kept watching for me. In the early morning of May 9, 1991, at 3:21 A.M. I had another projection, which was unconscious for the most part, even though I think I have a vague memory of it.

Jean was in the office adjoining the lab, sitting at a desk, writing out an order for a raw mill conveyor belt speed change. She sensed a warm, gentle, secure feeling and thought she was receiving an impression from her deceased "Grandma Thelma." Jean looked up from her work and saw my astral form floating in, trying to get her attention. Then I stood beside the desk, and rested my hand on the desk top. To Jean, my astral form appeared as I normally look, in color, but washed out and made up of vaporous, rather than solid, material. I floated above her a bit and said, "I can see you are busy with that belt change, so I'll come back later." Then I disappeared.

Either of these unconscious projections could be spontaneous or self-induced, because around those times I had been trying regularly to project to Jean at the lab. However, I did not keep detailed enough notes to determine if, on those two nights, I was consciously inducing an OBE.

I have experienced many OBEs from the middle part of the OBE continuum, including the branches that connect with the dream continuum. Along a branch to the dream continuum, starting at any one of the various types of dreams, at the end closest to the dream continuum, these experiences range from

OBE-like dreams, to dreamlike OBEs, to OBEs containing some dreamlike elements. Along the branches between the dream continuum and the OBE continuum, subjectively, the OBE appears only partially developed, and conscious awareness can easily shift back into the ordinary dream world or wake up to the physical world. These branches are where dreams can become lucid and turn into OBEs, with or without sensations and observation of the actual separation from the physical form.

Sometimes, when it appears as though an ordinary dream evolves into a lucid dream and then directly into an OBE, without a return of awareness to the physical body in the hypnopompic state, it is possible that that could be an unconscious OBE suddenly turning into a conscious OBE. In other words, what was being interpreted as a dream actually may have been an OBE.

At the waking end of the OBE continuum are fully conscious OBEs, which can also be either spontaneous or induced. Case study collections frequently contain experiences of people who are sleeping and suddenly find themselves out of their bodies.[17] My first spontaneous conscious OBE was the one described at the opening of this book, in which I found myself crawling across my cabin floor in astral form in the middle of the night.

Induced conscious OBEs can be either initiated by the subject or an outside influence, such as an experimental procedure, another person, such as a hypnotist, or an external event, such as sudden danger, serious injury, or a drug. It is possible to learn to self-induce conscious OBEs, and these are the ones emphasized throughout this book.

---

[17]See these books for more information on spontaneous OBEs: Susy Smith, *The Enigma of Out-of-Body Travel*; Celia Green, *Out of the Body Experiences*; Sylvan Muldoon and Hereward Carrington, *The Phenomena of Astral Projection*; H. F. Prevost Battersby, *Man Outside Himself: The Methods of Astral Projection*; Robert Crookall, *More Astral Projection*; Janet Bord, *Astral Projection: Understanding Your Psychic Double*; and Herbert B. Greenhouse, *The Astral Journey*.

All of these alternative states of consciousness—OBEs, lucid dreams, dual consciousness, transition state ESP, mental projection, and inspiration—appear to be possible from the hypnagogic and hypnopompic states. The intricacies of this labyrinth of consciousness are baffling! The dream continuum, the OBE continuum, and the other types of awareness appear to be connected to each other by a tangle of circuitous routes and shortcuts. Lucid dreams can lead to wakefulness, OBEs, or normal sleep, while OBEs can lead to ordinary dreams, the hypnopompic state, or other states of consciousness. The term OBE is applied to a variety of experiences, and a variety of terms refer to OBE-like experiences.

Many questions remain to be answered. An important one is whether or not mental projection, transition state ESP, and OBEs are all the same state of consciousness. Could OBEs actually be a special type of ESP characterized by mental imagery of occupancy of an "astral body" separating from the physical body and functioning on the "astral plane?" Both affirmative and negative conjectures are convincing.

It seems likely that OBEs and lucid dreams are different states of consciousness. The EEG studies discussed in chapter 1 showed that OBEs are different from dreams and are usually accompanied by a decrease in REMs, while researchers have determined that lucid dreams occur when REMs are at the peak of their activity. It is difficult to imagine that OBEs from the waking state are lucid dreams. Most importantly, the subjective experience of lucid dreaming differs from astral projection; by definition a lucid dreamer knows the experience is a dream, but astral projectors are usually convinced the experience is "real."[18]

Lucid dreams also appear to be different from transition state ESP, because immediately before and during the ESP episode there is no experiential awareness of ordinary dreaming,

---

[18]Sue Blackmore, "A Theory of Lucid Dreams and OBEs," in *Conscious Mind, Sleeping Brain: Perspectives on Lucid Dreaming*, Jayne Gackenbach and Stephen LaBerge, eds. (New York: Plenum Press, 1988), p. 374.

only hypnagogic imagery, but this may or may not be the same type of imagery as that of dreams. Transition state ESP seems to involve an external focus, lucid dreams an internal focus, but nobody really knows if OBEs are internal or external.

The tangled corridors of the hypnagogic and hypnopompic states, filled with open holes, dead ends, intersections, and crossovers to mysterious realms that have their own deceptive entrances and exits, entice us to search inward, outward, and beyond our familiar physical world—to explore the invisible worlds around us.

Chapter 5

Invisible Worlds

Where are the invisible worlds? In another universe? In the imagination? Here? Do the invisible worlds only exist in our minds during alternative states of consciousness? Are they clever illusions created by our brain chemistry for reasons of which we are still unaware? Or are they part of our external environment, a part of objective reality, which can be perceived by more than one person?

Some psychologists and scientific researchers present theories explaining the existence of the invisible worlds as internal mental phenomena, while others present equally plausible theories to the contrary, hypothesizing that the invisible worlds are external. They all have received justified criticism.[1] We still lack proof that the invisible worlds are internal or external, or that they exist at all.

An Esoteric Model of Reality

According to esoteric teachings, interspersed with the physical dimension, which we experience in everyday waking life, is a vast realm containing multiple worlds organized to enclose different types of reality and varying levels of spiritual development. These worlds are divided into seven major levels; the lowest is the physical plane, then the astral, and then the mental. Above these three are the causal, devachanic, buddhic, and

[1]H. J. Irwin, *Flight of Mind: A Psychological Study of the Out-of-Body Experience* (Metuchen, NJ: Scarecrow Press, 1985), pp. 219–259.

nirvanic planes, with the order and names varying according to different sources. Each major level is then subdivided further into seven sublevels, resulting in a total of forty-nine levels. Each higher level is closer to divine perfection than the one below it. With the coarsest substance composing the physical world, the matter composing each higher sublevel becomes finer and finer.[2]

Although esoteric writings refer to the seven major levels as planes, such as the physical plane or the astral plane, they indicate that rather than consisting of planes organized in a vertical arrangement in space, the various types of matter composing the invisible worlds interpenetrate one another and exist simultaneously in the same place, but with some levels extending beyond others.[3] The idea of levels refers to different reality systems made up of various kinds of matter, each with unique densities, particle size, and vibrations. Different esoteric and spiritualistic writers use different names to refer to planes of reality and classify them in various ways, but the basic structure is usually similar to the one given here.

Therefore, if esoterica is correct, the invisible worlds are right here, right now! We must use "clairvoyant" vision to see them. To "travel" from one plane or subdivision to another, it is necessary to shift awareness to a state of consciousness receptive to the new level and learn to function in the appropriate body for that level.[4] Esoteric teachings state that, preferably through the protection and guidance of a qualified teacher, almost anyone can learn to consciously enter and utilize the invisible worlds.

Esoteric philosophy teaches that the seventh and lowest major level is the physical world. "Above" the seventh level are the major levels 6, 5, and 4, etc., each interpenetrating those below and everything in them, except for the areas of some that extend beyond the others. The "closest" major level to the

---

[2]C. W. Leadbeater, *The Astral Plane* (Wheaton, IL: Theosophical Publishing House, 1977), pp. 16–17.

[3]Leadbeater, *The Astral Plane*, p. 15.

[4] *The Astral Plane*, p. 16.

physical world is 6, the astral plane, which is subdivided into its seven minor subdivisions also numbered 1 through 7, with 7 being the lowest.

The seventh subdivision of the astral plane is made up of the coarsest, densest astral matter and penetrates below the earth's surface. It is a dark, gloomy realm filled with horrifying images and much pain and sorrow. It is a place that attracts the least evolved, most evil beings.[5] This is the temporary abode of the newly dead and the earthbound, with the length of their stay depending upon the strength of their attachment to the material world, physical desires, and negative emotions such as hate, fear, or anger. (Of course, if the levels all interpenetrate each other, as esotericism says, then it is logical to assume that the other levels would pentrate below the earth's surface also, unless this is an example of an area of one extending beyond others.)

The minor subdivisions 6, 5, and 4 of the astral plane correspond closely to physical reality and contain the astral counterpart of every object in the physical world, with the upper parts of 5 and 4 becoming less and less material. All mineral, plant, animal, and human forms have counterparts on the astral plane, made up of astral matter.[6]

However, the astral plane extends far beyond these counterparts. It has locations that lack physical existence, and it contains reflections of the past and future as well as the present. Subdivisions 3, 2, and 1 are the heavenly worlds of all religions, so far removed from physical reality that they have little in common with it.[7]

DENIZENS OF INVISIBLE WORLDS

In the invisible worlds, we are not alone! According to esoteric literature, case studies, and my personal experience, a strange

[5]*The Astral Plane*, pp. 18, 30.
[6]*The Astral Plane*, pp. 18–21.
[7] *The Astral Plane*, p. 31.

mixture of entities inhabits the invisible worlds, existing in forms that appear as human, animal, and otherwise.

The simplest ones exist as amorphous clouds of nonphysical matter and lack individualization. The various individualized creatures roaming about the invisible worlds range from simple shapes of intelligent light forms, through a wide variety of more complex anatomic arrangements, to the most highly evolved celestial beings. Some appear as ordinary people, some as majestic beings of radiant matter clad in shimmering robes, and others as demonic villains posing menacing countenances and threatening gestures, or even attacking. The variety of forms seems endless.

According to many belief systems throughout the world and throughout time, the different kinds of entities occupy the different levels and subdivisions of the invisible worlds. Some are depicted as hideous monsters in horrible hells, delighting in the torment of humans. Others are seen as benevolent deities in glorious heavens, expecting appeasement from humans and bestowing blessings in return. Esoteric literature presents an elaborate hierarchy of beings at various levels of spiritual development to inhabit the invisible worlds and administer the proceedings of each plane.

The most basic forms are elemental essences, which are simple nebulous masses of different types and densities, awaiting individualization through the descent of spirit. Elemental essences exist as types pertaining to the three kingdoms of esoteric theory, the mineral, vegetable, and animal kingdoms. The elemental essences of each kingdom can be further classified by densities in the four catagories of elements—earth, water, air, or fire. Fire, which is another term for what traditional esoteric teachings call ether, is subdivided to include four densities of its own, giving a total of seven elements. The result is a septenary arrangement of seven elements on seven levels of reality. (The esoteric use of the terms "element" and "ether" is distinctive from the chemists'; the two usages should not be confused.)

Elemental essence is sensitive to thoughts and will temporarily take the form of any thought that happens to come in contact with it. These thought forms are called artificial elementals and soon dissipate back into the elemental essence, with their life span depending upon the clarity, intensity, and duration of the thought. A thought form may be sustained or strengthened by repetition of the thought, either by the originator or others. Artificial elementals are formed passively, as well as deliberately, by the thoughts of individual or collective entities in the physical and invisible worlds.

Composed of the same substances as elemental essences, but more highly organized, are what esotericism calls nature spirits, which include the often mentioned spirits of earth, water, air, and fire (ether). Nature spirits are individualized, intelligent astral entities known throughout esoteric writings as gnomes (earth), undines (water), sylphs (air), and salamanders (fire/ether).[8] These are the elves, goblins, gremlins, fairies, trolls, and other fantastic beings appearing in the folklore, legend, myth, poetry, and prose of all times and places. Normally, to humans on the physical level, nature spirits are invisible, but when they wish to be seen, they can materialize into a form perceptible to physical eyes. They are characterized as playfully mischievous for the most part, sometimes helpful, and occasionally malicious. Although their worlds occupy the same space as ours, their development is along a different path. They will never be human.

Humans can exist in the invisible worlds. According to general esoteric belief, the physical body has nonphysical counterparts, to be described in the next section, specifically designed to operate on different levels. Human inhabitants of the invisible worlds include the ethereal, astral, mental, and causal counterparts of those who also exist in physical form, those who have departed from physical life, and still others who are preparing to enter physical life. Animals, too, have their subliminal forms in the invisible worlds.

---

[8]See *The Astral Plane*, pp. 92–125 for references to elemental essences.

Other, mythical kinds of forms exist also, some humanoid, some animal-like, and some part-human and part-animal. Any of these beings may be at different stages of spiritual and intellectual development. Besides being highly developed in every way or lacking significant development of any kind, some may be advanced spiritually, but have little intelligence, while others may be highly intelligent evil beings. Whether astral entities are diabolical creatures of horror or god-like beings of magnificent beauty, they include those who are still insufficiently developed to exist on the physical plane, those who are between earthly lives, those who have advanced beyond the physical plane, and those who will never occupy the physical plane.

Esoteric teachings warn us that certain forms appearing as human or human-like are something entirely different, even if they have the exact personality features and mannerisms of a friend or loved one. Some of these impostors may be only thought forms, conjured up from elemental essences by humans or other entities. Others may be the discarded subliminal bodies of deceased persons, occupied by other entities. Also, many beings have the ability to appear on various levels in human form or any other form they may choose. In this category would belong the "familiars" of black magic and witchcraft.

The most highly evolved entities of the astral and mental planes are angelic forms of exquisite beauty. These exalted celestial beings have advanced far above evil, and are capable of only good thoughts and actions. Of similar status are the seven rulers of the seven elements of matter (earth, water, air, and the four grades of fire). The three highest rulers of the fire element are so far above humanity that we ignore them, but the other four are symbolized as the four kings in the Tarot deck, and referred to as the guardians of the four corners of the earth.

Although the highest astral plane subdivisions, 3, 2, and 1, occupy the same space as the lower subdivisions, they seem far removed from the physical world. The matter comprising these upper levels and their inhabitants is so fine that they are practically oblivious of the physical world. The dwellers within these heavenly worlds create their own thought-like surroundings—beautiful cities with well-designed buildings and colorful gardens, and countrysides with forests, lakes, and mountains. Although created mentally from extremely fine matter, these environments are substantial enough to exist in objective reality, perceptible to other entities on the upper astral plane, as well as those on the lower subdivisions who have developed sufficient clairvoyant vision.[9]

In the realms above the astral plane are beings so advanced that they are virtually beyond comprehension by our intellect and description by our language.[10]

Esoteric teachings describe a vast array of functions for this multitude of entities. Many of them are spirit guides, willing at a moment's notice to help anyone along the path of spiritual development; others are agents of a god, working to fulfill the divine will; and some are infused with evil, existing to carry out the intentions of black magicians. Most are struggling somewhere along the path of spiritual development, as are we.

INVISIBLE BODIES

According to esoteric belief, just as we possess a physical body which allows us to live and function on the physical plane, we possess other, nonphysical bodies which allow us to exist in the invisible worlds. These various forms coexist in the same space in the same manner as the different levels of reality which interpenetrate each other, but they can separate and operate as independent vehicles.

Ordinary physical matter composes the physical body, which is the densest of our forms. Considered to be a part of the physical body, the etheric body is made up of various grades of

---

[9] *The Astral Plane*, p. 32.

[10] C. W. Leadbeater, *The Devachanic Plane* (London: Theosophical Publishing Society, 1896).

ether and serves as a mold for the physical body.[11] The etheric body is also called the vital body, because it absorbs the life energy, *prana*, from the environment.

Finer than either physical or etheric matter, astral matter forms the astral body. Traditional esoteric writings describe the astral body as a more or less exact replica of the physical body, depending upon the development of the person.[12] Supposedly, the astral body of a highly evolved individual is well-defined with explicit detail, while that of an intellectually and spiritually less developed individual will be diffuse and vague. This seems contradictory, since, for example, evil entities can appear as exact imposters of others. But then, perhaps what we see is something other than their astral bodies.

The astral body has three functions: it transmits thought between the physical body and the higher bodies; it transforms emotions and desires into a form which we can experience; and it acts as a vehicle for independent action on the astral plane.[13] Because of its role in the formation of emotions and desires, the astral body is often referred to as the desire body.

The theory of repercussion states that damage done to the astral body is transferred to the physical body. For example, if a witch appears in astral form as a wolf, and the wolf is shot, the physical body will suffer a bullet wound. I have never experienced any firsthand evidence of repercussions.

According to some esoteric writers, psychic investigators, and experienced astral travelers, surrounding the astral double is an ovoid aura composed of fine, luminous matter from the astral plane and higher planes.[14] The aura extends past the physical body for about 6 to 18 inches around ordinary persons, and even

---

[11]*The Astral Plane*, p. 24.

[12]*The Astral Plane*, p. 40.

[13]Arthur E. Powell, *The Astral Body* (Wheaton, IL: Theosophical Publishing House, 1973), p. 23.

[14]For more information on this subject, please see the following titles: Susy Smith, *The Enigma of Out-of-Body Travel*; Arthur E. Powell, *The Astral Body*; Benjamin Walker, *Beyond the Body: The Human Double and the Astral Planes*;

farther around those who are highly evolved spiritually. Many of these writers agree that like thought forms, emotions and desires exist on the astral plane. They make the astral body and its aura frequently change appearance and brilliance as it takes on new shapes and colors with each passing mood. Physical health, intellect, and spiritual development are all reflected in the intricately layered, colorful patterns of the aura.

Even finer than the astral body is the matter composing the mental body of the lower mental plane. The mental body is the immortal part of a person that enters physical life and then, after death, returns to the upper levels. The mental body also changes appearance, but much more slowly than the astral body, taking on new characteristics with long term personality changes.

Still higher, on the upper mental plane, is the finest of all the forms, the causal body, which esoteric teachings consider to be the vehicle of the higher self. The causal body shows the changes accumulated during different physical incarnations, or lifetimes spent in the physical dimension.[15]

The ego, which in esoteric terminology comprises the true individual, is expressed in all these forms, each composed of the appropriate material to function on the particular level it was intended for. Perhaps the different states of consciousness (OBE, lucid dreams, transition state ESP, creative inspiration) are due to the functioning of these different "inner" bodies, and dual consciousness shows the ability for awareness to function simultaneously in more than one. Perhaps, with practice, the ability to consciously function in all the invisible bodies can be developed and controlled.

Different writers of the supernatural use different terminology for the anatomic forms that function on the various levels, but the scheme presented here is fairly representative of eso-

---

Herbert B. Greenhouse, *The Astral Journey*; Oliver Fox, *Astral Projection: A Record of Out-of-the-Body Experiences*; C. W. Leadbeater, *The Astral Plane*; and Joe H. Slate, *Psychic Phenomena*.

[15]*The Astral Plane*, p. 22.

teric, psychic, and spiritual beliefs. The astral body, also referred to as the soul body, body-of-light, phantom, astral double, and many other names, is the form with which we are mainly concerned in the OBE context.

CONTRASTING PERCEPTIONS

Although throughout my personal astral odyssey, many of the phenomena in the OBE world have appeared as esoterica describes, I have failed to see some of them, such as the complexity of the ovoid-shaped aura. Astral travelers, as well as clairvoyants, however, have allegedly seen it in all the colorful splendor claimed by esoteric teachings.

Whether or not the invisible worlds exist in external objective reality, as esotericism teaches, or internal subjective reality, as many others believe, part of the astral plane does appear to be a replica of our physical world. The houses, factories, and office buildings, sidewalks and traffic-filled streets, or natural landscapes look much like those we are familiar with in everyday waking life. Whether these locations are astral counterparts of the physical dimension, the actual physical locations seen through astral vision or a type of ESP, or figments of the imagination, remains a mystery. Whatever they are, during an OBE these areas of the astral world appear as substantial as the physical world—every bit as real as the paper holding these words. However, the "astral counterparts" are often a distorted version of physical reality, with objects added, missing, altered, or misplaced.

The astral counterpart of a familiar physical location may contain an extra object or two, with no physical counterpart(s) in the present physical location. Once, while out of my body in an OBE described fully in chapter 7, I found a framed print lying on my fireplace mantle. Physically, the print was not there, nor have I ever owned a print like that one.

Besides containing wayward objects, the astral world can have things left out. During another OBE, I glided downstairs to my living room. The living room was there, exactly where it was supposed to be, with its maple floor, textured walls, high ceiling, and large window, but all the furniture was gone. Of course, a few minutes later, when I went there physically, everything was present as usual.

Minor alterations are also common, such as when the astral counterpart of my bedroom window had a venetian blind, while the physical window had a shade. Another distortion is that an object may appear as a mirror image of its physical counterpart with right and left turned around. For example, during one astral adventure, my watch dial was reversed.

Sometimes astral objects are misplaced respective to physical objects, such as once when the quilt that was on my bed in physical reality appeared on my porch astrally.

All of the details of these OBEs are also related in later chapters.

Some of these quirks on the astral plane may result from our mental activity. Esoteric teachings inform us that because the elemental essences are sensitive to mental energy, thoughts and ideas acquire structure and substance, and temporarily exist on the astral plane much as physical objects exist more permanently on the physical plane. If this is true, then by reversing the process, maybe our minds can make astral objects disappear. So, on the astral plane, thinking about an object may cause it to appear and forgetting to think about it may cause it to fail to appear. This theory, however, is inadequate for most of these distortions; usually projectors realize it when something is added, missing, altered, or misplaced.

If thoughts are actual things composed of astral matter, they could have an even more significant impact upon the structures and events in the astral world. During OBEs our beliefs, emotions, attitudes, and expectations could create thought forms, which could affect the construction and phenomena of the astral world. Our personality traits could affect our behavior toward these created images as well as whatever objective images the astral world contains.

Another explanation for these strange distortions may be that astral consciousness is perceiving a past or future aspect of the physical environment, or an overlapping of more than one world, such as with dual consciousness.

Esoterica informs us that there are three reasons why we may fail to experience the astral plane exactly as they describe it. One reason is that it takes much experience to develop astral sight so that perceptions are accurate. Another reason is that many novices are too dazed, confused, or careless to interpret and remember what they experience in the astral world. Finally, due to some astral entities' extraordinary abilities and tendencies to deceive, we may be subjected to illusions.[16]

Sometimes, though, the astral counterparts of familiar places look confusing because they are viewed from unaccustomed perspectives. Since the astral body can operate in any position and from any vantage point, an inexperienced projector, or even an experienced one, can easily become disoriented, because every position feels normal and right-side-up. An ordinary place, which has been occupied almost every day for years, can look strange when viewed from the astral body lying on its side in midair; objects totally lose their familiarity and easily can be mistaken for something else.

Although most projectors experience an astral environment similar to or identical to their actual physical surroundings,[17] in the astral world it is possible to travel to mysterious areas that may or may not have physical counterparts. I have found myself projected to places completely alien to my conscious mind, and met strangers who, to my astonishment, recognized me. To this day the places, people, and reasons for going remain enigmatic.

If the astral world provides opportunities to travel through time as well as through space and reality levels, as many astral

---

[16]*The Astral Plane*, pp. 28–29.

[17]Irwin, *Flight of Mind*, p. 102.

travelers claim,[18] perhaps some trips to unfamiliar locations are visits to the past or future. I have had at least one such instance in which it appears as if I traveled to a place in the future—the time I projected to a gambling casino full of people enjoying themselves ten days before it opened.

There is also evidence that the dreary underworld, esoterica's seventh and lowest subdivision of the astral plane, may exist. Some projectors have encountered an area made of dark, dense, stagnant astral matter, like heavy, smothering fluid composing a region filled with swarming, demonic entities that torment those who pass through.[19] Although these vile creatures appear to do no actual harm, they annoy projectors by shoving, biting, blocking, mocking, and general harassment.

In general, much of the rest of the astral world appears brighter, in varying degrees, than the physical world. In the dark, where most things would be difficult to see physically, everything looks clear astrally. When the astral world is most brilliant, it looks like a composition of luminescent matter, where objects glow as if they emit rather than reflect light. Sunlight and natural objects, such as plants, rocks, and the sky, shimmer with a lustrous beauty unseen by physical eyes; colors take on rich vividness unimagined by an organic brain; and the entire atmosphere is charged with energized, scintillating vivacity.

Astral Adventures

Throughout the ages and throughout the material world, people have journeyed to the invisible worlds, and brought back mater-

---

[18]Herbert B. Greenhouse, *The Astral Journey* (Garden City, NY: Doubleday, 1975), pp. 18, 245, 320.

[19]The following books contain material on this "dreary underworld": Robert Crookall, *Out-of-the-Body Experiences: A Fourth Analysis*; Robert A. Monroe, *Journeys Out of the Body*; Herbert B. Greenhouse, *TYhe Astral Journey*; Douglas M. Baker, *Practical Techniques of Astral Projection*; and Yram, *Practical Astral Projection*.

ial for myth, fantasy, religion, and philosophy. Astral travel is a familiar theme found in ancient cultures, more recent recorded history, and primitive cultures of today, as well as modern societies.

Scientific research has found evidence indicating the universality of OBEs. Researchers estimate that about one in five to ten normal adults will experience the sensation of leaving their bodies at least once during a lifetime. Based upon analysis of over 70 different cultures throughout the world, studies approximate that 95 percent of them consider OBEs a valid supernormal experience.[20] Furthermore, independent reports from different cultures and individuals without contact with each other provide similar descriptions of the phenomena.[21]

Some people have difficulty accepting that it is natural to experience the sensation of having an astral double capable of existing apart from the physical body. Some are terrified if they become conscious of what seems like involuntary separation, believing they are going insane or dying, panicking at the thought of being unable to reenter their physical bodies, worrying about harmful effects on physical health, dreading the unknown, or fearing a different entity will take over their physical bodies while they are out, resulting in demonic possession.

Fear of attack by harmful astral entities is also present for some, and with good reason; projectors have been astrally attacked by creatures of varying descriptions. One time I was floating along, minding my own business, when I was grabbed and nearly captured by two humanoid astral entities. While I struggled to escape, I looked into one of the strangest faces I had ever seen—a furry animal face with a long snout and beady eyes!

The best defense against any panic situation appears to be to calm down, take a slow, deep breath, and relax. (Of course, it is much easier to tell you to do this than to actually do it my-

---

[20]D. Scott Rogo, "Traveling Light," *Human Behavior* (Oct. 1978): 37.

[21]Robert Crookall, *Out-of-the-Body Experiences: A Fourth Analysis* (Secaucus, NJ: Citadel Press, 1970), pp. 11–38.

self.) Try to be assured that the higher self knows how to handle all kinds of circumstances, and will safely return the astral body to the physical body as soon as any danger is perceived, whether it is real or imaginary. Usually, upon experiencing an intense emotion such as fear, the OBE will be terminated by automatic return to the physical body.

Perhaps I am too curious or overly confident, but based on personal experience and oral and written accounts of others, I believe that most of the above mentioned fears have little basis in reality. Many people have been out and back, some numerous times, without difficulty or known adverse side effects. Of course, proof of the complete safety of OBEs is lacking.

One survey seeking responses from persons who had experienced OBEs found that 85 percent of them reported pleasant feelings. Over half of the respondents considered the OBE joyful, and 43 percent thought it was the greatest experience they had ever had.[22]

Case studies of OBEs do include reports of feelings of fear, but they indicate many positive feelings as well, such as exaltation, exhilaration, vitality, and mental clarity. Projectors often report that while exteriorized they felt a new sense of freedom and a lack of interest in the physical body, and afterwards the elimination or significant reduction of the fear of death. One of the most predominant feelings during a fully conscious OBE is a sense of the reality of the experience.

If fear is absent, astral projection can be one of the most thrilling experiences of a lifetime, because the astral world is a wonderland full of beauty, magic, excitement, and surprises. The entire realm of the astral world offers learning opportunities beyond comparison with exclusively physical conscious experience.

The first time I voluntarily left my physical body and entered the astral plane fully alert, I was astonished that my consciousness actually could exist outside my physical form. As is

[22]D. Scott Rogo, *Leaving the Body* (Upper Saddle River, NJ: Prentice Hall, 1986), p. 18.

typical of others who have had even brief OBEs, I no longer *believed* I had a "soul," I *knew* it. I was amazed at how absolutely solid and real the astral plane appeared—as convincing as physical waking reality—and how I could experience my surroundings so vividly from a viewpoint away from the physical body. What a weird feeling that revelation presented!

The Astral Body

While experiencing a conscious OBE, most projectors occupy a nonphysical body.[23] It appears that encased within the physical body, beneath ordinary awareness, is an entirely different body, the astral body, just as magnificent and real as its physical counterpart, and capable of functioning independently as a vehicle in which to wander about the astral plane.

Sometimes, in astral form, when separated from the physical form, projectors are aware of being in a body with abilities far beyond those of the physical body. When projected, a person can actively participate, touch and move astral objects, walk around with the feeling of solidity beneath the feet, engage in conversations with astral inhabitants, or change location using various methods of mobility. Although extremely rare, there are documented cases of astral forms moving physical objects.[24]

Being in the astral body, separated from the physical body, generally feels just like being in the physical body. In both situations the body image is obtained from the interpretation of perceptions through various internal and external sense organs, which transmit tactile, kinesthetic, and visual information. Just as the physical body, the astral body can reach out with one hand and feel the texture and firmness of the other hand. The movement of an arm through space by exerting its muscles feels the same in the physical and astral bodies. It is possible to hold

---

[23]Irwin, *Flight of Mind*, p. 114.

[24]Greenhouse, *The Astral Journey*, pp. 56–65.

an astral hand in front of the astral eyes and observe it, but it changes form more readily than its physical counterpart. Proprioceptors, the internal senses that inform us of conditions such as hunger or discomfort and the positions and movements of the different parts of the body, function the same astrally as physically. When present, pain hurts the astral body just as much as the physical body. The astral body seems to have the same external senses the physical body has: vision, hearing, touch, smell, and taste.

Whether in physical or astral form, the body image resulting from a combination of these perceptions is accompanied further by the same psychological components: the spacial impression of occupying the body, the personal significance of self being the body, and the possessiveness of owning the body. In the astral body, just as in the physical body, it is possible for the individual to be aware of the appearance, position, and feeling of the body, as well as experience the emotional attachment resulting from the belief of occupancy, being, and ownership.

However, the structure, abilities, and senses of the astral body change frequently. The structure of the projected body takes on surprisingly different forms at different times. The abilities of the astral body vary also; sometimes it can easily perform actions that are difficult or impossible at other times. Often the astral senses operate exactly as the physical senses, but sometimes they are more limited, and at other times their capabilities surpass those of the physical body. The astral body's composition, performance, and functions change frequently and differ from its physical encasement in many ways, because it is designed to operate in the invisible worlds around us.

The majority of projectors report the existence of some type of astral body, and it manifests in a wide variety of morphological forms. Often it resembles a duplicate of the physical body, but appears to be composed of matter existing in a range of densities. Some projectors report that their astral forms consist of a ball of light, and a few say they have no astral body at all, only a point of consciousness.

The astral body probably acquired the name "body-of-light" because often it appears luminescent, usually either a brilliant gold or white, but occasionally other colors. At times, it looks like a glowing silhouette of a human body and lacks detail and solidity, while at other times it looks like a three-dimensional image of the physical body with an eerie glow. When near the physical form, or during dual consciousness, it sometimes appears as a flat, two-dimensional, glowing, ghostly humanoid abstract, that lacks solidity. The luminous form is much more elastic than the physical body, with the ability to stretch and bend in maneuvers that are impossible for organic structures.

Many times the projected double looks dull, feels substantial, and forms an exact replica of the physical body with every detail intact, including color, clothing, and the feel of solid flesh and bone. But the astral body can also have the look and feel of the physical body with a few details altered, sometimes in rather bizarre ways.

Regardless of how the astral body looks, its weight and density can change; sometimes it is heavy and dense, other times misty and light.

With rare exceptions of nudity, the astral body appears clothed in a variety of ways, usually in the projector's normal style, often corresponding to what the projector is actually wearing, a similar article of clothing, or another outfit actually owned by the projector. Occasionally the astral body is covered with long, flowing robes, conforming to images common in spiritualism. Normally, a departure from the immediate vicinity of the sleeping physical form is accompanied by an appropriate change of attire—apparently most projectors dislike wandering too far in the nude or in pajamas, nightgowns, or underwear. Most of the time, the choice of garments and dressing of the astral form take place unconsciously.

Many times I have paid attention to how my astral body is dressed and noticed that it is usually wearing clothing identical to or similar to items from my physical wardrobe, but it is often an outfit other than what my physical body has on at the time.

Once I did go outside in my pajamas (astrally), but I was at a secluded cabin, away from people. Oddly, the pajamas were not the same ones I wore to bed. Sometimes my astral body wears clothes that I have physically worn out and thrown away. During a few projections, my astral body was cloaked in beautiful diaphanous gowns that shimmered with astral luminosity; they created a fashion statement only strived for by earthly garment manufacturers.

Often it seems as if the astral body is made up of the finer, lighter, more diffuse astral material described by esoterics, material different from what we are accustomed to physically. When the astral double is weightless it can float, frolic about, dart from place to place, and perform midair acrobatics. Walls and closed doors seldom present a barrier to this diffuse form because it has the ghostly ability to pass through apparently solid objects.

At other times, the astral body feels so heavy and laden with matter that it is limited to physical laws, being confined to the ground or encountering resistance when trying to pass through solid material.

Some astral projecters claim that while exteriorzed they experience synesthesia, or trans-sensate phenomena, in which their astral senses have multiple functions, such as the ability to feel a color, see a musical tone, or hear a light. Others say their astral vision functions from any part of the astral body, has a visual field of 360 degrees, or can detect an object from all sides, inside as well as outside.

The first time I intentionally opened the eyes of my astral body, I thought I was opening my physical eyes, because the sensation felt identical. Sometimes, in the early phases of projection, I still find it difficult to distinguish which eyes are opening. During some projections, the astral world looks dim, blurry, or misty, but at other times, astral vision is as clear as perfect physical vision. Occasionally the astral body's sense of sight is more powerful; my astral eyes have had the ability to see through solid objects. Sometimes objects on the astral plane look brighter than their physical counterparts, glowing as if they emit their own light rather than reflect light from another source.

The astral world is full of sounds, some strange and others ordinary.

From my experience and from reading case studies, I have learned that it is common for certain noises to be present, often described as humming, buzzing, or rushing, like the wind blowing through trees. Since many of my projections took place from a forest, I could have been listening to an astral wind blowing through astral trees, or these could have been the physical sounds normally present there. They could also have had some other source. Sometimes I have heard buzzing, roaring, and high-pitched whirring, but at other times these noises have been absent, or they may have been present and I failed to notice them.

On the astral plane, I have heard the everyday commotion that we identify with the physical world, such as human conversation, barking dogs, and roaring engines. I have also heard ordinary sounds distorted with a strange, eerie, off-key resonance; my voice and my piano have sounded tinny and out of tune.

During several projections I noticed an acute sense of smell, such as when I went through ceilings and entered attics. The musty old smells prevailed with the same redolence in the astral attics.

The astral body can experience tactile sensations just as the physical body can. The feeling of the wind blowing in my face as I soar through the astral world is just as real as when a physical wind blows against my skin. My astral hands can feel rough and smooth textures just as readily as my physical hands can.

My astral nerves are sensitive to cold and heat, as when I touched a cool, moist rock, or when the astral counterpart of the atmosphere inside my cabin felt stuffy and hot. Usually, though, the astral environment seems to be at just the right temperature. Even when in astral form and wearing only a shirt and jeans, I felt perfectly comfortable flying through a brisk Dakota winter night.

I have felt both hunger and thirst in my astral form while in the OBE environment, with these impulses corresponding to how my physical body felt at the same times.

Besides senses similar to those of the physical body, the astral body has instinctual senses and other senses unique to more diffuse forms. The ability to fly and pass through solid objects came to me automatically, although at first it took some practice to gain control. When passing slowly through objects, my astral body experiences a peculiar sensation that I can best describe as molecular tingling, as if I can feel each molecule of my astral flesh vibrating and brushing against the particles of whatever I am passing through. When passing through quickly, I feel nothing at all; the objects present no more resistance than air.

Some of the astral senses operate unconsciously. It appears as if an instinctual part of the astral body is always aware of the condition of the physical body, with this information possibly being transmitted through the silver cord. Apparently, if anything disturbs the physical body or requires consciousness to return to it, the inner senses are immediately alerted and the astral body automatically returns, no matter how vast the distance between the two.

The astral body moves around much more freely than the physical body, having at its disposal several methods of mobility.

It can walk upon a solid foundation, just as the physical body can; the required muscle movements and balance feel exactly the same. Even though other methods are faster and more exciting, I often prefer walking because it enables detailed observation of the interesting and surprising astral environment. When the composition of the astral body is diffuse and light, it can take large, bouncing steps, resembling those of the astronauts that walked on the moon.

If walking is too slow, but a normal perspective is desired, the astral body can maintain an upright position and glide along a few inches above the surface.

Flying, of course, is faster. Sometimes the astral double can fly through the air easily, without the support of wings, airplane, or spacecraft. A wide variety of speeds and altitudes is available.

When conditions are favorable, all that is necessary to initiate flying is to think about it, and the astral body will soar upward effortlessly. This fantastic double can hover near the ceiling in a room or high in the sky, where it is possible to keenly observe objects and entities below. For an even greater thrill, it can fly up and away, across the landscape, to enjoy the scenery from an eagle's point of view.

It is amazing how different the world looks when viewed from heights to which we are unaccustomed. When skimming along a few hundred feet above treetop level, it is easy to lose our sense of direction. We can get lost without the normal perspective of familiar signs and landmarks along sidewalks, streets, or roadways. Buildings can lose their identity if little more than the rooftops are seen.

It is exciting to cruise at an altitude of a couple of thousand feet, confident of the power that holds the astral body up and propels it through the sky with such speed that the wind presses against the astral flesh as it rushes along. No carnival ride compares to the thrill of looking down at the landscape as it rolls by below, with its hills, forests, and prominent landmarks. It looks like the view from a small airplane, but is more panoramic since it is unobstructed by wings, window frames, or panels. Astral flight is also more pleasant because it is tranquil, without the engine noise.

The astral body can go much higher than an airplane; it can attain altitudes so high that the earth's surface looks like a living geographical map. I have never stayed at such extreme heights for longer than a brief moment, but that was long enough to get an impressive global view that offered an alarming perspective of the planet's limitations and vulnerabilities.

Besides walking, gliding, floating, or flying, the astral double can accelerate to incredible speeds that obliterate the distinction of objects, with everything rushing by in a blur of subdued color. Sometimes it looks and feels as if a powerful outer force propels the astral body through a narrow tunnel composed of a cloudy atmosphere. The outer force seems to control the speed, direction, and often the destination. In this manner, astral travelers can span great distances within a brief moment or two, sometimes to another city or town, sometimes to the other side of the planet, and sometimes to fanciful realms populated with strangers or exotic astral entities.

As incredible as these speeds are, the astral body has even greater capabilities. It is possible to reach a destination just by thinking about it; the thought of a place or a person occurs and the astral body can be instantaneously placed there, without any sensation of travel.

ASTRAL ENCOUNTERS

Whatever the astral world is and wherever it exists, whether in each individual brain or as part of a system of exterior invisible worlds, it is a busy place, populated with many active inhabitants in various forms. Spiritualists proclaim that just as we can enter the invisible worlds and travel about, astral entities can enter the physical domain and often do for various purposes, such as communication from the dead, personal guidance, or harassment. Persons who have developed clairvoyance or clairaudience (or both) can detect astral beings and sometimes communicate with them. Projectors often encounter strange and interesting entities in the astral world, and throughout my astral odyssey experiences I have witnessed some of the categories of nonphysical beings mentioned in esoteric writings.

Most astral entities detected by projectors and psychics, either on the astral or physical plane, have been human-like in form: friends, relatives, associates, famous personalities, and strangers to the conscious mind. I have seen "astral forms" of a few familiar people and many strangers, as well as animals, myth-like creatures, and abstract forms. During OBEs, I have seen forms of humans and animals who could have been astral or physical, and during the hypnagogic or hypnopompic states I have seen others who may have been astral forms either in the astral world or the physical world, depending upon which world my consciousness was perceiving.

The first time I consciously approached beings on the astral plane, I was in an unfamiliar, though ordinary appearing house whose ordinary appearing occupants were strangers to my conscious memory. I thought it was quite likely that I was invisible, but I was wrong. To my surprise and embarrassment, the people in the house not only saw me, but they recognized me and spoke to me! To this day I have not determined who they are or why I projected there.

During my attempts to astrally project to my friend Judi, I succeeded twice; in two OBEs I astrally stood by her bedside as she slept. There is an enigma, however. Was I gazing down at her astral form or her physical form, and was my astral form actually in Judi's bedroom, or was I on the "astral plane?"

During another OBE, upon returning to my bedroom from an astral journey, I encountered a young man (a stranger), standing near my bed as if watching over my physical body. I assumed he was a guardian angel of mine, or a helper of some kind, but I failed to get much information from him.

The most impressive being I have ever seen during any of my astral projections (or during my physical life) appeared one night after I floated out my upstairs bedroom window in astral form. I clearly saw, standing on my porch roof, a figure that looked like depictions of Jesus Christ.

Most of the human-like entities I have observed on the astral plane, however, have appeared as ordinary people going about their business in an ordinary world, populating the streets, parks, and buildings of the astral plane. They converse, drive cars, wear business suits or other appropriate attire, prepare meals, play slot machines, stroll through parks, and perform many other activities, much as we do in the physical world. Perhaps they are physical beings in the physical world, seen from an astral perspective.

Many of the beings mentioned in the chapters on my OBEs or in accounts of others could be regular inhabitants of the astral world, the astral counterparts of physical beings, or they could be physical forms seen from an astral viewpoint. Others are definitely nonphysical. Astral forms observed psychically from a physical viewpoint could also be either dwellers of the astral plane or the projected astral doubles of physically incarnate persons. Perhaps entities encountered during OBEs or through clairvoyant or clairaudient perception are thought forms, either of the projector or others. It is also possibile that some or all of them are imaginary.

When, from the astral double, an individual's own physical form is viewed, it is impossible to know if it is the genuine physical form or a mental image, or if it is seen from an astral world or from an exteriorized viewpoint in the physical world. It is hard to believe that the "physical form" viewed would be an "astral counterpart" when the person is "in" the astral counterpart, a few feet away. Whatever the truth is, to the astral projector it certainly looks like the actual physical body lying there, breathing quietly, sound asleep, and it can really give people the creeps to see themselves this way.

Often, if it is a waking projection during injury, the projector calmly and painlessly views the physical body undergoing the traumatic event, feeling little concern even when the physical body appears to be writhing and screaming in great torment. An exception to this is the case of Sylvan Muldoon, when his projected astral double experienced prolonged agony as his physical body was being electrocuted in a childhood accident, which he survived.[25]

Anesthetized surgical patients often leave their physical bodies and watch their operations from above, and afterward shock doctors and nurses with accurate accounts of what was done and said during the procedure.

If it is possible for persons in astral form to view their own physical bodies lying or writhing beneath them, or undergoing surgery, it appears logical to be able to view the physical bodies of others from the OBE environment.

---

[25]Sylvan J. Muldoon & Hereward Carrington, *The Projection of the Astral Body* (London: Rider, 1951; York Beach, ME: Samuel Weiser, 1977), pp. 259–261.

During OBEs I have also seen human-like forms that I know were not physical. One time, shortly after I left my physical body and passed through my bedroom wall, I saw the shadowy, translucent forms of several men engaged in a fistfight in my living room. Their movements were realistic as they parried and threw punches, and their grunts and the smack of flesh hitting flesh were audible. I have occasionally wondered whether they were hypnopompic images, dream elements, thought forms, or some type of astral entities.

Whether they are astral beings, physical beings, or the astral counterparts of physical beings, many of the human forms encountered during OBEs look and act just as humans do in waking physical reality; they perform their various tasks much as we do as we go about our daily lives. They each have their own unique features, build, hair color, style of dress, and mannerisms, just as people we see when we are in normal physical consciousness.

Animals, too, are observed during astral projection. I have seen my dog and cats while I was out of my body and they looked normal, solid, and three-dimensional, sometimes responding to me in their usual manner and other times appearing to be unaware of my presence. Most of the time when I have observed my pets from astral form, as when I have astrally observed some humans, it was impossible to determine whether I was seeing their astral, physical, or imaginary bodies. On one occasion, however, my cats accompanied me on an astral journey, so I assume they had to have been either thought forms or astral forms.

It may be possible for astral forms of animals to be detected from the physical plane. Once, from hypnagogic consciousness, I sensed the presence of my black cat, Zephyr, who had been gone for several days. I was lying in bed and felt him jump up on the foot of the bed in his usual spot, lie down, and dig his claws into the covers, as cats do when they relax. I was relieved and happy he was safely home again, back from wherever he had gone, but I wondered how he had gotten into the cabin, since both doors were closed. When I sat up to welcome him back, the spot was empty. To this day, I have never seen Zephyr again, either astrally or physically, but this experience gave me hope that departed cats may have astral forms that live on somewhere.

The most frightening creatures I have ever seen in the astral environment were the ones I mentioned earlier in this chapter, in the section titled "Astral Adventures." These were the two monstrosities with human bodies and furry animal faces, who tried to abduct me. They were unlike any of the familiar creatures evolved on our physical planet Earth.

Even further removed from ordinary biological forms, however, were some that dropped by my cabin late one balmy night. I was in bed, aware either in the hypnagogic state or astral form, when I saw what appeared to be entities that had neither human nor animal form. Four or five glowing golden spheres, each about four inches in diameter, floated through my window into my room. Although they appeared to be simple globes of light, they behaved as though they had intelligence, purpose, and will. As they floated from the window to the space above my bed, I sensed that they were friendly and peaceful, so I sat up to get a better look at them. They gracefully danced in the air around me, lightly landing upon my arms, then slowly bouncing away and back again. After a few moments, the shining globes disappeared out the window and into the dark woods, as silently as they had entered.

* * * * * * *

Down through the ages, we have amassed many impressions of the invisible worlds and the entities that inhabit them. Much of what has been learned from esoteric traditions is supplemented by reports from those who pushed beyond preconceived limits and ventured away from the familiar constraints of the physical dimension. We still question, however, whether the invisible worlds and their inhabitants are part of a master plan of reality, whether they are chaotic collisions of realms randomly imposed upon one another, or whether they are only imaginary.

Perhaps anyone can cross the boundary between worlds and embark upon an astral odyssey. If more people learn to self-induce OBEs, using the methods described in the next chapter, or similar methods, someday we may solve the mystery.

Chapter 6

Between Worlds

Can anyone who wants to actually visit invisible worlds? Where is the boundary between the physical world and the astral world? How do we get from one side of that boundary to the other? The crossing between worlds is hazy, intangible, and elusive, but it is approachable through the junctions and byways of consciousness found in the hypnagogic and hypnopompic states. Chapter 4 showed us that within the transition states between waking and sleeping are enigmatic shifts of awareness that can take us to and from dream worlds, to the expanded awareness of creative inspiration, mental projection, transition state ESP, dual consciousness, and lucid dreams, or to the astral plane. Although we all frequently pass through this mental labyrinth, we are usually oblivious of it, and we have only limited studies, confusing nomenclature, numerous and incomplete systems of classification, and few reliable facts upon which to base our knowledge. We need hypotheses that can be tested by repeatable experiments that result in clear definitions and fundamental principles upon which to base practical applications that can increase human knowledge.

It is paradoxical that modern scientists know more about the external physical world and how to manipulate it than they know about the imaginations that create the complex technologies dominating today's world. We have learned much about the psychology, anatomy, and physiology of the brain, but we understand little of the life force that animates it. We know how to travel to outer space, but we have much to learn about traveling through our inner selves.

Somewhere along the interdimensional continuums of consciousness, in the evasive and transitory hypnagogic and hypnopompic states, is the border between worlds. Delicately balanced at a point between waking and sleeping is the level of consciousness that holds the key to the astral world. It is extremely rare for a person to deliberately use that key, but I believe most people can learn astral projection if they are aware of its existence and have an idea of where to begin. Contemporary researchers are amassing study after study verifying that persons can be trained to reach and recognize the state of consciousness in which it is possible to release a part of the self and experience existence from an exterior location.[1]

Although self-induced OBEs are extremeiy rare, spontaneous OBEs are somewhat more common. Occasionally, individuals suddenly awaken and find themselves out of their physical bodies, floating in astral form, wondering why and how they got there. This happened to Ben, a person who is admirable in both physical and spiritual forms, in his spontaneous conscious OBE late May 26 or early May 27, 1993.

In the darkest hours of night and in some stage of seemingly dreamless sleep, Ben somehow unintentionally crossed the dividing line between our physical world and the astral world. Awareness returned, but he was unsure if he was awake or asleep.

Ben was aware of lying on his back in bed. He looked up and saw above him, floating only inches away, his face, neck, and shoulders, which were bare, as was his physical form. He could clearly see his astral body, because it shined with "ethereal light," a steel blue luminescence which emitted from an indeterminable source and cast an eerie glow upon and within the levitated form. As Ben looked up into the face of his astral double, the astral eyes were open, looking down at him. The shoulders were darker and the lower part of the body disappeared down into shadow.

---

[1]D. Scott Rogo, *Leaving the Body* (New York: Prentice Hall, 1986), p. 15.

Then, instantaneously, he was in the glowing image! Ben looked down at his sleeping physical face on the pillow. It looked normal, appearing solid and dull, lacking the blue radiance. As he looked down at his sleeping face, a teardrop fell out of his astral eye and onto his closed physical eyelid. He felt a teardrop splash on his eye, and "awoke" crying, wondering why he was crying. The glowing image was gone.

Why does the astral body sometimes involuntarily separate from the physical body? What causes the astral body to dissociate from its physical enclosure? How can the process be learned? Numerous occult, spiritualistic, mystical, and metaphysical writings explain methods of astral projection. Unfortunately many of them, especially earlier ones, are secretive, providing vague and incomplete instructions, only hinting at "inside information" too powerful for the general public, or too dangerous if learned by anyone with evil intentions.[2] Probably originating within mystical systems of yoga and prehistorical religious traditions, this information supposedly has been known and handed down since ancient times by select groups of theologians and occultists.

Although according to older writings it is preferable to learn astral projection under the careful guidance of a qualified expert,[3] it is possible through self-instruction. It appears there are always gurus, masters, and teachers who profess to have superior knowledge of the astral world and who claim that theirs are the only safe, reliable techniques to consciously and voluntarily leave the physical body. Often they warn about the possiblility of dire consequences if a beginner fails to follow their instructions exactly.

Some writers have indicated that astral projection is generally acceptable and fairly safe for most people, but discourage its

---

[2]Ophiel, *The Art & Practice of Astral Projection* (York Beach, ME: Samuel Weiser, 1977), pp. 15–17.

[3]Benjamin Walker, *Beyond the Body* (London: Routledge & Kegan Paul, 1974), pp. 118–120.

practice by those with heart disease, illness, "nervous" temperament, mental or emotional instability, lack of self-control, an immoral nature, or a tendency to consume drugs or alcohol.[4] The possible dangers that they point out include heart failure, hysteria, insanity, coma, congestion, cerebral hemorrhage, paralysis, headaches, dizziness, hypochondria, fainting, hallucinations, nightmares, loss of memory, attack by hostile astral entities, severance of the silver cord, illness or injury to the astral body, repercussion of injury to the astral body upon the physical body, disruption of the connection of the soul to the psyche, entry of harmful astral entities into the physical domain, spirit obsession, becoming the victim of lower forces, excessive preoccupation with astral projection, loss of interest in physical life, and death. This impressive and formidable list has no scientific research upon which to base any part of it. We do know, based upon statistical analysis, that perhaps millions of people have had spontaneous or induced OBEs and returned safely with no obvious harmful effects.

Different in nature is another risk—ridicule and ostracism if OBEs are mentioned to narrow-minded people or anyone who would use knowledge of such activity against another. Similar to such misfortune, and hopefully rare, is a case discussed by Herbert Greenhouse in *The Astral Journey*.[5] A young college student mentioned her OBE to an ignorant resident physician, who immediately had her taken by police to a mental institution. The trauma of the experience inhibited further development of her psychic growth.

Since the publication of works by three of the 20th century's most highly acclaimed adepts, Oliver Fox, Sylvan Mul-

---

[4]For more guidelines on astral projection, please see Yram, *Practical Astral Projection*; Benjamin Walker, *Beyond the Body: The Human Double and the Astral Planes*; Oliver Fox, *Astral Projection: A Record of Out-of-the-Body Experiences*; and Sylvan Muldoon and Hereward Carrington, *The Projection of the Astral Body*.

[5]Herbert Greenhouse, *The Astral Journey* (Garden City, NY: Doubleday, 1975), pp. 308–310.

doon, and Robert Monroe, many books, too numerous to list, are available giving explicit instructions for voluntary OBEs.

METHODS OF INDUCING OBES

Many methods of learning to self-induce conscious OBEs are found in the bibliography. These methods vary in their success for different individuals and at different times. Most of the methods applied to voluntary self-induction of OBEs are centered upon training the mind to stay alert in either the hypnagogic or hypnopompic state, starting from waking, partial waking, or dreaming. The trick is to allow the body to sleep and keep the mind alert, perfectly balanced at the correct point between wakefulness and sleep. I believe that most persons with the desire and enough persistence can learn to leave their physical bodies by using one or more of these methods, which can be modified or combined to compensate for individual differences and preferences.

One type of method involves "creating," by mental visualization, an "astral form," placing it in the external environment, and then projecting consciousness into it.

After consciousness is transferred to the astral form, it may then drift away from the physical body. Some writers disclose exotic magical rituals used to manifest the astral form.[6] I have never tried these methods, but they are plausible—Ben may have unconsciously and spontaneously created his astral form, then projected his consciousness into it. If it can happen spontaneously, why not voluntarily?

However, it is also possible that the astral form already exists in coincidence with the physical body, and all that is required is to exteriorize it and transfer consciousness into it, or si-

[6]For more on exotic magtical rituals, read these books: Ophiel, *The Art and Practice of Astral Projection*; and Melita Denning and Osborne Phillips, *The Llewellyn Practical Guide to Astral Projection*.

multaneously separate the astral form with consciousness from the physical form. Many methods take the latter approach.

Some of these methods utilize the invocation of astral inhabitants to assist the projector out of the body and guide the journey through the invisible worlds. I have had some success this way, and so have others I have talked with and read about.

One time, when I was lying in bed, at the balance point between sleeping and waking, attempting to project, I felt astral hands push against my back and move my astral body forward, into a sitting position, out of my physical form. On this particular occasion, I had requested help from "spirit guides," but such assistance may be unsolicited!

A long-time friend of mine, Lyla, told me she had in her house a "spirit" friend, a huge, masculine entity that looked like a typical white-sheeted "ghost." He tried to persuade her to leave her body one night. After she declined, he attempted to grab her hand and pull her out, but Lyla became frightened, not of him, but of leaving her body. After Lyla's astral scream, the big billowy entity disappeared, reassuring her that we have contol over how nonphysical personalities behave toward us.

In the literature are many examples of "helpers" who have been readily available to projectors. Often, though, they seem to be away when assistance is requested.

Esoteric teachings have long considered the pineal gland to be important in initiating supernormal phenomena of all kinds, including OBEs. The pineal body is shaped like a tiny pine cone and located in the center of the skull, directly behind the eyes. The French philosopher and mathematician, Descartes, considered it to be the "seat of the rational soul," and it has often been referred to as the "third eye." Interestingly, in many reptiles the pineal gland is located near the top of the head, and in some has formed a structure resembling a rudimentary third eye with a simple lens and photoreceptors. Although there is much conjecture, nobody knows for sure the function of the pineal gland in humans, but in other animals it actually does function to regulate activities related to darkness and light, such as wakefulness and sleep, or behavior and coloration based upon seasonal changes, which result from differences in the amount of day-light.

In supernatural disciplines, the pineal gland is employed in some methods to induce OBEs. After physical relaxation, concentration upon the pineal gland is supposed to activate the "crown of the head" chakra, the most powerful of the seven chakras, which serve as energy centers, or points of connection between the physical and astral bodies. When the chakra at the top of the cranium is activated, energy is directed to raise the vibration level of the astral body, allowing it to separate from its physical constraint.

It may be wise to avoid all OBE induction methods that attempt to activate the chakras. Most sources containing information on these chakras, or energy centers, warn that it is extremely dangerous to arouse the chakras prematurely, which may "raise the kundalini" before one is sufficiently developed spiritually or psychically. According to D. Scott Rogo, there is some evidence from yoga students attempting to "raise the kundalini" by practicing cross-breathing techniques that these warnings should be taken seriously, to avoid resulting psychological and physiological disturbances.[7]

Some of the most commonly described methods to induce exteriorization are those that use projection from lucid dreams. They use autosuggestion for an OBE, applied with some combination of the four steps in chapter 3: dream recall, interpretation, induction, and intervention. Dream projection methods make use of a wide variety of techniques in the application of each step, and are among the most successful.

Another way to reach the type of consciousness conducive to voluntary OBEs is to stay aware in the hypnagogic state. Different hypnagogic techniques are applied by incorporating autosuggestion, focusing on internal or external images, or using magical rituals. Some hypnagogic methods are commonly referred to as trance, meditation, and self-hypnosis.

---

[7]Rogo, *Leaving the Body*, pp. 83–84.

Hypnotism by someone else or listening to specially prepared tapes can also be successful in producing the necessary state.

Other useful techniques stimulate alertness in the hypnopompic state. As soon as waking consciousness begins to arouse, it is prevented from waking up entirely or going back to sleep. As discussed in chapter 4, this intermediate awareness may automatically become conducive to the state necessary to produce a conscious OBE.

Many OBE induction techniques are based upon the philosophy of magic. Magical rituals can be applied to any type of projection method and be made up of specific postures, positions, motions, chanting, mantras, mental visualizations, or symbols. The combinations and variations seem endless. Besides magical rituals, or in conjuction with them, are many different relaxation procedures, breathing exercises,[8] and concentration practices. Some methods even recommend special diets or ascetic life styles, devoid of materialism, desire, and attachments, to enhance their success.

Crossing the Boundary

As with other aspects of astral projection, there are many varying and sometimes conflicting opinions concerning the actual process of separating the astral body from the physical body.

To allow exit of the astral body, the most commonly recommended posture for the physical body is lying on its back, but evidence indicates that any comfortable arrangement in which total relaxation is possible will suffice for voluntary induction. As seen in chapter 4, involuntary projection may take place while engaged in ordinary activities, such as walking out of a restaurant, sitting on a swing, or riding in a car.

---

[8]Cross-breathing exercises, a specific technique used in yoga, should be avoided when inducing OBEs, because they may accidentally "raise the kundalini." See footnote 7 on page 145.

Although some sources imply that subdued illumination is necessary for projection of the astral body, it can be accomplished in other kinds of light, including bright sunlight.

OBE literature contains many contradictions concerning the state of physical health necessary for the easiest exteriorization of the astral form. Some sources recommend near perfect health and fitness, while others say the astral form separates more readily from a physically weakened condition. Contrary to what many authors claim, the condition of the physical body can be clinically dead, debilitated by illness or injury, or in excellent health, and the astral body is capable of conscious projection.

The actual separation of the astral form from the physical body can take place in many different ways. One OBE book may describe a process and imply it is the only way, while another will describe a totally different mode of separation. Both processes may be successful. It could be possible that the astral body can leave the physical form through the solar plexus, head, feet, or separate from all points at once.

Many books on OBEs give explicit descriptions of the route taken by the astral body as it leaves the physical body. One of the most common examples provided is that from a physically reclining posture, the astral body rises upward while parallel to its counterpart. My experience has been that the astral body can leave the physical form in any direction. One of the things that surprised me most during my first conscious separation was my astral body dropped straight down through the bed and floor and landed on the ground underneath my bedroom.

According to reports, the process of separation can be accompanied by many different phenomena. It is quite common for a brief period of unconsciousness to intervene, but if the projector remains conscious during any part of the separation, numerous peculiar experiences are possible.

Audial and visual effects are common. Unusual sounds may be present, such as ringing in the ears, buzzing, rushing, humming, or even musical tones, phrases, or songs. At a certain point, when it seems possible to see through closed eyelids, visual images may appear in the form of humans, frightening monsters, special effects of light, weird patterns, tunnels, or anything else.

Strange tactile and kinesthetic sensations may be felt, such as invisible hands pushing or pulling, or energy forces moving the astral form, causing it to tip, sway, spin, jerk, or bob up and down. Tingling, shaking, vibrations, numbness, paralysis, or catalepsy may also be experienced temporarily. Coolness or warmth may also be sensed.

A few projectors have described feeling as though the entire self rushed into the head, or they experienced pressure within the brain, and then these sensations were relieved at the sound of a "click" or a "pop" at the instant the astral form was released.

Sometimes, despite arduous and prolonged effort, the astral body remains fixed tightly within the physical encasement. Quite often, when strenuous efforts to separate are ceased, the astral form gently lifts out as if on its own. At other times it seems as if a powerful outside energy propels it out and away from its physical double.

Some projectors experience confusion, pain, fear, or distress with many of the separation phenomena, but I have always felt perfectly at ease with them, except for frustration when the astral form refuses to dislodge from its physical enclosure.

The most dramatic separation phenomenon I have experienced is the vibrations. They literally feel as though an electric current is flowing through the body. I have found that I can easily control them with mental effort—smooth them out, move them to different parts of my body, slow them down, or speed them up. I have had many OBEs start out with these vibrations, and others in which this curious phenomenon was absent. Although they feel definite and powerful, for me they produce no pain or discomfort. On the contrary, they feel rather soothing and are a reliable indicator that I am mentally and physically prepared for an OBE.

The projector can also remain unconscious during the entire separation, and awaken to awareness in the exteriorized astral body, hovering or standing near the sleeping physical body. Unconscious separation can also take place from a dream, in which case the projector suddenly becomes lucid in a dream and then aware in the astral body, in an astral environment similar to or continuous with the dream locale.

Separation can also take place automatically and be a total surprise, such as when a projector sits up, gets out of bed, and walks away, and then suddenly realizes it is the astral form being occupied and the physical form is still lying in bed asleep.

After the astral and physical bodies are separated, they are still connected by the "silver cord." While some projectors describe the cord as appearing cylindrical, others see it as a tape, ribbon, thread, or rope made up of several strands. Some perceive it as a light beam, or an extremely fine filament resembling a spider web. It is often seen with pulsating light streaming along its length between the projected double and the physical form. It is highly elastic and appears to be made of the same material as the astral body.

There are also many descriptions concerning the attachment of the silver cord. One writer may insist that it emanates from the physical solar plexus to some point on the astral body, while another says the astral and physical heads are connected.

The only time I studied the silver cord subjectively, I felt behind my neck, a commonly described point of attachment, to see if it was there. Sure enough, it was! It felt cylindrical, smooth, and firm, with a diameter of an inch or so. Before it connected to my astral body, it branched into many finer segments and entered at numerous points on my neck and upper back.

It could be possible that just as the astral form can separate from many points of the physical body, the cord can connect the two forms in a variety of ways. As I have said previously, the astral plane is full of surprises. This may be one reason why the literature is full of contradictions.

Return to the Physical Side

People who have never experienced a conscious projection may wonder how to get back inside the physical body. From my experience, this has never been a problem; return is almost always automatic. For me, it is a greater problem to remain exteriorized for longer time periods than to get back to physical existence.

Shock, fear, or any intense emotion will usually cause the double to automatically return, as will any disturbance in the vicinity of the physical body. According to my experiences, as well as written and verbal accounts by others, an exterior force, or an unconscious control, seems to suddenly bring the astral body back into coincidence with its material form. If a projector wants to return, all that appears necessary is to think about the desire to go back to the physical form and, no matter how far the astral double has ventured, the projection is automatically terminated.

However, if a projector did find it impossible to return, how would anyone ever know?

Return of the astral body and consciousness to the physical body can take place in several different ways.

The slowest return is when the astral form is near the physical body. The ghostly double has a natural affinity for its physical enclosure, and reunion occurs automatically, with perfect realignment of the astral parts to the physical parts. It is possible to remain calm and relaxed and observe the two forms reunite. I have watched my glowing astral parts line up with their physical counterparts, and then disappear into them.

When it functions, the mysterious exterior force quickly pulls the astral body back to the physical body. The projector may feel a tug on the back, or some other place on the exteriorized double, and then has the sensation of moving through a hazy, tunnel-like structure, back to the location of the physical body. This method of return can occur at incredible speeds across vast distances, or take place swiftly from one end of the house to another, with the double pulled painlessly through walls, furniture, appliances, or any other obstacle between it and its physical counterpart.

When the astral form is in the same room or house as the physical form, return may take place semi-instantaneously. Awareness flashes back to the physical body, but there is a momentary pause when the two forms unite, as though consciousness is briefly suspended at the border between worlds. Dual consciousness is experienced as the astral world and physical world are superimposed, and then the astral world fades away while the physical world comes into focus.

Sometimes return to the physical body occurs instantaneously. The astral double may be anywhere, in the same room as the physical body or exploring distant realms, when suddenly consciousness is located in the physical brain, the physical eyes open, and the astral world is gone.

During the reunion of the astral double with the physical form, some projectors experience shock, temporary paralysis, catalepsy, and sounds or visions similar to separation phenomena.

Although it is common to retain full consciousness from the astral plane through the return to the physical world, occasionally there is a brief unconscious interval between the two states. After return, with concentration, the correct balance between wakefulness and sleep can be maintained so that the astral form can separate again. It is also possible to go from an OBE into a dream state, and then wake up normally or experience a false awakening.

Specific Procedures to Project the Astral Body

When I first succeeded at learning to voluntarily and consciously leave my body, I used autosuggestion and a modified composite of techniques described by Sylvan Muldoon in *The Projection of the Astral Body*, Hugh Callaway, who wrote under the pen name Oliver Fox, in *Astral Projection: A Record of Out-*

of-the-Body Experiences, and Robert Monroe in *Journeys Out of the Body*. Here are five specific procedures I have used to successfully induce OBEs.

Procedure One

To apply this procedure, the first one I succceeded with, I lie down in bed as usual, in any comfortable position, covered up enough to keep warm. I close my eyes.

To begin physical and mental relaxation, I take several long, slow, deep breaths, inhaling until my lungs are nearly full and exhaling until my lungs are completely relaxed. While inhaling, I imagine *prana*, or psychic energy, flowing into and permeating my entire body, and while exhaling, I imagine all daily stress flowing outward.

To deepen mental relaxation and induce a trance-like condition, I slowly count backwards from 10 or 20, concentrating on each number in turn. With each number, I imagine my mind descending to a deeper, more relaxed state of consciousness. By the time I reach zero, my mind is usually calm and comparatively free from daily concerns.

To deepen physical relaxation, I do a progressive muscle relaxation exercise, starting with my feet and progressing to the top of my head. I flex the muscles of my toes, noticing the feeling of tension this causes, then allow them to relax, paying attention to the difference in feeling. Then I similarly flex and relax my lower leg mucscles, then my thighs, hips, hands, arms, torso, neck, face and forehead. When every muscle group is relaxed, I silently acknowledge how pleasant the feeling of total relaxation is.

With mind and body in a deep state of relaxation, I continue to the next part of the procedure, which is the simultaneous application of three techniques: autosuggestion for an OBE, visualization of a black screen, and imagination of vibrations.

For the autosuggestion part of this triad, I tell myself over and over that I will leave my body. I think about the feeling of my astral form separating from its physical enclosure, and then the feeling of being out and traveling around in the astral world. Notice that I only think of the *feelings*. If any other emotions arise, I suppress them and think about the feelings of leaving my body.

While imagining these feelings, I visualize a black screen behind my eyes. I focus my inner vision upon the blackness, and if any hypnagogic images intervene, I "think" them away so that my mental screen remains black.

While applying autosuggestion and visualizing the black screen, I imagine vibrations emitting from a point six feet away from the top of my head and at an angle of about 30 degrees above the line of my body axis. If the vertex of the angle is at the top of the head, the first side of the angle is an extension of the body axis away from the head, and the second side, directly above, forms the 30 degree angle. The point is six feet away from the vertex, on the second side of the angle. I imagine the vibrations entering my head and spreading to the rest of my body.[9]

Usually, I fall asleep during the simultaneous application of these three techniques. However, when I begin to awaken, sometimes my thoughts are still focused on my attempt to have an OBE, and vibrations are surging through my body. As mentioned previously, they feel just like an electrical current, but to me they are painless. When the vibrations are strong, it is possible to separate in astral form from my physical body.

Sometimes, after starting Procedure One, I fall asleep, enter an ordinary dream which becomes lucid, then project from the lucid dream. Also, as discussed in chapter 4, I can go from a lucid dream to the hypnopompic state, and then to an OBE.

Procedure Two

I have another procedure that sometimes works well in the hypnopompic state. Upon waking, before consciousness has returned entirely to the physical world, I relax, and sink back to-

---

[9]I read about this technique in *Journeys Out of the Body* by Robert Monroe (Garden City, NY: Anchor Press/Doubleday, 1973).

ward slumber, concentrating on the desire for astral projection and the feelings of astral projection. I imagine the feeling of my inner self rocking back and forth, forward and backward, while holding my physical body still. I "rock" faster and faster, and soon the feeling of inner movement automatically changes into the same vibrations as produced in Procedure One. Then I am in the effective state of consciousness to have an OBE.

Sometimes after attempting Procedure One and failing because of faltering concentration or falling asleep, I have succeeded in inducing an OBE with Procedure Two.

Procedure Three

I tried this procedure because often, even though the vibrational state is reached, it is difficult to release the astral form from its physical confinement. I have discovered that dissociation can be easier from a lucid dream.

To use Procedure Three, I start out the same as for Procedure One. I take several deep breaths, count backwards from 10 or 20, going to a more relaxed mental state with each number, then do the progressive relaxation exercise. While mentally and physically relaxed, I provide myself with autosuggestions to have a lucid dream and project astrally upon attainment of lucidity.

Sometimes, while implementing this method, I have fallen asleep during the first steps, but have obtained a lucid dream anyway, and proceeded to an OBE, either directly or via the hypnopompic state.

Procedure Four

Another approach to the state of consciousness conducive to OBEs is directly from physical waking consciousness into the hypnagogic state. By monitoring mental phenomena during the hypnagogic state, I have automatically encountered the correct state of consciousness for an OBE, either directly or from a lucid dream formed in the presence of waking consciousness. This procedure can be tricky, because with it, the vibrations usually are absent. When it has been successful, I either have effortlessly separated in my astral form, or gotten up thinking I was in my physical form when actually I was in astral form.

The hypnagogic procedure can be enhanced by using the deep breathing, counting, and relaxation techniques of Procedure One, and then observing passage through the hypnagogic state while passively contemplating having an OBE.

Procedure Five

The hypnopompic state can also be used to automatically attain the state of consciousness required for astral projection. I use the techniques previously discussed (deep breathing, mental and physical relaxation, autosuggestion) to interject awareness into the hypnopompic state, then the conditions may be automatically available to proceed to an OBE, just as in the hypnagogic state.

After acquiring some success with these procedures, I incorporated autosuggestion into them to project to specific places or strive for specific goals while in astral form, such as studying the structure of the astral body, attempting specific capabilities, or searching for astral entities.

To increase the success of any of these procedures to induce OBEs, it is beneficial to saturate the conscious and subconscious minds with the topic of astral projection as much as possible by reading, talking, and thinking about it at all convenient times during waking hours, as well as concentrating on it in the hypnagogic and hypnopompic states.

Fantasize about traveling astrally to any place you want to go, any earthly location, planet, star, or invisible realm, or seeing anyone you want to see, any friend, relative, lover, or cosmic entity. Fantasy with intense, vivid, and detailed mental imagery develops theta brain waves, and people with more theta waves have a greater tendency for OBEs.[10]

---

[10]Rogo, *Leaving the Body*, pp. 13–14.

Think about astral projection, imagine it, but most importantly, will it. Saturation at the conscious and subconscious levels will influence the unconscious and superconscious so that ordinary dreams about astral projection may appear, along with more lucid dreams and false awakenings, or perhaps a spontaneous OBE, indicating the time is near for an actual, voluntary, consciously controlled OBE. When it happens, it is a certainty.

Since applying these procedures and finding that they actually do promote conscious voluntary OBEs, I have had conscious spontaneous OBEs more frequently. They most commonly arise from lucid dreams or false awakenings.

Once the conducive state of consciousness is reached for an OBE, I find it is usually necessary to deliberately separate or eject from the physical body in astral form. Sometimes I just mentally express the desire to float upward, and the astral body obeys; other times I roll out, either to the left or right; and occasionally I emerge through the top of my head. A few times, when these techniques failed, I succeeded in moving one part out, such as an arm, and the rest of the astral form followed until it was completely released. At times my astral body has exteriorized without any conscious effort, as if it were suddenly dropped down or hurled outward, and at other times it has remained confined within physical bounds, despite the use of all these techniques.

* * * * * * *

Remember, these methods may take time to be effective. Weeks or months may pass, with these procedures resulting in nothing but a good night's sleep, a restful nap, or submission to wandering thoughts. I have no idea what to assume would be normal, but I would expect from three weeks to a couple of months may be necessary, or maybe less for someone who happens to have a lifestyle particularly suited to this type of development. I believe OBEs are like any other skill or mental discipline—the more effort put into achievement, the greater the development of ability.

Throughout the next three chapters are detailed records of my odyssey into the invisible worlds, which I reached through the application of these procedures. Based upon actual notes carefully written after each OBE, each account tells of my passage from the physical world to the astral world, what I saw, thought, felt, and did, and how I returned. Since it was sometimes inconvenient to immediately record the information into the journal, a few slight errors may have occured in the times and dates, but the majority of them are accurate.

With practice and determination, these methods work. When they do, previously held ideas about self, reality and the nature of the universe change permanently.

Knowledge obscures belief.

Chapter 7

The Cabin Projections

I first learned to consciously leave my body when I lived in a secluded cabin in the woods near the small town of Keystone and only a few miles from Mt. Rushmore, in the Black Hills of South Dakota. Life at my little cabin proved to be more enlightening every day. I lived in an environment imbued with nature, where I watched the seasons' changes reflected by the woodland creatures, the sky, and the forest. While there, I found it easy to focus inward and explore previously ignored states of consciousness.

Nestled in the trees on a hillside, along a bumpy, hilly, rut-filled road, the rustic cabin, covered with cedar shake siding and a green roof, blended well with its surroundings. Being a humble abode, it had no running water or indoor plumbing. I stoked up a wood burning stove and fireplace to keep the main room warm in the winter, but sometimes, even with both fires blazing, it got so cold in the adjoining kitchen that the water in my dog's dish froze solid.

A description of the layout of the cabin and its surroundings will facilitate the understanding of events covered in this chapter.

The cabin is nearly hidden in a thick growth of tall pine trees interspersed with aspen, birch, and oak. Chokecherry and raspberry bushes, and, during the growing season, ferns, wild flowers, and poison ivy cover the forest floor. The narrow dirt road passes beyond the cabin for a short distance before the driveway branches off in a sharp left turn and doubles back to the cabin. After the driveway branches off, the road continues up the hill, curving left for about fifty or sixty feet, where another road, actually more like a trail, branches off to the left and doubles back across a ridge above the cabin.

The cabin, remote and peaceful in the tranquility of the forest, is a modest, but well cared for structure. If you stood in front of it, facing it, you would see a porch running all the way across the front and halfway around the right side, where it ends at a doorway that leads into the kitchen. A roof covers all of the porch except on the left end, where it is open to make a sun deck.

The main entrance is centered in front. If you opened the heavy wooden door and entered, you would be standing in the knotty pine paneled living room and facing the dark brown and black, smooth-brick fireplace on the opposite wall. On each side of the fireplace is a four-paned barn sash window. To the left of the fireplace, in the wall perpendicular to the one you are facing, is a doorway leading into the bedroom where I usually slept. Also in this side wall, but closer, is another doorway leading into the spare bedroom, which has bunk beds built into the wall it shares with the first bedroom. To the right of the fireplace, in the other wall perpendicular to the one facing, is a doorway leading into the kitchen, and from the kitchen a Dutch door leads back onto the section of the porch that runs along the side of the cabin. On each side of the front door is a six-paned window and to the immediate right is the wood burning stove.

During the years I lived there, I usually worked at night, and often it was nearly dawn when I bounced over the rocks and through the ruts of the steep road home. Sometimes, I also worked days, so my sleeping hours were irregular. Most of my OBEs occured in midmorning or during the afternoon. Following is a chronological account of those experiences.

MAY 5, 1978, 9:15 A.M.

I lay down in bed, took several long, slow, deep breaths, and counted backwards from ten to one, imagining myself going into a deeper, more inward state of consciousness with each number.

I cleared my mind and relaxed each part of my body, one part at a time, starting with my toes and continuing upward, tensing and relaxing each muscle group in succession until I flexed my frontalis muscle (forehead), and then let every muscle slacken. My entire body felt limp and calm.

I mentally told myself, over and over, I would leave my body, and to keep my mind from wandering, I concentrated on an imaginary black screen behind my eyelids and forehead. Whenever unrelated mental images formed, I refocused on the blank screen. At the same time, I imagined vibrations coming from a point in space six feet from my head and 30 degrees above my body axis, a technique described by Robert Monroe.[1]

After a while, I dozed off. I passed in and out of a dream state several times, but remembered my goal when my consciousness came closer to waking. Then I managed to hold the hypnopompic state.

The vibrations began. The sensation felt as if an electric current was running through my entire body, causing every cell to tingle with energy, a feeling much like that experienced when a limb "goes to sleep," only not unpleasant at all. The vibrations were erratic, jerky, growing intense and then faint. I kept my eyes closed and tried to speed them up and smooth them out; I discovered that it was easy to control them.

I wondered how to go about leaving my body, and decided to see if I could just move an arm out. With my eyes still closed, I lifted my arm, which moved easily, but it was impossible to determine whether it was my astral or physical arm that I was controlling. Suddenly, I fell downward, out of my body, through the bed and floor, and onto the ground beneath my cabin. Somehow, I landed on my hands and knees. Startled, I opened my eyes, and through the dimness clearly saw damp soil, rocks, and debris, mostly consisting of pine cone cores left by squirrels. I

---

[1]Robert A. Monroe, *Journeys Out of the Body* (Garden City, NY: Anchor/Doubleday, 1973), p. 212.

reached out and ran my hand over one of the rocks, amazed at how real it felt; it was hard, cold, moist, and rough.

I decided to attempt to move out from beneath the cabin to see how the "astral world" above looked, but I wanted to avoid rising straight up, because I was concerned that I might reenter my physical body and terminate the OBE. I thought it would be preferable to move up diagonally at a forty-five degree angle, so I would pass through the floor and wall and hopefully be positioned outside my bedroom window. As soon as I conceptualized my intentions, I rose effortlessly along the intended path.

When I emerged from beneath the cabin, I passed back into the dream I had been having earlier. The only change in the dream was the location; instead of occurring in a dream world detached from other realities, it was taking place outside my bedroom window, superimposed upon the "astral environment." I apologized to my friends in the dream for my brief absence, and continued the chimerical drama from where it had left off, until the telephone rang, jolting me to physical consciousness. It was 10:45 A.M.

The difference between the OBE and the dream was vivid; I was precisely aware of the nature of the dream drama superimposed upon the "astral image" of my cabin from outside my bedroom. The OBE was just like being awake, only I knew my physical body was unconscious on my bed, while another part of me saw, felt, and functioned under the cabin. Either a nonmaterial part of my being was actually beneath the cabin, or my subconscious mind created a convincing illusion. After a brief moment of lucidity upon first entering the dream, the dream drama became an ordinary dream in which I passively played my part, accepting it as reality at the time it was happening.

MAY 18, 1978, 8:00 A.M.

After being up since early morning, I lay down to self-induce astral projection. Soft rain drenched the forest, and thick fog smothered the hills and treetops outside my window.

I relaxed each part of my body, starting from my feet and working up to my head as before. When all of my muscles were relaxed, I kept my eyes closed and "focused" on the blackness behind my eyelids, while I thought about astral projection. Unintentionally, I fell asleep.

I dreamed about huge earth-moving machines roaring up the road and over the hillsides, pushing down tender young trees, crushing wildflowers, and plowing up the earth to build a web of new roads for a major housing development. I was deeply disturbed as I watched them tear up and destroy the natural beauty of the land surrounding my cabin, and I was sad to lose my peace and solitude.

Suddenly, the dream became lucid, and I entered the hypnopompic state. I felt intense vibrations throughout my entire body, the feeling like an electrical shock, only it was soothing and energizing. At the same time, in my head, I heard a buzzing, roaring noise that sounded like a continuation of the clamor of the road equipment in my dream. I concentrated on leaving my body by imagining my consciousness in my astral body, inside my physical body, pushing upward and out.

I felt my inner being exit through the top of my head, as if my consciouness was in a new body that had the ability to slip out of the old one. I passed easily through the knotty pine wall at the head of my bed.

I floated in midair in my living room for a few moments, and looked at the familiar, but hazy, furnishings. When I tried to move, I flew around the room randomly, without control over destination or position. I tried to steady myself and remain upright, but I tipped and swayed, and bounced away, as if swept by an exterior force. Then I suddenly changed direction and darted to a different part of the room, turning and flipping through the air.

I was hurled into the adjoining kitchen, and decided to try to go outside. As soon as the thought formed, I shot directly through the wall, and found myself outside, floating at roof level, next to my cabin.

I quit zigzagging from place to place. My vision had cleared considerably. I looked around and studied this astral environment, or physical environment seen from an astral condition, or unique level of consciousness, or whatever it was.

I was astonished by the vividness of the colors and the splendor of the woods surrounding my cabin. The new spring-green leaves on the aspen trees and chokecherry bushes shimmered with rich color that radiated from within, and bright sunshine reflected from the rain drops that still clung to the leaves. The pine needles, too, had a more intense color, although it was darker, and the clusters of slender shafts held even more drops sparkling in the sunshine in a myriad of tiny, bright globes.

I remembered the thick fog that had covered the hills when I lay down in bed. Instantaneously, at the thought of my body lying in bed, I zapped back into my physical form, wishing I could stay out longer and see more.

I felt the warm feather bed beneath me and the pile of quilts on top of me. I held still and kept my eyes closed; my body was still vibrating. I wanted to project again, so I tried to roll out, as if turning over in bed and leaving my physical body behind, but my material form had a firm grasp on its astral double. I struggled to roll out, and after a few minutes, gave up.

I decided to just lie back and experience the vibrations, study them, and concentrate on how they felt. Suddenly, without trying, I was out again, floating beside my bed. I felt weightless, no longer confined by gravity, the bed, and the quilts.

I cautiously half opened one eye and saw what looked like a French door in front of me. My cabin did not have French doors, so I wondered if I was entering another dream, although I knew my physical body was a few feet away, unconscious, while I floated in another dimension.

I wanted to maintain the lucidity, so I looked at my hands[2] and saw two rather shapeless, semi transparent, glowing arms

---

[2]This had been suggested to me by a friend who read Carlos Castaneda's books.

that ended like formless paws, lacking the detail of physical arms and hands. I was surprised by the bright, whitish-gold light emanating from my astral arms. Unintentionally, I began to reenter my physical body, so I decided to try to get back in one part at a time, to see if I could watch the astral and physical parts reunite.

My thoughts were back in my physical brain, from where I could see my gleaming astral legs hovering above the covers over my physical legs. I stretched my leg to see which would move.

My consciousness returned to my astral body, which slipped through the wall at the foot of my bed, and went into the closet, where I briefly saw clothes hanging as I passed through to the outside of the cabin. Several people were standing around out there, and I had the impression they were involved in a dream, my dream, a dream that had been missing the star character, me.

Suddenly, I was back in my bed where I had left off—getting into my body. I watched my golden, indistinct astral arm line up with the position of my physical arm and disappear, and then there I was, in an ordinary wakeful state; lying in bed. I opened my physical eyes and looked at my watch—9:40 A.M. I looked out the window. In the hour and 40 minutes since I had fallen asleep, the fog had cleared, and the morning sun was shining brightly, reflecting off the rain drops still clinging to the aspens and pines outside my cabin, just as I had seen astrally.

As I lay in bed, pondering the experience, I realized that if I was floating on my side, near my bed, body axis parallel to the floor, and facing the windows, the double barn sash windows, with their small panes of glass, would look like a French door, especially if I was convinced I was in an upright position.

What impressed me most about this experience was that out of my body I would roll around out of control, sometimes upside down, other times sideways, and once in a while even right side up. The strange thing was that every position *felt* right side up, which made viewpoint and perspective confusing. I was amazed that I could become so disoriented in my own cabin, where I had been living for most of the previous five years.

While out of my body, vision was blurry with intermittent periods of extreme clarity. The trees were quite clear, but the most vivid image was that of the double barn sash windows, with the wood framing the panes perfectly in focus and in color. Even though it was the most vivid image, I failed to recognize it simply because I was unaccustomed to looking at my windows from that position in space.

I experienced no fear whatsoever of dying, demons, inability to return, or any negative feelings that some people have encountered during OBEs. I felt just the opposite—freedom, exhilaration, curiosity, excitement, and enthusiasm all at once. I wanted to go places, see my physical body from the outside, see my astral body and other things, visit people, and explore that "different" world, or alternative state of consciousness, all at the same time.

May 21, 1978, Midmorning

I was wide awake, lying in bed, and decided to see if I could produce the vibrations. After the relaxation procedure and a short time of concentrating on the blackness, my body felt as though it was shaking, much like involuntary shivering in the cold, although I was quite warm, snuggled on my feather bed under the heavy quilts. I relaxed, and the convulsions smoothed out, until they felt like a mild electric shock traveling through every cell of my body.

I imagined myself in my astral body, separate from my physical body, lifting out and away, but the more I concentrated, the heavier and denser I felt. Finally, though, after persisting, I succeeded! I floated out sideways, to the left side of the bed—the side next to the wall—and drifted down. I landed on the floor, under the bed and against the wall, from where I could clearly see dust and clumps of dog and cat hair covering the floorboards.

I wanted to rise upward and look around, and an instant later I was floating above the bed, looking down at Shunka, my German shepherd-type dog, as he jumped up onto the bed, turned around a couple of times, and lay down. I was looking at the foot of the bed, where Shunka lay, and failed to see my physical body, which was covered with blankets and quilts; actually, I just neglected to pay much attention to it.

I wanted to go exploring, so I flew out the bedroom door, eagerly anticipating the discovery of an invisible world, an interesting new realm, or a higher plane of existence, but only got as far as the kitchen, where I was floating above the counter near the Dutch door. I looked around, trying to analyze and comprehend this strange state of being, when my attention was drawn to an object on the floor, a red, rounded article about five inches in diameter that appeared to be a crumpled piece of paper. I wondered if I had forgotten to pick up a shopping bag or something.

Suddenly, against my conscious will, I was swiftly pulled right through walls and furnishings, back to my bed. I was in my physical body. I looked at my watch so I could record the time in my notes, but the numbers were blurred, and although I tried hard, it was impossible to bring them into focus; they also looked out of sequence, so I concentrated on the hands, which were a little clearer, though it was difficult to distinguish the long one from the short one. At best I could read the time as 5:10, but I knew that was wrong, because I was aware that I had lain down in midmorning and had only been in bed for a short while.

I lay my head back down on the pillow and was surprised to feel that the vibrations were still present. To experiment, I decided to see if I could direct them to different parts of my body. First, I concentrated them into my head, where they made my scalp and brain tingle. Then I directed them downward. I felt them travel down my right arm into my hand, where they became particularly intense, as though my hand was "asleep" from having the circulation cut off.

A few seconds later, I "awakened," although I had felt as if I had been fully awake during this entire experience. At the point of total return to physical reality, however, I felt a definite shift from an alternative state of consciousness to "ordinary waking." My hand felt normal. If the circulation had been cut off, it was too soon to have had time to resume normalcy, and furthermore, it was across my chest with no pressure on it from anywhere.

I remembered my watch, and looked at it again; this time it clearly read 10:40. Five minutes earlier it would have said 10:35, which happens to be the mirror image of 5:10, disregarding the sizes of the hands, which were impossible to differentiate when I "looked" earlier. The positions and angles of the hands showing these times are exact mirror images of each other—amazing!

I got up and went to the kitchen to see if there was anything on the floor; all I could see was the "clay tile" linoleum and the Navajo design rug. Then I thought that perhaps I had become disoriented in space again and seen something on a wall or the ceiling from a position that made it seem like the floor. I carefully looked at the items on my kitchen walls and shelves to see if I could find anything that looked like the "crumpled red paper" I saw during the OBE. I noticed the picture on the calendar; it was a large red flower with many layers of petals separated by dark shading where they overlapped. I squinted my eyes and forced them out of focus to blur my vision, then studied the image of the big red flower; it looked exactly like what I thought I had seen on the floor while out of my body.

June 6, 1978, 8:00 a.m.

I slowly awakened from normal slumber, and instead of thinking about the day ahead, I decided to return to the deeper stages of the hypnopompic state and try to induce an OBE. I was already deeply relaxed, so I skipped the counting and relaxation exercises. To loosen my astral body, I "rocked" my inner self by holding my physical body still and mentally moving quickly back and forth in a rocking motion, creating a sensation much like "imaginary rocking"

Soon I felt the vibrations. For a short while, I simply rocked with the vibrations and hoped I would find myself floating somewhere, but my consciousness remained united with my physical body. I tried to float out, but failed, and then I tried to roll out onto the floor. I remained in my organic form, but the vibrations continued. I tried to exit through my head, and then through my feet, but stayed firmly connected to the material world. Disappointed, I dozed off for a while.

When I began to awaken, I closed my eyes again and rocked my inner self. Within minutes the vibrations returned. I tried to drop out of my body, felt a downward shift, and then had the impression of packed cotton surrounding me. For a moment, part of my consciousness was inside my mattress, prevented from going any farther, while another part was in my physical head. Then my cognizance was unified in "normal" physical reality again.

I decided to try once more to exteriorize through my head. Again, I experienced dual consciousness, the impression of being both in my body and out of it at the same time. Part of my conscious awareness was in my physical form lying in bed, while another part was in my astral form standing upright, front pressed against the wall at the head of my bed. I tried to float through the wall, but felt both as if my body was plastered against the wood and lying in bed at the same time. I felt the cool knotty pine paneling against the length of my astral body, but the resistance of the wood was too powerful to allow me to pass effortlessly through the wall, as I had done before.

I thought perhaps I could pass through if I pushed only my hands through first, then my arms, then followed through entirely. (In retrospect, I wondered why I was so intent on going through the wall; it probably would have been easier to just walk out through the doorway). I pressed my palms against the wall. It felt cool and solid, as before, but then the resistance dissolved and my hands went through, followed by my arms. I felt around and could feel wood and empty spaces. The wall was of normal thickness, so I presumed that I had reached into my upright piano, which was in the living room, against the other side of the wall. Part of my awareness still remained in the physical portion of my being, lying in bed.

Suddenly I was through the wall and inside my piano, surrounded by wires and the complicated wooden mechanisms of hammers and levers that comprise its inner workings. My consciousness was entirely in my astral form.

From inside the piano I could vaguely see through it, out into the living room, where three or four shadow-like forms of men were having a fistfight. They were three dimensional and appeared semisolid, formed from shades of gray, smoky-looking material. I heard them grunting and hitting and saw them swing at each other and fall down. They seemed to pass through the furniture without disturbing it, rather than crash into it. I wondered whether they were dream images or impressions from some other source, but at that moment I was too preoccupied with getting out of the piano to give the matter much consideration. Before I could go any farther, however, I "awoke" in the physical world.

The lingering vibrations faded completely. I opened my eyes and listened; the living room, as well as the rest of the cabin, was quiet. It was 9:30 A.M.

JUNE 13, 1978, 9:00 A.M.

I was lying in bed and wanted to project. Before trying, however, I decided to carefully construct a plan, so that hopefully I could obtain more control and better orientation. I resolved to stay calm and proceed slowly, one step at a time, and carefully observe my environment, myself, and my abilities in the astral world. At first, instead of passing through "solid" objects, floating, flying, or performing "aerogymnastics" in my astral form, I planned to simply walk down my road and study existence from an exteriorized point of view. Although I assumed that amazing feats would be much more entertaining and exciting than simple walking, I believed my strategy would enable me to become accustomed to the astral environment gradually and develop more effectual control.

I closed my eyes and took several slow, deep breaths; I relaxed each muscle group; I used autosuggestion to mentally imprint my intention to attain the vibrational condition and leave my body. Then I counted backwards from twenty, visualizing each number while imagining my body and mind sinking into a deeper state of relaxation. After I got to zero, I focused on the blackness, while I concentrated upon my desire to project. Within a few minutes, I was asleep.

The next thing I was aware of was awakening from a dream with the desire to project still in my mind. Before I was completely awake, I began rocking my inner body, mentally stretching outward with each forward movement, much like imagining the action of making a swing go higher. The vibrations were absent, but I heard a high-pitched humming sound that seemed to originate inside my cranium. Then I was in my astral body, outside my physical form.

I was floating on the left side of my physical body, so to avoid reentering it, I rolled over to the left, and found myself partly in the wall and partly in the small space of a couple of inches between the bed and the wall. Even though I held my eyes closed, I could perceive my surroundings; either they appeared as a blurry picture that spontaneously formed in my mind, or I could see through my eyelids to some extent. I tried to determine the best way to counteract the predicament I was in, because from my location it was inconceivable to simply take a walk according to the plan I had devised.

Suddenly, I dropped down and landed on the ground beneath my cabin. The left side of my face struck a rock and hurt for a few seconds, until I thought of exploring my environment. I felt around and could feel other rocks, cool and jagged, along with dirt and debris that I ascertained to be pine needles and pieces of pine cones left by squirrels.

I opened my eyes to search for a way out and saw an area of light about six feet away. It slowly formed the rectangular shape of my bedroom window, about six feet away from my physical body. I was back in the material world.

I wanted to project again, so I imagined forcefully pushing outward with my inner self, hoping to propel my astral body out. It slipped away easily, this time positioned on the right side of my bed, where there was enough room to walk. I managed to stand up on the floor beside the bed and take a few steps toward the doorway. It was quite easy to maintain my balance and remain upright, so I continued walking out of the bedroom, through the living room and kitchen, to the Dutch door.

I grasped the doorknob, pulled the heavy wooden door open, and as it swung inward, the screen door fell outward and landed flat on the porch with a crash. This seemed peculiar, but I refused to allow it to distract me; I just walked over it, across the porch, and onto the driveway, proceeding strictly according to my plan.

I walked along the driveway, which was only a dirt trail. Since I was barefoot, the hard, rough ground, pine cones, and sharp rocks hurt my feet as I walked over them, until I stopped thinking about the pain and gazed at the beauty surrounding me.

The sun shone down brilliantly on the forest, lighting my path as I walked along in my yellow pajamas. Oh-oh. This was too real. I wondered if I actually was sleepwalking and worried about passersby seeing me out wandering around clad in my pajamas. Then I remembered I had worn my blue ones to bed, so I felt somewhat reassured that I was in my astral body and quite certain I would be invisible to anyone on the physical plane that might happen by. However, everything looked and felt so authentic that a few doubts lingered. I was appreciably reassured when I felt my astral body drift up into the air a few inches, land lightly, and then bounce and float upward slightly with each step, just as the astronauts did when they walked on the moon.

The long driveway extended before me. At its end, I could see the junction where the road split off to the right and doubled back down the hill. I intended to turn left at the end of the driveway, walk along the road where it continued up the hill for a short distance, then turn left again and take the trail that branched off and doubled back along the ridge above my cabin.

A steep bank separates that trail from the driveway; I impulsively decided to take a shortcut by climbing up it. As I scrambled up the slope, I grabbed the protruding roots of some raspberry bushes that grew in the loose, rocky dirt, and effortlessly swung up to the trail, almost taking flight. That reaffirmed my belief that I was in astral form.

I followed the trail, slowly bouncing along in the floating strides of an easy astral stroll. It was an unusually warm late spring morning, and the sunshine on the profusion of fresh green leaves was absolutely resplendent. A gentle breeze stroked the aspens, and made them shimmer with light as each leaf cast a brilliant, dancing nimbus. I walked on for what seemed like a half mile or so.

I heard men's voices back in the trees, so I stopped and listened carefully. I was unable to distinguish their words, but their speech inflections and a mental image gave me the impression that the men were African American. I wondered if they were actual physical persons present in the woods, or if they were astral entities. Whichever they were, I felt self-conscious in my pajamas.

I thought about my physical body back at the cabin, and immediately had the intuitive impression that I was going to be pulled back to it, although I wanted to stay out longer.

Before the exterior power carried me away, however, I wanted to look at my hands. I held the left one in front of my eyes. It looked remarkably different from the physical hands that I know so well; my astral hand was covered with smooth, pallid white skin, and a tiny thumb and an excessively long, slender index finger protruded from the thin, narrow palm. The other fingers were slightly shorter, but also unnaturally long and thin. I definitely prefer my physical hands!

A strong force, opposing my conscious will, pulled me backwards. I was confident that it was going to return me to my physical body, so I relaxed and allowed it to sweep me away. With no effort arising from my conscious will, my astral body assumed a horizontal position on its back and began moving head first in the direction of the cabin. I felt as though I was rushing through space at tremendous speed; my surroundings appeared as a gossamer atmosphere of pale blue streaming past in a blur. It seemed to take an inordinate amount of time, considering the short distance and high rate of speed at which I appeared to be traveling. Finally I was back in my bed, conscious, but not fully awake, in the hypnopompic state.

As I lay there, I relaxed for a moment and analyzed the astral adventure. I felt drowzy and dull, but I wanted to get up to record the OBE in my journal. As I got out of bed, I felt strange sensations; my skin tingled, my mind was groggy, my body nearly defied gravity.

I felt slightly dizzy and unstable as I walked to the kitchen to boil water for tea. I noticed that my stove looked different; small scraps paper on which were written notes from LeeAnn, a friend of mine, were taped to the ledge that rises behind the burners. Since in physical reality I had not seen these notes posted on my stove, and as far as I knew, LeeAnn had not been to my cabin, I suspected that I was in some type of dream or alternative state of consciousness.

I went back to my bedroom, and LeeAnn was there, also present in the illusion, preparing coffee in a phantasmagorical kitchen superimposed upon my bedroom. She was scooping coffee from a large coffee can into the perculator and asked, "You make a full pot, don't you?"

I told her that I was making tea, but that coffee would be fine instead, and that was when I actually awakened to a normal waking state of consciousness.

I looked at my watch—10:40 A.M. I got up and went to the kitchen, and of course, the stove and screen door were normal. Then I looked into the mirror and confirmed that there was no mark where the rock had struck my face; serious doubts arose about the theory of repercussion. I went outside, onto the porch, and gazed into the hushed serenity of the spring forest. The morning was bright and sunny, unusually warm for this time of year, just as it had been during my astral walk. Later, I walked to the embankment and saw the raspberry roots protuding, just as they had before, on the astral plane, or in my mind, or wherever I had seen them earlier.

June 21, 1978, Between 6:00 and 10:00 A.M.

I had gone to bed, exhausted, shortly before midnight and had gotten up at 4:30 A.M. I lay down around 6:00 A.M., sleepy, but not as physically exhausted. I relaxed by counting backwards and gave myself suggestions about various matters, including one about having an OBE during this sleep period. I immediately went to sleep, and the next thing I was aware of was my consciousness emerging from a normal dream; I was still partially asleep, in the hypnopompic state.

Although the vibrations were absent, I rocked internally, back and forth and side to side, then slipped easily out of my body sideways and floated above the right side of my bed. I looked down at my calico cat, Tanya, lying on the bed, oblivious to my astral form watching her. Unintentionally, I turned a somersault in the air and gently landed back inside my body.

I opened my eyes and saw the window, and wondered if I was seeing through astral or physical eyes. I thought I was still in the hypnopompic state, so I tried to leave my body by projecting through the wall at the head of my bed, but remained firmly attached within my physical form.

As soon as I stopped trying to exteriorize, I floated out on my back, horizontal to my physical body, but my astral head was positioned above my physical feet. At the time this seemed perfectly normal, so I sailed backwards, hoping to exit out the window.

I had the sensation of moving rapidly backwards, but it seemed as if instead of entering new surroundings, my immediate environment, the closet at the foot of my bed, was moving with me. Suddenly I felt hungry, and instantly was back in my body, fully awake in physical consciousness. I was hungry, but turned over and immediately went back to sleep—ordinary sleep.

JUNE 30, 1978, 1:30 P.M.

I lay down in bed, counted backwards from twenty, and still felt tense, so I counted from twenty again. Then I relaxed each part of my body successively as described previously. I concentrated on keeping my consciousness aware and my body relaxed, but soon fell asleep.

My next impression was that I was sitting at the table in the main room, writing. The cabin was stifling, so I got up to open the door for air. I fumbled with the hook, unable to unhook it. Then I tried to flip the light switch beside the hook, but the room remained dim. Why had I been writing in the dark?

Suddenly I understood—I was in an alternative state of consciousness! With the excitement of this discovery, but wondering whether I was in a dream world or the astral world, I found myself standing outside on the porch for a brief moment, and then back in bed, conscious of my impending awakening, but still in the hypnopompic state.

I rocked my inner self, attempting to leave my body, and the vibrations started, which, to my surprise, made me feel cold. A high-pitched humming noise whirred inside my head.

I half-opened my eyes, barely enough to see the room; my body became calm, and the humming stopped. I shut my eyes and rocked some more, only two or three times, and the vibrating and humming started again.

I began to project from my head and pass through the wall at the head of my bed, eager to explore the astral plane, but then returned. The vibrations faded again, so I rocked a couple of times to strengthen them. After their intensity increased, I tried to float upward, and then I tried to roll out to the right side of the bed, but I felt confined within my physical form. The vibrations stopped, and I immediately entered normal waking consciouness.

During this episode, the door beside the table where I had "dreamed" I was writing actually was open.

I reasoned that my surprise, excitement, and enthusiasm over being either in a lucid dream or outside my body may have broken the relaxed mental condition necessary to maintain the precariously balanced state of consciousness conducive to OBEs, so I reaffirmed my determination to remain calm the next time I became aware in the hypnagogic or hypnopompic state and entered an invisible world.

JULY 2, 1978, 8:00 A.M.

I lay down, counted backwards from twenty, completed the relaxation exercise, dozed off, and awakend with my body vibrating. I pushed outward in my astral body. Then I discovered that I was standing beside my bed, and, with blurred vision, was surveying the bedroom. I avoided looking at my physical body, because I was concerned that the sight of it may turn my thoughts to it and cause my astral form to reenter it before I utilized this opportunity to explore the astral world.

I jumped up into the air a couple feet, and gently landed standing up. I jumped up again, this time going as high as the ceiling, and came down firmly on my feet once more. With increased exertion, I jumped again, and shot up through the ceiling and the roof, and ended up floating about one hundred feet above my cabin.

My vision had cleared considerably. I circled in a horizontal position and looked down at my roof, which was in various stages of repair. It was divided into neat rectangles of different colors—tan where the underlying boards were exposed, black where fresh tar paper had been nailed down, and green where the asphalt roll shingles had been attached.

I decided to try to go to California and visit my aunts, Patti and Midge, so I stopped circling, attained a vertical position, and concentrated on my wish. Soon I felt I was accelerating at a high rate of speed, but all I could see was a dark, shadowy cloudiness. When I stopped, I was back in my bed, "awakening" in my physical body.

The hypnopompic state lingered; I felt deeply relaxed, alert, and focused inward, away from physical reality. I "felt" for the vibrations and they started again, but I found it impossible to exit my physical body. The vibrations faded and resumed a few times as I slipped in and out of the hypnopompic state for a while. Then I went to sleep until 9:30, when I awakened to normal physical consciousness.

JULY 9, 1978, 3:00 OR 3:30 P.M.

I had gotten home sometime after dawn and entered the cabin through the kitchen door, as usual. I slept most of the day. I had *not* been on the front porch at all since the previous day.

I got up for a while, but then I lay back down to meditate. I took several long, slow deep breaths, completed the counting and relaxation procedures, and asked my higher self for a problem solving dream concerning a specific problem I had. Soon I was asleep. I dreamed that people were in my cabin, and the dirt road had been replaced by an asphalt highway paralleled by a jogging trail for expanding tourism and a growing population.

That dream turned into a more vivid one in which I was in nearby Rapid City, driving my parents' blue Chevy down a picturesque boulevard, a street that I used almost every day in physical reality, but usually in my own car. I was speeding and looked at the speedometer to see how fast I was going—sixty miles per hour! I glanced up at the rearview mirror, and it reflected the flashing red lights of a patrol car, so I pulled over and stopped at a corner where there were so many garbage cans sitting out on the street that there was only room for one car to park. The police car behind me had to take a left, turn around, and come back, so while it was gone, I turned right and sped two blocks to a street that heads out of town.

I was speeding up the hill at the edge of town, and the scene before me filled me with shock and instant dread. Directly in my path were several Native American boys who had fallen off their bicycles and were lying in the middle of the highway. I swerved, barely missed them, and kept going. I looked into the mirror to see if the cops were pursuing me, and hoped that if they were, they would see the boys in time. All I saw were the little Native Americans picking up their bicycles and moving to the side of the road.

I drove on, much slower, extremely grateful that the youngsters were uninjured, and then I noticed, down in a gulch to my right, a beautiful little pond surrounded by scattered trees. I looked down at the clear blue water and thought about how interesting it would be to project into that pond sometime during an OBE.

Then I realized that I was in a dream and that from such lucidity I could induce an OBE.

I sensed my astral body; it contained my consciousness and emerged from its physical counterpart. With blurred vision, I flew out of the bedroom and floated erratically around the living room, tossing and turning about, flipping over, darting here and there, completely out of control.

I noticed a four-foot-long, white metalic object next to me that looked familiar, so I reached out, turned it over, and discovered that it was the grow light hanging above my plants. Adjacent to the light was one of the six-paned windows that looked out upon the porch. I willed myself out the window, but remained in the living room. I extended my arms above my head in a diving posture and flew out. I was on the porch, next to the window, contemplating going through the porch roof to a point above the cabin, when my attention was drawn to a four-paned window I saw in the roof.

Actually, I had mentioned to the carpenters who were repairing my shingles that I was considering having a skylight built in the porch roof so my plants could get more sunshine. I thought perhaps they had done so while I was at work the previous day. I noted that it would be something interesting to verify later, after I returned to the physical plane, to confirm whether a new window actually had been installed.

As I floated there, looking at the four-paned window, I had a rushing, tingling feeling followed by a brief blackout, and when I opened my eyes again, I was looking directly at a six-paned window. I was in my body, fully awake, looking at my bedroom window. The time was 4:30.

All of the windows in the cabin had six panes, except for the two located in the wall directly opposite the window I flew out of. The two four-paned windows flanked the fireplace. Later, when I went outside to look at the porch roof, most of it was normal, with no window, but one end of it had been almost torn down to make the sun deck. Some of the two-by-fours were still up, and gave the impression of wooden frames suspended above the porch. I was struck by a powerful sense of deja vu when I observed my open porch roof after seeing a window in it from an astral perspective, but I wondered why I had seen a four-paned window.

I looked into the window I had flown out of, and I could plainly see the four-paned window in the opposite wall, as well as the reflection in it of the porch behind me. If my astral body had been in a horizontal position, perpendicular to the window, with my head next to it, and I tipped my head to look upward, I would have seen the four-paned window, and I could have easily misinterpreted its placement, since astrally I am often unaware of my position in space, but fully aware of my location. In this instance, I was confused even more, because the part of the porch roof viewed during the OBE actually had been almost entirely removed since I had last seen it physically.

AUGUST 19, 1978, 2:40 P.M.

I lay down in bed for a nap, took some deep breaths, counted backwards, and presented the autosuggestion that I would become aware of dreaming and project from a lucid dream, either directly or indirectly via the hypnopompic state.

I dreamed I was at work, washing my hands under a sink faucet, when I realized there was no water running out. Gradually, I became aware of the absurdity that I had been washing my hands as usual, but with no water. It occurred to me that I was dreaming.

My consciousness shifted from the dream scene to my physical body in bed. The vibrations were surging through my body, so I tried everything to get out, floating out, rolling out, rocking out, and shooting out through my head, but I remained anchored in the physical world. When I stopped trying and relaxed, I slipped out with ease, able to actually feel my exit from every part of my body. Although I did not know if I was sensing with my astral or physical nerves, it felt like the sensation of pulling an arm from a sweater sleeve, only the perception involved my entire body.

When I was completely separated and in my astral body, I walked from my bedroom into the living room and stopped in front of the fireplace. I floated up to look down upon the mantle. Two pictures were lying face up, side by side, on the right end of the mantle. One was a still life of flowers, which in physical reality hung on the wall to the left of the fireplace, and the other one, which I had never seen before, was a framed print, in dark, somber colors, of an old woman looking at a picture hanging on a wall. I wondered if the old woman was an image of me in the future. I picked up both pictures and floated down to the floor to take a closer look. I walked into the kitchen while studying the print of the old woman, trying to discern the somewhat vague details and memorize them.

From the kitchen, I could see through the heavy wooden Dutch door, which was closed, onto the porch beyond, where my quilt lay in a heap on the porch floor. I thought it was strange, because I knew that in physical reality the quilt was on the bed, covering my physical body.

I turned around and took the pictures back to the living room, memorizing the features of the elderly woman as best I could. I placed both pictures on the mantle and returned to the kitchen, where I stopped at the door, debating whether to open it or pass through the solid wood. I thought it would be interesting to attempt to open it, to determine what would happen if I succeeded, because on a previous astral journey, I did open it and the screen door fell down. Then I decided to pass through it instead, so I could concentrate on the sensation of going through a solid object.

I moved forward, slowly, with ease, and carefully pushed through the heavy Dutch door, feeling the particles of wood fiber brush against the astral matter, or astral energy, or whatever it is that composes my astral body. There was no resistance, just a feeling like a gentle tingling against my skin and through my hair.

After I had passed through, onto the porch, I saw the quilt lying there as before. The orange and white patterns on the blocks were identical to my quilt in physical reality, but, unlike the "real quilt," the misplaced astral quilt had a brown wool, striped or plaid lining. I accepted it as just another one of those astral quirks, for I knew that the physical counterpart of this quilt was actually on my bed.

I wanted to venture somewhere, but had no previously planned destination, so I paused briefly before setting out. I decided to fly up through the porch roof and choose a direction from above the cabin. I willed myself upward, and remained grounded. Then I tried to jump, but my astral body had become extremely heavy, incapable of levitation. I relaxed and was pulled back to my bed, into my physical body. I opened my physical eyes and saw the quilt on the bed, exactly where it was supposed to be. It was 4:00 P.M.

SEPTEMBER 14, 1978, BETWEEN 1:00 A.M. AND 5:00 A.M.

I was sleeping in the lower bunkbed in the spare bedroom, next to the room in which I normally slept. I had gone to bed with the intention of normal sleep and was awakened by a telephone call at 1:00 A.M. I had difficulty returning to sleep, but just concentrated on relaxing, instead of devising autosuggestions to leave my body. For the previous month, however, I had been trying persistently to induce an OBE by concentrating on obtaining conscious awareness in dreams, but had failed.

When I finally did get back to sleep, I dreamed that someone stole my car. I was angry and upset, and then relieved as the knowledge that it was only a dream penetrated my brain. The dream became lucid, but an instant later I achieved awareness lying in bed in the hypnopompic state.

I willed myself to astrally move upward, through the ceiling, and immediately I was in my astral body, rising above my physical body. I rose through the ceiling and up into the attic, where I could clearly see the rafters and boards forming the structure of my roof. The points of hundreds of nails poked through the roof boards, where they had held down the old wooden shingles. I was acutely aware of the acrid smell lingering after the previous rodent tenants, which my cats had proficiently evicted. (In physical reality, I had been spending many long hours up there, cleaning and insulating, so I knew the environment well).

I continued to rise, and wondered if I would feel all those sharp nails puncture my astral skin. After I passed painlessly through the roof, I entered a thick fog and had the sensation of traveling extremely fast, unaware of my direction, destination, or the source of the energy that carried me forth.

Suddenly, a scene lit up all around me, and my vision became clear. It was a bright, sunny day, and I was walking down the steps of a concrete porch on the front of a modest, neatly kept, 1950s style house that, to my conscious knowledge, I had never seen before. From the bottom of the steps, I walked down a short walkway and turned right to follow a sidewalk.

I was walking along for a few yards, enjoying the warm air, when I came to a small flower garden bordering the sidewalk and containing white flowers, some of which had begun to wither. I stopped and bent over to examine a few of the fresh ones more closely; the beautiful flowers looked like small moonflowers, about two inches in diameter. I thought I must come back to this place in physical reality to see if they were actually there, that is, if I ever could ascertain where I was, or if it actually existed. As I gazed down upon the delicate white petals, a soft wind brushed against my face and riffled through my hair.

I walked on for about half a block in what appeared to be a quiet residential neighborhood of small wood frame houses, similar to the one from which I had begun my stroll. At the end of the sidewalk I turned right, for no apparent reason, and walked up an alley for about another block. I approached the back of a gray and white house built upon a hill and designed as a split level, with the garage below the main floor. I stood before the open garage door, hesitating, and then decided to enter and see if there were any people inside. I felt like an intruder.

I walked into the garage. On the right I saw an opened door and a room beyond. It was a bathroom, where a middle-aged man was sitting on the toilet. He was heavy set and wore only an undershirt and boxer shorts pulled down around his knees. I was extremely embarrased at having walked in on him, and wished I had just kept going down the alley, but then I thought I was probably invisible anyway; at least I hoped so.

The man stood, pulled up his shorts, shuffled out, and, to my dismay, looked directly at me. "Well," I thought regrettably, "so much for being invisible." I was tense, and wondered what the most appropriate action would be. I felt self-conscious, because I totally lacked any knowledge of astral etiquette. Then, to my amazement, he smiled at me and said, "Well, what are *you* doing here?" as if he knew me.

I remained silent, being at a complete loss for words, because I was overwhelmed at not only being discovered, but recognized. A woman, also middle-aged, thinner, with short, dark brown curly hair, and wearing a plain cotton dress, came down a short stairway that led from inside the house. I presumed she was his wife. She saw me, too.

I was perplexed, so I just rested my hand against the seat of a blue, lightweight bicycle that was parked next to the wall. As I stood there, trying to decide whether to go to another location on the astral plane, return to my body, or stay and visit with these people, I glanced down at the bicycle seat where the black covering was wrapped around the back to attach underneath. I ran my hand along the folds of the inner rim, and could distinctly feel the rough vinyl. I decided to leave and walked out.

An outside stairway led up to an apartment, so, undaunted and still curious, I entered.

I walked into a small kitchen, decorated with warm, brilliant hues of red and orange, where another middle-aged woman was preparing a meal. She had red hair, red lipstick, a rather large, stocky build, and was wearing a light blue apron. I stood nearby, but she failed to notice me. I waved my arms at her, and she just went on with her work, as if she was alone. Wondering if I had become invisible, I tapped on the reddish-orange counter. She looked straight at me and asked a question, something like, "Are you still making the Queen's bed?" I answered, "No."

I felt uncomfortable, because I had intended to only observe, and had not expected people to see me, recognize me, and even question me, so I willed myself back to my body. A powerful force pulled me through the front of the house and into a busy street. I felt the turbulence from the speeding traffic buffeting against my skin, and some of the cars passed right through my astral form. I wondered why I could feel the rushing air, but not the impact of the motor vehicles.

Then I was speeding through what appeared to be a black tunnel. Powerless to proceed by my own volition, I was propelled on and on through the narrow, abysmal darkness. I closed my eyes, and felt the intense, black atmosphere rush by. After a while, I seriously wondered if I would ever get back to my body, because considering the high velocity and excessive amount of time I had been traveling, I reasoned that I must have projected far away and, besides, I had been out of my body for a longer period than ever before. And, since this was the first time I willed myself back to physical reality, I wasn't sure if it would work.

I sped further through the seemingly infinite blackness, and eventually opened my eyes to see if my surroundings had improved. I was still encompassed by the dark channel, and still being swept away to an unknown destination. As I catapulted through the black void, I looked down at my astral body and saw a luminous, white replica of my physical body.

Finally, I stopped. The tunnel had vanished and I was floating near my bed, so, a bit relieved, I wriggled into my physical body. I could see the parts of my astral body and move them to merge with their physical counterparts. When everything was aligned, I returned to consciousness in physical reality.

I could tell that my physical body had remained still for quite a while, because I was warmly snuggled under a pile of quilts. That bunkbed was so cold that after any movement, it took considerable time to warm up the new place, and I was warm all over, with my gold striped cat, Taffy, curled up against my side, sound asleep.

This OBE differed from previous projections, because I went to an environment completely alien to my physical consciousness, and I felt I was able to stay out of my body indefinitely. Although to me the people were strangers, they apparently knew me, and accepted my astral intrusion calmly with a matter-of-fact attitude. Wherever the neatly kept, modest neighborhood was, it was daylight, but when I returned to my physical body, velvety darkness pressed against the outside of the cabin windows.

NOVEMBER 23, 1978, 1:00 P.M.

I had been napping, drifting in and out of dreams and awakening intermittently. During one dream, a printed page magically appeared, suspended before my eyes. I could discern the black print against the white background fairly well, and although some letters were blurry, I could partially comprehend a paragraph that told about one of my past lives. (I have no definite beliefs concerning reincarnation.) As I concentrated on holding a particular word in focus and comprehending its meaning, I realized this experience was a dream and appreciated how marvelous it was to receive a message in this manner.

The page faded away, and I acquired hypnopompic consciousness in my physical body, which was vibrating with a high-pitched humming in my head. I tried to project, but had difficulty exiting in my astral form. After a few attempts, I moved slightly out of alignment with my physical form, and my astral body began slowly rotating, parallel to the plane of the bed, head to foot, foot to head, with my waist as a pivot, in a counterclockwise motion. I relaxed, and the momentum increased. One of my cats, Tanya, and my dog, Shunka, were lying beside me, but my gyrating double spun through them without the slightest resistance. The whirling motion accelerated to an incredible velocity, and astonished, I wondered what would happen next. My astral body continued spinning, around and around, with no indication of doing otherwise, until eventually I became bored. I wanted to project somewhere.

The spinning ended; my astral double rolled to the right and fell through the mattress. I was under the bed, floating belly down, parallel to the floor, where I could see the floorboards and wall panels clearly. I was about to pass head first through the wall separating the bedrooms, when I felt something bump my upper back. Instantaneously, I was back in my body, fully awake, in normal physical consciousness. It was almost 1:30 P.M.

DECEMBER 22, 1978, 2:45–3:50 P.M.

I took five or six slow, deep breaths, and began the relaxation exercise, but before I proceeded past my waist, I fell asleep. After a while, I awakened, realized what had happened, and continued the relaxation. Again, I fell asleep.

I had a false awakening dream, in which I dreamed I had gotten up and gone to the kitchen to prepare dinner, but then I realized I was actually in bed asleep. Upon this realization, I entered the hypnopompic state, with the sensation of mild vibrations pervading my body.

I tried to project, but my physical form had a firm grasp on its astral counterpart; I tried to float upward and sink downward, to no avail. After a while, I ceased these efforts, relaxed, and allowed the vibrations to continue without my conscious intervention, hoping that separation would occur automatically, as it had on several previous occasions. My astral double remained imbedded within its material enclosure.

Then I decided to take advantage of the present situation and experiment with the vibrations. I imagined them speeding up, and they oscillated at a much higher frequency. Then I directed them to various parts of my body by just "thinking" them to my head, feet, thorax, and evenly distributed again. Although I had control over the speed and placement of the vibrations, it was impossible to move so much as a finger out of my body.

When I tried even harder to project again, I felt as if I entered a semiopaque borderline awareness, where the hypnopompic state, a dream world, and an OBE merged. Between short lapses of consciousness, I floated, head first, through the ceiling and up into the attic. I looked down and saw Shunka and the cats lying on the bed, and my brother, Jim, sitting in a chair, watching television in my bedroom. (Jim was miles away, and I never had a T.V. in the cabin bedroom.)

I emerged from that peculiar fusion of worlds to the hypnopompic state. The vibrations were still intense, but instead of leaving my body completely or totally awakening to physical reality, I entered another dream projection in which the same dream images of Jim and the television set merged with another dreamlike OBE. For a few minutes, my awareness fluctuated back and forth, between the projection dream state and the hypnopompic state accompanied by vibrations, and then I awoke to normal physical consciousness.

February 9, 1979, Afternoon

The previous night I visited (physically) one of my most unique and interesting friends, Pat, who had developed, along with other impressive talents, the ability of automatic writing. An entity who calls itself "Doctor Heath" often sends messages and advice through her, and Pat devotes much time to using such communications and other psychic gifts to help others. I asked the doctor if he could furnish some advice on astral projection, and, as the pencil in Pat's hand moved across the paper with a will of its own, I received the following, reprinted here verbatim, with the incomplete sentences typical of messages from Doctor Heath's dimension:

> "You're experiencing the difference between really leaving your body. Your attachment to body is great. Let go of the body feeling. You will go to higher levels as soon as you do. Trust your spirit to be free and move free without body attachments."
>
> "Don't I do this?" I asked.
>
> "No. Vibrations are to release totally the body. Believe light can beam you up and out. Your light. INNER LIGHT. Yes. Will give you energy for your light to bring you forth. Ask your guides to be of energy service to you. Energize yourself thru them then will you beam up and thru your body. You are ready for this but needed help in understanding the difference."

As I drifted through the hypnagogic state, I pondered the message and decided to heed the advice, but then dropped off to sleep. I dreamed that a young man and woman, whom I had never seen before, were walking up the road to my cabin. The long-haired man was carrying a small child, and the woman was chasing after a brown beagle-type puppy that had strayed off the road and was bounding toward my cabin. I stood at the door, watching, and told the young woman it was fortunate that Shunka was inside, because he probably would have attacked the puppy if he had been out. As I spoke, the dream became lucid, and I entered the hypnopompic state, with the vibrations vigorously pulsating through my body.

I tried to project, asking spirit guides, if they were present, to help. I passed swiftly through the hypnopompic state and into physical consciousness, and the vibrations ceased.

FEBRUARY 13, 1979, 2:45–4:00 P.M.

I lay down, took ten or so deep breaths, began relaxing each part of my body, but went to sleep before I finished. From sleep, I entered a series of false awakenings.

I dreamed that I awoke when a friend, a male dream character, dropped in to visit. As he stepped into the bedroom where I was sleeping, half of a ragged old quilt fell off the bed, and he threw it into the wood stove, glad it had finally fallen apart.

As my quilt smoldered in the stove, I realized I was dreaming, and "awakened" to another false awakening, this time believing he had actually arrived. I wondered which room he was in, so I checked the spare bedroom, believing he might be sleeping in there. The lower bunk was freshly made up with the covers turned back, empty.

I began to awaken, understanding that I had entered another dream, but I lapsed into still another false awakening. In the new dream, I got up and went into the spare bedroom again. On the top bunk, my cat, Tanya, was in bed, covered up, with her head on the pillow. On the bottom bunk was the quilt from the first dream, unscorched and completely intact. I petted Tanya's head and told her she was a good cat, and then returned to my own bed.

I began to wake up again, realizing that this, too, was a dream. I entered the hypnopompic state, and the vibrations were strong, so I asked my spirit guides to help me get out of my body. The vibrations continued as I tried to move myself out, unsuccessfully. Then I tried to exteriorize without a body feeling, though I failed to imagine exactly what that was like.

I remained enclosed within my material form, so I concentrated on the vibrations, increasing their speed at will. I asked my spirit guides to direct the correct amount of energy into the vibrations, and I mentally expressed my desire to project to acquire knowledge that would be beneficial to me, as well as to others. Then, lying flat on my back, I relaxed.

After a brief moment, to my astonishment, I felt a pair of hands clutch my back and slowly raise me to a sitting posture. My arms were in the position they would be in if I was seated in an arm chair, resting them on the chair arms. They were relaxed and comfortably floating.

My eyes were open while the firm astral hands positioned my body, but, as in some other instances, I was unable to ascertain whether I was seeing astrally or physically. Then, to my bewilderment, I noticed a fringe of my own hair hanging in front of my eyes, but I saw a grotesque mutation of any locks that I had ever seen before; each filament had hundreds of other shafts branching from it along both sides. The branches were very short, and all were nearly the same length; they gave the impression of a structure more similar to feathers than to human hair. Beyond my outlandishly modified astral tresses, I discerned my bedroom, which looked normal; the warm glow of the pine paneling was subdued by the pale winter daylight streaming in through the windows.

I still felt the hands, which were against my back, near the region of my waist and partially encompassing my sides. The invisible hands gently lay me back down, slightly diagonal to where I had been lying before. The sensation of pressure where the hands of the unknown astral entity had held my body faded away.

As I lay in bed, fully awake in physical consciousness, I realized that it was my astral body that had been sat up, although while the hands were lifting me, their strength and touch produced such a definite sensation that it felt exactly as though they were moving my physical body.

February 16, 1979, Afternoon

I took ten or so deep breaths, relaxed each part of my body, implemented autosuggestions for astral projection, and fell asleep.

Later I awoke, quivering with vibrations, and called upon the spirit guides for assistance to leave my body, but I returned to sleep instead, and had what I believed to be a dream of astral projection.

I dreamed I was hovering above the hillside behind my cabin, gazing at the scene below. My cabin and the encompassing woods, bare and brittle in their own winter slumber, were shrouded with twilight, but I could distinctly ascertain the landmarks below. Silver highlights defined the rocks and trees, as if they were drenched by the light of a full moon. The glow spilled over upon the dry, lifeless mat covering the forest floor. I saw Taffy roaming through the shadows and pools of light below, her golden fur acting as protective coloration against the tawny winter foliage below the towering pines.

I awoke, physically, as the late afternoon sun sunk behind the ridge. I stepped out of the bedroom, and Taffy greeted me from the living room, where she had been curled up in the chair in front of the fireplace, lost in her own dreamland, perhaps chasing mice, climbing trees, or roaming through a winter forest.

I believed that during this "projection," my awareness was functioning on one of the branches between the dream continuum and the OBE continuum. Although the images were vivid, I lacked the distinct impression of actually being there; I felt I was either partially awake in a dream or partially asleep in an OBE.

FEBRUARY 28, 1979, BEFORE DAWN

I had gone to bed late, tired, and fallen asleep immediately. Later, I awoke with an incredible thirst. I thought about some bottles of juice that were in the lower cabinet of my kitchen cupboard. The cool, tart juice was just what I wanted to relieve my parched throat and mouth.

However, it was freezing in the cabin, and I felt too tired and comfortable to leave my warm, cozy bed, so I went back to sleep.

Later, I woke up again, even thirstier; I just had to get up and have a drink of juice. Hopefully, it would not be frozen. I threw the covers back and got out of bed.

I walked into the living room and groped in the darkness for the chain dangling from the ceiling light. I listened—I heard a loud rushing noise. It sounded as if a strong wind gusted out of the night, blowing heavy rain or sleet against the cabin. Finally, I found the light chain and pulled it, but the room remained dark. I thought perhaps the storm had knocked out the power.

I found my way to the kitchen and flipped the wall switch, and after repeated tries, became frustrated by the ineffective click. The darkness of the woodland night persevered. Determined to quench my thirst, I opened the cupboard, sat down crosslegged on the floor in front of it, and felt around inside, on the left, for the bottles. They were gone. After further searching, I discovered them on the right, the opposite side of the shelf from where they should have been. I pulled them out; my eyes became accustomed to the dark; and I sat there, trying to decide which kind to have.

Suddenly, I was pulled through the air, back to my bed. I opened my eyes, and I was lying in bed, thirstier than ever. Outside the barn sash windows, the stars twinkled brightly through the calm forest in the dark, cold night. Perhaps the "storm" had only been those strange noises peculiar to the astral world.

As I lay there enjoying the tranquility of my rustic little haven, I had no idea that circumstances were about to disrupt my life and set me on a new path, away from my beloved cabin in the woods.

Chapter 8

The Storefront House

Although my physical residence changed, my astral odyssey continued. In the spring of 1979, I rented an old house that many years before had a store on the ground floor with living quarters upstairs. It still had the false front, hence the name, storefront house; to this day, that is how some local people refer to it.

My new home was located in a small town, situated along an interstate highway, which passes along the edge of the community, about a block northeast of the storefront house. My life was changing as fast as the traffic speeding along the nearby interstate; I was in the process of taking new directions in relationships, career goals, and lifestyle, which were all in turmoil at once, but I escaped back to my cabin whenever I could find the time. The following OBE took place during a weekend when I had gone back to find some peace and solitude in the quiet of the woods.

September 9, 1979, 1:30–3:00 P.M.

After lounging on the deck since morning, reading and sunning, I decided to go inside where it was much cooler, lie down, meditate for a while, and take a nap. As I passed from the hot sun deck into the cool, dim cabin, I thought about astral projection and considered that sunbathing may have helped to induce it before, although I had not recorded specific notes of that fact.

While lying in bed meditating, I visualized the package of notebook paper on my table, empty pages that I wanted to fill with dream studies and accounts of OBEs. I skipped the previously discussed techniques, which had brought surprising success followed by disappointing failure, because I had applied them numerous times without results.

After meditating for a while and dropping off to sleep, I dreamed that a professor was lecturing in an outdoor setting, where tall shade trees stood on a wide, manicured lawn, a setting that resembled a campus or a park. A large crowd had gathered to listen. The professor stood on a wooden structure that resembled a pavilion, or a balcony, or perhaps a gazebo. The distinguished looking speaker was handsome—young, slender, dark-haired—and wore a gray suit and glasses. I was intrigued by his topic; it seemed to pertain directly to my life, but the words slipped away before my memory could grasp them.

My astute professor was interrupted by the roaring and chugging of a motor vehicle stuggling up the steep, rocky road to my cabin and bumping noisily over rocks and ruts. Shunka leaped off the bed, growled and barked ferociously, dependably fulfilling his self-appointed role as the overtly enthusiastic protector. I threw the covers off and got up, teasingly saying, "Get 'em, Shunka, get 'em," while he got more excited and ran out of the bedroom, his paws losing traction on the bare areas of the wood floor as he barked emphatically at the metallic "monster" infringing upon his territory.

I noticed that my voice sounded strange; it had a quavering, hollow ring, and I wondered if the present action was actually taking place, or if I had been talking in my sleep and hearing my voice as I entered the hypnopompic state, or if I was silently dreaming the entire incident.

I hurried to the kitchen to hook the door in case someone actually was dropping by, because all I had on was my blue-flowered long johns. (In physical reality I was wearing my swimsuit covered with a black T-shirt.) I had difficulty finding the hook, and the door casing cast a luminous golden glow, instead of the dark red-brown color I had recently painted it. (It *had been* a gold color before I repainted it.) I concentrated intensely on putting my hand exactly where the hook should have been, found it, and hooked the door.

I stood in the kitchen and wondered if I was physically awake or out wandering around in my astral body. I decided to test the situation by determining if I could fly through the wall to the outside of the cabin. To my surprise, I swiftly floated out and hovered a few feet from the woodpile.

The atmosphere was "charged" with a pervasive type of energy; I could sense a strong force like static electricity in the air around me. I decided to relax, remain passive, and see if an exterior power would propel me to a new location.

I felt a tug on my upper back, and then my astral body was coursing rapidly through a blue-gray foggy blur. I thought about the time I ended up at the house of those people who seemed to know me, although they were strangers to me, and I wondered if I was going back to that modest astral neighborhood, or to a similar situation.

Then I stopped; the blue "tunnel" had disappeared. I was back in my bed. I wanted to project again, so I pushed out through my head. As I passed through the wall at the head of my bed, I wanted to open my eyes, but I was concerned that my physical eyes would open and result in another return to my body. Then I thought, "My astral vision will fade in through my eyelids."

It did! A view of the inside of the wall came into focus, and my eyes felt open, although I had held them shut. I could see two-by-fours and the dark side of the knotty pine paneling as I slipped through and emerged in the living room, where I stood before my piano. (I had moved only a few belongings from the cabin to the storefront house, which was partially furnished when I moved in.)

The piano keyboard was open, so I stepped closer to see if I could play it while in astral form. I remained standing, bent over the bench, and reached out to find the correct keys to play Beethoven's "Fur Elise." I found them easily, but when I struck them, the piano sounded tinny and dreadfully out of tune. I started over several times, because I knew my piano was tuned to pitch, but each time I played, it was just as dissonant. Puzzled, I gave up and floated to the kitchen.

I stood in the middle of my kitchen and remembered the astral experience I had had the previous year, in which I jumped up into the air several times, and went higher each time. I decided to try that again. I jumped up a few inches, came down, jumped up a few inches again, and on the third jump, I soared high above my cabin. I wanted to fly somewhere, but I drifted back down into the kitchen.

I tried again. First, I only jumped up a couple of feet and came down in slow motion. Then I jumped part way through the ceiling, and landed softly on my feet. Next I jumped as hard as I could, shot upward, glimpsed my attic on the way through, and ended up hovering high in the air above my cabin. I looked down and saw the little green kitchen roof attached to the larger roof of the main structure.

I darted about in the bright blue, sunny sky, doing flips, turns, and barrel rolls, soaring and diving above my cabin. I flew toward the southeast, and watched the trees below glitter in the sunlight.

I stopped. I was floating next to and slightly above a railing, almost identical to the cabin porch railing, except that the one in the astral world had a structure attached to it. The structure was made of a wooden platform, about two feet by two feet, supported with two-by-fours nailed to a post against the railing. I alighted on the platform, from where I saw rusty nails, some pulling loose, holding it to the weathered and splintered post. It appeared too rickety for the weight of a human physical body, but readily supported my astral double. The railing was stained brown, just like the porch railing in the physical dimension, but the board I was crouched on was plain weathered wood.

I had the "paranormal knowledge" that there was a beach, or some type of open space or recreational area behind me, as I faced the railing, and houses to the left and right, with my immediate surroundings and the houses built within a thick grove of trees. Without actually seeing the open area or houses, I intuitively sensed that they were there.

I looked down at some leaves scattered on the ground—already they flaunted shades of orange and red, an autumnal prelude in the warm glow of the late summer sun. The leaves vanished, and I was back in my body, opening my eyes as the vibrations faded away.

NOVEMBER 1, 1979, 6:00–7:00 A.M.

I was sleeping in an upstairs bedroom in the storefront house, when I awoke early and decided to try to project. I rocked internally and drifted into the hypnagogic state, concentrating on leaving my body.

After a brief period of unconsciousness, I entered the hypnopompic state and felt my body vibrating, so, just by willing it, I easily moved out of my physical body, upward, through the ceiling, and above the house.

Mentally, I expressed the desire to pay an astral visit to Cara, one of my closest and most precious friends, who lived a short distance away. Cara is intelligent, practical, inquisitive, and well educated, and together we have often experimented with psychic phenomena. She was aware that I might attempt to visit her in astral form.

An invisible force lurched me backward, away from Cara's house, but in spite of such a powerful contrary influence, I tried to force my astral body forward, and soon fell softly onto the ground.

I looked around. I was sitting in a field, next to a barbed-wire fence, with tall dried grass and weeds tangled around me. I saw that I was still wearing my blue pajamas.

I zapped back into my body, sensed the vibrations for a few seconds, and then awakened physically. I looked at my watch—it was almost 7:00—and I realized that Cara would be just arriving at her place of employment, which was in the opposite direction from my house. I wondered what would have happened if I had allowed the astral force to pull me in that direction, as it had begun to do, before I insistently intervened with my conscious effort to travel to Cara's house.

DECEMBER 19, 1979, 3:30–5:20 A.M.

Shunka awoke me at 3:30, pleading desperately for a short walk. After getting up and dutifully allowing him to drag me around the back yard in the frozen darkness of the crisp wintery night, I lay in bed for a long time, wide awake, but trying to go back to sleep. Then I assumed I had dozed off, because I had the sensation of awakening to the music of the clock radio alarm, which I actually had set for 5:30. I relaxed and contemplated how pleasantly it gently faded into my awareness. I listened to the soft music and became even more relaxed. I decided to try to leave my body.

Immediately, I floated with ease, up from the bed, and paused next to the ceiling, where I put my hands against the plaster to observe how it would feel as I went through. I felt slight resistance as my diffuse astral form mingled with the material forming the ceiling, and then passed into a tiny room above, which puzzled me, because my bedroom was on the top floor. I presumed that the small enclosure must be an attic. (I have never physically seen the attic in the storefront house.) Although it was dark, I could see that the walls enclosing the small area were constructed of many narrow, unpainted boards.

I rose farther upward, through the roof, and was surprised to discover that I could still hear the radio as clearly as before. I wondered if it was physical music perceived by the sensing of sound traveling up the silver cord, or if it was astral music perceived by my astral hearing.

I decided it would be interesting to explore the astral features, or entities if any were present, in an old building that was originally designed and used as a hotel, but at that time housed an antique shop in a portion of the ground level. It was only half a block away. One of the owners, Dot, who is one of my favorite and most spirited friends, lived in the house next door, and we had discussed the "intriguing ghosts" that may still be wandering around in the rather spooky old building.

I flew to the northeast, toward the interstate highway, over my house, then over Dot's house. The antique shop in the old wooden hotel was on the other side of Dot's house, but, when I saw the posts holding up the northeast side of the porch, I realized I had gone a little too far. I was on the side of the shop facing the interstate highway; I flew away from the building, over the railing of the stairway leading up to the porch.

I saw another antique shop across a street, in a big, old, yellow wood frame house. Neither the street nor the house were present in physical reality—if there actually had been an antique shop there, it would have been in the middle of the interstate highway.

The picturesque Victorian style house had a strange aura of familiarity. I flew through the wall into the front room, which was full of antiques: furniture, dishes, nicknacks, pictures, etc., and some partially unpacked cardboard boxes, which were open on a sofa. Crumpled newspapers, which apparently had been used for packing, were scattered around on the floor, sofa, and in the boxes.

A woman, whom I presumed to be the owner of the house, entered from a room beyond the front room. She had dark hair and appeared to be in her forties. She looked directly at me, seemed to recognize me, and asked why I was there so early, since they were not open yet. I answered, but forgot what I said. Then she remarked about thirty women coming over at 10:00 for a club or a meeting of some kind. I told her I had to return to my house and get ready for work.

I entered an adjoining room, where I viewed a shocking sight—lying asleep on a cot was an ancient, bony, shriveled up, white-haired woman, who looked as if she was barely clinging to the fragile remnants of a life that must have begun a century ago. I flew out the side wall that faced the old hotel building on the other side of the street.

I paused before crossing the street, and sat on a branch up in a huge, leafless tree beside the house, and gazed out over the barren winter landscape. I looked down at my astral body; I was wearing blue jeans and a red wool turtleneck sweater that, in physical reality, I had discarded years ago. The early morning sun felt warm for that time of year.

The dark-haired woman walked outside, looked up at me, and spoke to me about something I didn't understand. I felt I had to leave, so I flew back "across the street," and floated in the air beside another tree, next to the old hotel building. I felt unusually warm air radiating up from the ground. Then I flew over the hotel, over Dot's house, and drifted down into my bedroom.

I saw my bed below, covered with a striped quilt, however, I failed to notice my physical body, which would have been buried under a pile of bedding. I had a striped quilt like the one I saw, but it was on a bed in another room.

Suddenly, my vision narrowed to a small window on the upper right; everything was black except the dim gray light of dawn, sneaking in through the window. I was back in my body, lying in bed, from where I could see out a small window. Outside was the predawn darkness of a cold winter morning. The clock radio was silent. I got up and switched on the light. The clock said 5:20. While I hurriedly dressed in the frigid old house, the radio alarm began playing as usual, at 5:30.

I lived in the storefront house for another year, during which I turned my attention away from my astral odyssey and concentrated more on material matters. At the end of 1979, I moved to Rapid City, a larger town, where I had purchased a house more conveniently located. I often referred to it as my town house, to differentiate it from my cabin. Even though my goals, for the most part, diverted my path away from the invisible worlds, a few months after moving into my town house, I had an astral adventure more profound than I had ever imagined possible.

Chapter 9

The Town House

The old two-story town house faces north, with a roofed front porch overhung by the branches of black walnut trees that provide enough shade to make the porch swing enjoyable on even the hottest of days. (Many of the passages in this book were conceptualized on that swing.)

Inside, on the main floor, the front half is a living room and the back half is divided into the kitchen and dining room, with a small bathroom and porch room attached to the rear. Just beyond the front entrance and to the right is the staircase leading to the second floor.

All three bedrooms are upstairs. The two front bedrooms each have a set of double windows overlooking the porch roof. There is a small bedroom in back, in the southeast corner of the upstairs, and the main bathroom in the southwest corner.

I had attempted astral projection only occasionally during the previous year, but, to my conscious awareness, for the most part I had remained attentive to the material world with normal interludes of dream consciousness.

I had read Paul Twitchell's book, *Eckankar*,[1] which frequently mentions astral guides, or spiritual travelers, as Twitchell calls them. Supposedly, these are beneficent entities on the astral plane that can be summoned when help is desired by anyone seeking the spiritual path. The spiritual travelers are highly developed and are also referred to as "masters."

---

[1]Paul Twitchell, *Eckankar: The Key to Secret Worlds*, (San Diego, CA: Illuminated Way Press, 1969).

SOMETIME IN 1981, THE MIDDLE OF THE NIGHT

I was sleeping in the northwest front bedroom and partially awakened in the hypnopompic state, with vibrations pulsating throughout my body. I made an effort to rise in my astral body while keeping my physical body still, and after a few moments, I simply flew out the window, surprised to find myself in my astral body so suddenly.

I hovered a foot or so above the west end of the porch roof and, as an experiment, mentally demanded, to no one in particular, "Show me my master!" Then, to my amazement and delight, I saw a figure standing at the other end of the porch roof.

I was fascinated, with my total attention drawn to the apparition. I saw that he was a long-haired man wearing a loose-fitting robe draped over his shoulders and tied at the waist, with the sleeves hanging down in relaxed folds. The mystical being glowed with a serene, blue luminescence, which encompassed the entire vision. I looked at him—enthralled—and realized that he had the features depicted in pictures of Jesus Christ. He stood there, facing me, with his arms held out, slightly raised from his sides.

My heart was filled with an overpowering feeling of happiness and love, emotions more intense than any I had ever felt before, either on the astral or the physical plane.

I was helplessly drawn to him and knelt at his feet, where I wept with huge, wrenching sobs that came from the most remote depths of my soul. I experienced an emotional reaction that was completely beyond my control or understanding. A flood of tears sprang from my eyes and washed down my face.

Before I could speak, listen, or do anything else, I was back in my body, awakening in my bed. My eyes were dry, but I could feel the aftermath of the powerful emotions lingering within.

I was astounded! At most I had expected an average spirit guide, but this experience bewildered me, and I wondered why it had happened to me. I accepted the apparition as Jesus, though, because of the overwhelming nature of my emotional response, and trusted that my higher self could ascertain a holy presence. But, of course, I could have been wrong.

To this day, that astral encounter still puzzles me more than any of the others. Although I allowed the events of my life to pursue a course away from astral projection, I have never forgotten the beautiful figure that appeared on my porch roof. During occasional moments when life seems insignificant, or in times of desperation, thoughts of that apparition bring the peace of mind and inner strength necessary to continue, assured of the constant presence of divine guidance and purpose.

FEBRUARY 7, 1990, THE MIDDLE OF THE NIGHT

Throughout the busy decade of the 1980s, amid a steady progression of achievements and upheavals, I had occasionally rearranged my house and, for the previous several years, had utilized the back bedroom in the southeast corner of the house as my sleeping quarters. On this particular night, I had gone to sleep concentrating on astrally visiting Judi, who lived about ten miles northwest of town in a housing development. She was expecting me. We had planned to attempt travel on the astral plane together, in a mutual projection, to help determine whether the OBE world is objective or subjective, because a primary criterion for objectivity is phenomena experienced by more than one person.

Sometime during the night, I left my body and floated through the spare bedroom in the front part of my house, in the northeast corner. I continued through the double windows, and observed the internal wooden framework as I passed to the outside. From my front yard, I flew across the street and down the alley. I stopped above some garbage cans, where I saw a black and white cat rummaging around, and I wondered if it was my cat, Sylvester.

I remembered my intention to project to Judi's house, so I flew away toward the northwest, over the buildings and out of my neighborhood. I was high in the air, in complete control, cruising slowly enough to observe the sights below. I looked down upon the familiar hills, partially covered with dark jigsaw patches of native ponderosa pine, the trees that cause the hills to appear black from a distance. Then I looked ahead and saw the lights of the cement plant twinkling in the darkness.

I felt an attraction pull me closer to the cement plant, where I had previously been employed in the laboratory. I knew current employees who might be working the graveyard shift, and I was concerned that I could be delayed if I allowed my astral form to become distracted from my original goal. I resolved to continue my journey to Judi's house.

I stopped and hovered above the hills to study the vista and to determine whether the best route to Judi's house was to the right or to the left of the cement plant. I knew she lived somewhere on the other side of the plant, but without following roads and with seeing the landscape from an unfamiliar perspective, I was confused about the exact location of her house relative to my position and the cement plant.

After a brief hesitation, I chose to go right, and as I turned and flew onward, I concentrated on a mental image of Judi's house.

An invisible force instantly transported me to her bedroom, where I stood on the left side of the bed in almost complete darkness, and looked down at her. She was sound asleep, lying partially on her stomach and right side; I saw the back of her curly blond head and her right hand sticking out from under the comforter.

I wondered how I could awaken her to the plane of consciousness I was experiencing to tell her I was present in astral form. I put my right hand over her right hand, and instantly became aware in my physical body, back home in my own bed.

I immediately reentered astral consciousness, by just willing it, with the intention to return to Judi's. I sprang out of my physical body and flew out the south window of my bedroom and into my backyard, where I had a dreamlike experience of conversing with my next door neighbor, Mary. This state of consciousness appeared to be the merging of an OBE with a dream on a branch between the OBE continuum and the dream continuum, from which I soon awakened, in bed, in physical reality.

Later, in physical reality, Judi confirmed that her bedroom was very dark and that she often sleeps in the position I described, but she had had no awareness of my astral presence.

When I asked her how she wanted me to awaken her next time, she suggested that I try to rouse the dogs, who slept on the bed with her, to see if they could perceive my astral presence and bark to let her know I was there.

APRIL 17, 1990, EARLY MORNING

I awakened in the predawn stillness. I tossed and turned for a long time, trying to return to sleep. Eventually, I decided to forget about sleeping and use the time as an opportunity to experiment with astral projection. I took some deep breaths, relaxed, and visualized numbers, counting backward from ten.

After I relaxed for a while, in a state I assumed to be light hypnagogic consciousness, I decided to see what would happen if I simply tried to get up. I pushed the covers back and stood next to the bed, wondering whether I was in my astral or physical body; I felt just as I ordinarily do when performing these movements in physical waking. I flew out my south bedroom window, confirming that I was in my astral body.

As I sailed through the indigo sky over my neighborhood, I discovered a surprising phenomenon—I was carrying my two striped gray cats, Moriah and Merlin, one in each arm! I was amused that they could travel astrally with me, never having considered this as a possibility before. I truly enjoyed having them along. I considered it plausible that if cats are proficient astral travelers, mine naturally would accompany me, because these two, especially Merlin, like to have me pick them up and carry them around the house. Often when I go for walks, all three of my cats trail along behind, enjoying the quaint old neighborhood in which we live. Sylvester, the most athletic of the feline trio, will even jog with me for short distances.

I flew along, clutching my fuzzy companions, and sought the direction to Judi's house. My concentration and control were poor. I ended up in several foggy, dreamlike locations, most of the details of which I failed to retain.

At one point, I arrived in an unfamiliar bedroom, where a man, whom I knew casually, or someone that looked like him, sat up in bed and conversed with me, telling me he had overindulged at a party and was suffering from a hangover. I left and flew around some more, searching for the way to Judi's.

I ventured through the nighttime quietude, still clinging to Moriah and Merlin. I continued to concentrate on Judi's house by creating a mental image of her front yard, driveway, and door, but I kept landing in ambiguous settings that somewhat resembled homes of friends, where vague, dreamlike elements interfered with perspicuous perception. After much traveling, frustration, and brief intermittent returns to my body, during which I lost track of the cats, I wound up back in my bed, in the hypnopompic state.

To my bewilderment, I saw a pleasant-looking young man standing next to my vanity, watching me. Although he appeared solid, his features looked slightly out of focus. I could see that he was of medium height and build with medium length, thick brown hair, full lips, and large, gentle-looking dark eyes. He was wearing a light-colored shirt and dark slacks. I presumed he was a nonphysical entity, but I wondered who he was and what he was doing in my bedroom in the middle of the night!

I asked him if he was one of my spirit guides, and he said, "yes," and something else—I don't know what—that made me believe that his primary function was something else. I asked him if he could help me straighten out my life, and he told me he was only there to help me sleep. He gave me a little friendship hug, and then he walked across the room and stopped next to the closet, where a pretty young woman stood. She had long, dark hair and was wearing a flowing robe, fashioned from material so wondrously beautiful that it seemed to be woven from pure white satin and light. The young man embraced her and gave her a long, passionate kiss.

"Oh well," I thought, feeling a little disappointed, "so much for spirit guides." I flew out the window again, even more determined to get to Judi's house.

I flew to the northwest, over the hills, and approached the cement plant. This time I was amused to find my black and white cat, Sylvester, in my arms. I tried to avoid the cement plant by concentrating on Judi's house, but was drawn into the laboratory, where, once again, the situation became dreamlike.

A fire was burning somewhere in the plant. People were excited and dashing about, anxiously trying to extinguish the blaze and get the belching machanical giants running properly again. An instant later, I was outside, watching from the shadows behind a concrete wall near the front of the plant. Then, just as suddenly, I was back inside the building that contained the lab. I walked through a doorway and saw the graffiti scratched into the chipped green-painted surface of the metal door.

I clung to Sylvester, who was struggling to get out of my arms; he does not like to be carried as much as the other two do. I refused to let him down, however, because I was unsure if he could safely find his way home by himself. Of course, I had no proof that he was actually there, or, for that matter, that I was, but to avoid any risk of his getting lost, I held him firmly and told him to settle down. I tried to leave the plant by concentrating on Judi's house.

An energy force whisked me away to the northwest, toward my intended destination, while Sylvester relaxed and appeared to enjoy the ride.

When I slowed enough to distinguish my surroundings, I saw that I was in a town with old fashioned buildings, like those of frontier towns in the late 1800s. I was on a premises containing aisles and tables, but I was unable to determine if I was inside one of the buildings, or in a courtyard connected to one of them, or situated between two of them. It appeared to be the inside of a large complex of rooms, because I could see through openings that may have been windows overlooking the street outside, but at the same time the area itself had the quality of openess, with small trees or large plants growing here and there.

The color red dominated the decor; red draperies formed cascading partitions, or the walls were red, or both, and shiny metal and brightly colored lights lined the aisles and walls. The furniture and light fixtures looked antique, but in excellent condition, in the style of the 1800s or early 1900s. The room through which I walked had similar rooms adjoining for as far as I could see. A few people, all strangers to me, were wandering around, some of them dining at the tables. I held Sylvester tightly, wondering what would become of him if he escaped from my grasp.

I concentrated intensively on Judi's house, and a moment later I was standing in her bedroom, on the right side of her bed, gazing down at her. She was sound asleep, lying on her right side, turned over slightly on her stomach. All I could see was her head on the pillow and the position of her body under the covers.

I remembered that I had agreed to arouse the dogs if I returned astrally, and I started to search for them at the foot of the bed, when I stopped and thought—Sylvester! It occured to me that the dogs might get excited if they saw Sylvester, and he might panic if they barked at him. I stood there in a quandary and wondered what the possible consequences of an astral cat and dog fight would be, but I never found out, because Sylvester was saved by the bell. My alarm went off, jarring me back into the physical world.

Less than three weeks later, on May 6, Judi and I went to Deadwood, South Dakota, which is only about an hour's drive from home. We walked into one of the new gambling casinos, The Gold Dust, one in which I had never been before, and I was astounded by what I saw—it looked like the place I had projected to on April 17. The colors were predominently red, some furnishings looked antique, and colorfully lit slot machines formed aisles. Potted trees were placed decoratively about and intricate Victorian style light fixtures hung from the ceiling. Large mirrors lined the two side walls, and gave the illusion of similar adjoining rooms. I let my eyes go out of focus and looked around—this made it look and feel exactly like the place I had projected to almost three weeks earlier.

Later, I learned that the Gold Dust had opened on April 27, 1990, ten days *after* my OBE there!

(The cement plant ran smoothly that night. All three cats have been accounted for in physical reality and show no signs of damage from their astral odyssey.)

April 22, 1990, THE MIDDLE OF THE NIGHT

As I lingered in the hypnagogic state before falling to sleep, I concentrated on inducing a lucid dream, intending to astrally project from the dream and proceed to Judi's house.

I had a dream that a man, with whom I was somewhat acquainted on an impersonal basis in physical reality, owned a hardware store. In the dream I was employed by the store, where the situation became frustrating, with stock shortages, misplaced merchandise, and angry customers, and I was relieved that it was only a dream. At that thought, the dream became lucid.

I willed myself upward, out of the hardware store, and blasted up into the sky. Below, I could see the roof of the store moving farther and farther away, becoming smaller and smaller until it disappeared. As I continued my rapid ascent, the features of the landscape blended together—individual trees became forests, individual hills became mountain ranges, pastures and fields became plains. Up I went, higher and still higher; I saw the Great Lakes come into view, followed by the West Coast. Soon I saw the entire continental United States below me, exactly as though I was viewing a living map in natural tones of green, brown, and tan. I looked down, fascinated with the live, animated earth below, so engrossed by its realism that I forgot all about going to Judi's house.

Without intending to, I descended back into the hardware store and continued the dream for a while, and then I projected upward again, just as before. I soared through the upper atmosphere, viewed the entire U.S., and lapsed into sleep consciousness, without a thought of Judi and our plan to project together.

Although I had long before developed an understanding of and appreciation for ecosystems, I awoke with an urgent realization of the irreplaceable value of our planet as a self-contained unit, a fragile, intraconnected system of geophysical and biochemical processes absolutely vital to our physical existence, and so vulnerable to misuse due to human ignorance and carelessness.

April 23, 1990, THE MIDDLE OF THE NIGHT

Still determined to attempt a mutual OBE, I had gone to bed in my usual bedroom in the back southeast corner of the house, again concentrating on attaining dream awareness and projecting astrally to Judi's house.

I emerged from a dream, the details of which are lost to my conscious memory, and became aware in my astral form, in the spare bedroom in the front part of my house. I was floating about midway between the floor and ceiling, looking down at the rug on the floor beside the bed, and the chest of drawers in front of the double windows. I flew out the closed window, lost consciousness, and awoke in my bed.

May 1, 1990, VERY EARLY A.M.

I was asleep in bed, dreaming a dream that had been in progress for a long time. I had just entered a new scene in which I was standing next to a long wooden bar in a roughly constructed room that looked like a deserted Old West saloon. I walked around the end of the bar and peered behind it. Suddenly, from a hidden alcove, a man dressed in a cowboy outfit appeared—in one swift motion he knelt down on one knee, drew his revolver from his holster, and aimed it directly at me. My heart contracted in fear; I anticipated the deafening "bang" and a bullet ripping through my flesh. My immediate reaction was to duck out of the way. I dropped to the floor, rolled to my left, and faced him to determine if I was out of the pistol's sights. I awoke instantly, staring intently at the brazen desperado to anticipate where he would aim next.

I was in bed, alert in the hypnopompic state, lying on my left side, and the cowboy was still in front of me! Astounded, I watched him float about a foot above the left side of my bed as clearly as he had appeared in my dream, clad in his hat, western shirt and vest, chaps, and boots, aiming his six-shooter directly at my head. His image quickly shifted from an entity that appeared as solid flesh and blood to a light form composed of golden light, and then it faded until only a glowing outline remained, which broke apart, sparkled for a moment, then disappeared, leaving me amazed and alone in my dark bedroom, with my heart frantically thumping.

May 3, 1990, 6:15 a.m.

I had gone to bed concentrating on forming a lucid dream to induce an OBE. As my consciousness slipped into the hypnagogic state, I suggested to myself that I dream about swimming, recognize the dream as the induced dream when it occurred, and instead of floating only in the dream, actually float out of my body. I planned my route—through the wall at the head of my bed, through the spare bedroom, through the front of my house, and then on to Judi's house.[2] I entered deep, seemingly dreamless slumber.

[2]This approach was an idea I obtained from reading Sylvan J. Muldoon and Hereward Carrington's book, *The Projection of the Astral Body* (York Beach, ME: Samuel Weiser, 1977), pp. 158–165.

I awoke at dawn. Since plenty of time remained before I had to get up, I decided to relax and try to maintain consciousness in the hypnagogic state, hoping to induce an OBE. Soon I fell asleep.

I dreamed I was strolling along a quaint, shop-lined sidewalk in a part of Rapid City of which I had previously been totally unaware. I was amazed that the small city I grew up in could have such a significant area without my realization. The fanciful business district, located in the north part of town, consisted of rows of beautiful old brick and stone buildings with elegantly crafted wooden doors and window frames, some painted with richly colored enamel and others stained in natural tones. Many people were bustling about the sidewalks and going in and out of the various boutiques, galleries, taverns, and restaurants situated in the buildings.

I paused to study the intricate architecture of an especially attractive reddish-brown brick building with black bricks forming decorative borders around the door and window frames, which were painted a rich burgundy. I suddenly understood that I was in a dreamworld. I awakened to what I believed was ordinary physical consciousness, but it turned out to be a false awakening dream.

I dreamed that I was in the house where I grew up. I was lying in bed, trying to induce an OBE, when all of a sudden into my reverie blasted clangorous rock music, with a screaming electric lead guitar, booming base, and throbbing drums beating out a fast rhythm. Actually, it was a powerful, compelling composition, audaciously beautiful in its brilliant originality, but it disrupted my concentration. I was jolted awake, again into what I believed was physical reality, but it was actually another false awakening dream.

In the dream, I was still in the bedroom where I slept when I was a youngster, living with my parents, but it had become silent. Searching for the source of the rock and roll fantasia, I looked down and saw, on the floor, two stereo speakers with wires leading through the floor and down into the basement.

Anger shot through my brain—it was impossible to experiment with astral projection amid that racket! I suspected that my brother, Jim, had put those speakers in my room, so I got up to investigate and headed down the stairs to the basement, where his room was. Sure enough, he had an elaborate new sound system down there and had wired speakers to my room. Then my anger vanished instantly, as I appreciated his thoughtfulness and efforts.

When Jim saw me coming down the stairs, he gestured to the floor and said, "There's your duck." A live mallard hen was sitting on the floor. I had no use for the duck, so I went back upstairs. I stood at the doorway in the back of the house and gazed out at the neighborhood.

I noticed that in place of the 1950s style tract houses that characterize the south part of town where my parents built their home, there were beautiful old brick buildings, similar to the ones in the first dream of this false awakening series. I was studying a two-story yellow brick house with cream-colored trim, appreciating the quality masonry of the large, smooth rectangular bricks, when it occurred to me that this, too, was a dream. The scene of the elegant buildings shimmered away.

I began to awaken where I actually was, in my house, this time lying in bed, on my back. I held onto the hypnopompic state; the vibrations were in my head. Immediately, I tried to exit from my body through the top of my head and pass through the route I had previously planned—backwards, through the front bedroom, and out the window, where I would be on the roof of the front porch. I felt immobile, unable to free my astral body from the hold of my physical body. I tried pushing against the mattress with both arms, to no avail. Then I relaxed and just thought about my astral body floating upward, out and above the physical counterpart. It worked!

I envisioned my astral body, which was lying on its back a few inches above my physical body, and imagined it moving horizontally along the preplanned route. My consciousness split—my ephemeral self started floating headfirst through the wall at the head of my bed, while my material self lay on the bed. I was conscious in both my physical and astral bodies at the same time, experiencing dual consciousness.

With my physical eyes, which may have been closed, and looking "through" the eyelids, I saw the back of my astral body, shimmering in the darkness, about a foot above my physical body. The nebulous phantom was slowly moving away, toward the wall at the head of the bed. I studied my exteriorized form from a physical viewpoint, using what seemed like my physical eyes and brain; my astral double appeared as a pale gold, luminescent replica of my physical body, with hazy edges. Beholding my astral form was like looking at a glowing light bulb in a semitransparent fixture—the bulb can be seen, but its edges are a blur of dispersion. The bright radiance that my double emitted prevented me from determining all the details of its attire. Though I vaguely discerned a gossamer gown rippling in soft, airy waves, draped from head to ankle—it may have been only an illusion created by the ethereal glow.

From the eyes and mind of my astral self, I saw the ceiling above my bed as I floated on my back, and I sensed the momentum and slight pressure as my weightless form began to pass through the wall.

I felt as if I was equally situated in both bodies at the same time and simultaneously perceived the world from two locations.

Unconsciousness briefly intervened, and then I became intuitively aware of floating above my front yard. All I could see was a blurred, gauzy mass of white surrounding me. I thought that by this time Judi would be at her job, installing or repairing telephones on the airforce base about ten miles to the northeast, so I mentally expressed the desire to go to her.

An energy force swept me to the northeast at high velocity. When my speed decreased, I was cruising at a height of about 100 feet and the sights became clearer; I saw the shopping mall and surrounding businesses pass by beneath me and to my right. Soon, I came to a site where a small group of men and women dressed in denims, workshirts, and hardhats were clustered, installing wires in a cubical concrete enclosure, which was just large enough to contain them and allow enough space in which to work. I stopped, but Judi was not among them. They failed to acknowledge my presence, so I flew on, still aided by an astral force that was propelling me.

As I was carried along, I decided to reach around to the back of my head to determine if I could find the "silver cord" mentioned so frequently in astral projection literature. It was there! I touched a solid, hard cord that felt like a stiff garden hose when the water is running with full force. I ran my hand along the surface of the peculiar tube attached to my body, and attempted to fathom its dimensions. To my surprise, I felt a network of cords; the main cord, which was about an inch or so in diameter, protruded from the base of my brain for several inches before smaller cords branched off and attached to different locations on the back of my head, neck, and upper back.

The astral cord appeared to lack surface sensory receptors, because when my hand touched it, the only sensation I perceived was coming from my hand. Touching the cord felt like touching an inanimate object.

Reassured that the accounts of the silver cord had credence in astral reality, I decided to study my hands. When I first looked, my fingers appeared much too thin, almost as talons with narrow, pointed nails. That image lasted for only a moment before my hands changed into their natural shape, although they looked younger and plumper than my physical hands. They appeared to be composed of solid, ordinary-looking flesh with a dull, rosy, light tan color.

While I examined my hands, I noticed blue cuffs at my wrists, and I wondered what clothing my astral body was wearing. I was about to look when my consciousness became hazy.

The astral journey began to acquire the semblance of a dream, in which I was visiting at a house that I believed could be the home of a friend I see far too little of in physical reality, Lyla, who lives near the area to which I had projected. After a short period of vague interaction there, I again formed the thought of projecting to Judi, and again lost consciousness.

Next, I had the impression of being in a large, busy, foreign city, crowded with multi-storied buildings, people, and traffic. I was walking along a sidewalk in a park or city square, close to a noisy, congested street. I gazed beyond the immediate environment and noticed a huge castle built upon a hill on the horizon. A bluish mist prevailed around the ancient estate, and cast a blue tint on the massive stone walls.

A slender, good-looking man with fashionably styled, short, silver-white hair and a neatly trimmed matching beard stood nearby, smiling pleasantly and watching me. He was wearing a well-tailored gray suit and looked quite distinguished. I had no recollection of ever seeing him before, but I walked over to him and asked if this was London. He said it was.

After a brief conversation with him, I felt concerned for the safety of my physical body, because I had the impression that I had been away for a long time. I wished to return and instantly awakened, lying in bed.

I looked at my clock—6:30 A.M. I realized that Judi would not have been at work so early and that I should have attempted to project to her house. I tried to remember the conversation with the man in the gray suit, but, like castles in the clouds, it eluded me.

MAY 4 OR 5, 1990, AROUND MIDNIGHT———

I lay down in bed, although I felt energetic, and concentrated on staying awake enough to observe hypnagogic images change into sleep. I also hoped to recognize the conscious state conducive to OBEs. I had attempted such experimentation on other occasions and learned that it is extremely difficult for me, because first I usually lose control of my thoughts, and then I lose comprehension of my thoughts, and finally I egress through the hypnagogic state into oblivion.

I was lying on my left side (which is objectionable to some experts on astral projection) with Moriah curled up against my stomach and Sylvester snuggled against my back. I concentrated intensively, endeavoring to preserve awareness and monitor my mental processes, while simultaneously inhibiting waking consciousness enough to enter the hypnagogic state. After an hour or two, I was still in control, and I felt I could easily slip out of my body simply by willing it.

I partially sat up, astrally, and despite efforts to move away, remained stationary. Even though the room was dark, I could clearly see Moriah sitting against me, blocking the way. I had a close-up view of his gray striped fur. I tried to go through him, because I had passed through pets before when I was projected in astral form, but he was an effective barrier. I turned to go the other way, but Sylvester was sitting there, blocking my exit from that direction. I lay down and instantly returned to "normal" waking consciousness. Both cats were sound asleep in their places, as snug as could be.

May 27, 1990, 10:00 P.M.

After moving Sylvester and Moriah to a different room and closing my bedroom door, I lay down to explore the dimensions of the mind. I closed my eyes, took three long, slow, deep breaths, counted backwards from ten to one, and visualized my physical body reclining with my astral body hovering above it. While endeavoring to hold that vision, I paid as close attention as I could to my conscious state without falling asleep.

Several times my awareness became deeply immersed in the hypnagogic state, and several times I was distracted by a little fluttering noise in the window shade, just to my left. I did my best to ignore it, telling myself that window shades cannot make noise; it must be a breeze or something. I continued in this manner for over an hour.

The room felt too warm, so I threw off all the covers but the sheet. I changed positions several times. My concentration began slipping. Something in the shade kept fluttering—perhaps it was a large insect that might fly into my face while I slept. I had to go to the bathroom. Finally, I did get up and go to the bathroom.

When I lay back down, I again completed the breathing, counting, relaxation, and visualization procedures. I lay in bed for a long time, monitoring my consciousness, thinking about astral projection, bringing my thoughts back under control when they began to wander, and refocusing them when they became hazy. I felt fully awake.

A fairly loud bumping noise sounded from downstairs, and startled me to alertness. My heart jumped; I lay still and listened intensely. All was quiet. I decided to get up, go down, and investigate.

I left my bed and stood up. I could clearly see the bedroom cloaked in dim gray light. I took a step toward the doorway, lost my balance, and fell against a small bookcase to my right, beside my bed. The force of the impact bounced me upward, to my left, and my head went through the sloped ceiling, which runs along about two-thirds the length of my bedroom, conforming to the roofline where there is no attic. I floated back down and realized I had separated from my physical body.

For reaffirmation that I was in astral form, I poked my head back through the ceiling. I peered through the shadows and viewed the dark, rough, wooden framework of the roof. My astral vision penetrated the layers of various materials, from the inner surface of the unpainted boards to the spaces where faint light squeezed in between the shingles. The piquant smell of old wood wafted around me.

I pulled my head back into the room and stood there, deciding which route to take outside, and chose to fly out the south window. As I slowly passed through, I saw pale, diffuse light sifting through venetian blinds that covered this window and the one next to it. I realized that the blinds were an illusion, because in physical reality, only a shade covers that window. There are, however, double windows there, but only one shows from inside; the other one is covered by a closet that was built during a previous remodeling job. I wondered where the venetian blinds had come from.

After passing through the window, I floated above my back yard, where below me I glimpsed the lawn, fence, and narrow sidewalk leading to the garage. I thought about Judi and wished strongly to go to her, and then, carried by "astral energy" that seemed boundless, I accelerated in the direction of her house.

I was traveling so fast that all I could distinguish was a dark gray blur rushing by, and all I could sense was a feeling of motion. Suddenly, as if by a will power other than my own, I was slowed down, and I had the sensation of being turned to the right. I began flying fast again, in a new direction, directed and powered by a mysterious consciousness. This was puzzling, but I decided to go along with it and see what would happen.

As I flew along, I felt the soft spring air blow against my face and through my hair. A small white building loomed ahead, in my path, and I passed through the corner of it without feeling it or seeing anything inside. I clasped my hands around my wrists to see if they were solid—I was amazed at how firm my astral flesh and bones felt, as solid and real as their physical counterparts. I focused on the thought of Judi and felt my direction change again.

I flew on, enjoying the fresh astral breeze, and the sensation of swift flight, gliding through the night. Finally I arrived at a house which resembled Judi's, so I intentionally slowed down and swooped along the front, turned on my side to get a better view. The house was the same size and style as Judi's, but had a construction of darkly stained wood built onto the front, like an added on porch built around the door. That house did not look like Judi's, so I continued on to the next one, which was white, or light blue or gray. Judi's house was green, so I knew that was not it. I passed through the bare branches of a tree that was growing next to a low white fence or wooden partition along the front, knowing Judi did not have such a tree or structure.

Disappointed, I formed a mental image of Judi and flew on, speeding up again with my vision reduced to a blur. After a short distance, I abruptly slowed down; I was inside a large building that resembled a garage or repair shop with a dozen or so vehicles, perhaps fewer, parked inside. I stopped and floated above them, trying to ascertain where I was, when I heard boyish voices below, next to a van. I was drawn helplessly in that direction.

I approached the van; what I thought was one of the boys grabbed my leg and pulled me down. I felt a hand reach up and yank the front of my shirt, as if the boy was trying to wrestle me to the floor. The clenched fist tearing at my clothing drew my attention to what I was wearing, a blue sweatshirt that buttoned at the neck, unlike any I own, and blue jeans.

The first assailant moved up to get a stronger grip on my shirt, and a second one seized my legs. As I frantically tried to break loose by kicking and pushing them away, I looked down and saw an entity with a humanoid body about the size of an 8-year-old, but that is where the resemblance to humanity ended. I looked directly into the beady black eyes of a creature with a hideous face, covered with black fur and dominated by a protruding snout that curved downward like that of an elephant seal. Its black nose looked shiny and wet, and long, coarse whiskers bristled against me.

The attack startled me, but I was confident that I had more power than those astral imps. I was quite certain that if they proved to be a true threat, all I had to do was return to the physical plane where they would be unable to pursue me for long; hopefully, if they succeeded in following me across the border between worlds, they would soon disintegrate, as the pistol-packing cowboy did on a previous occasion.

Instantaneously, I returned to my physical body, sat up in bed, and immediately turned on the light. I was relieved to gaze about my quiet, peaceful bedroom and see that I was alone. It was 12:45 A.M.

JUNE 27, 1990, 7:15 A.M.

I had gone to sleep concentrating on astral projection and awakened from a dream about bears outside the windows of a classroom. I began to go back to sleep. My awareness wavered near the sleep end of the hypnagogic range when I remembered that I wanted to project, so I relaxed and easily shifted to the correct balance between waking and sleeping.

Next, I was aware of walking down my stairway, wondering if I was in physical or astral form. I stepped down to where my stairs make a ninety degree turn. Instead of a normal size step, the turn has a square area about three feet on each side. I tried to stop there to see if I could pass through the wall to verify that I was in my astral body, but instead of stopping, I glided down the rest of the stairway, becoming assured that I was, indeed, in astral form.

I stepped into the living room. At first glance, it appeared to be empty; all the furniture, rugs, pictures, and tapestries were gone. Then I gazed across the vacant expanse of the maple floor and saw, at the opposite end of the room, in front of the fireplace, one misplaced piece of furniture, an antique vanity with a tall, oval mirror, which in physical reality was in my bedroom, about five feet from the right side of my bed.

I decided against going to Judi's house, believing that she probably would have left for work, because early morning had lapsed.

I looked across the living room at the vanity while I considered possible places to explore, but before I reached a decision, I was absorbed into the physical dimension. I was lying in bed, with my eyes open, focused upon the antique vanity in my bedroom.

October 14, 1990, 7:00–7:30 a.m.

I had been awake since before dawn with a horrible stomach ache, so finally, wondering why I had waited so long, I closed my eyes and lay back to meditate on the love and healing power of the higher self in an attempt to relieve my discomfort. Soon I was in the hypnagogic state, contemplating astral projection and the prospect of floating through my bedroom wall.

I kept my physical eyes closed, but with only the slightest effort, opened my astral eyes. I could feel my physical eyelids closed against my eyeballs, but I could see through the layers of tissue and gaze at the bedroom surrounding me, with the pallid morning light creeping in around the edges of the shades.

I prolonged the hypnagogic state, feeling in perfect control of my state of consciousness and able to sustain the ideal balance between waking and sleeping.

I wanted to leave my body, so I attempted to float out and roll out, but remained connected within my organic structure. I felt too heavy and dense to defy gravity. Finally, I decided to throw back the covers and get out of bed, reasoning that since I was in the hypnagogic state, perhaps my astral body would be the vehicle leaving.

I felt exactly as I do when physically getting up and wondered if I actually was. I walked over to my south window and flew out, delighted to be in astral form after all. (I advise extreme caution to anyone who may try this; people who were actually sleepwalking have been seriously injured doing things like this. It is *always* best to try a safer test first. Although I didn't write it down, I was probably floating before I took off.)

I was a few feet above my back yard, suspended in the soft morning light, when something compelled me to fly to the southeast, although I had no conscious intention to embark in that direction. I wanted to go to Judi's house in the opposite direction, so I turned and went northwest instead. I doubted if she would be home; it was more likely that she would be having breakfast somewhere or be on her way to work. I concentrated on Judi instead of on her house, hoping I would be drawn to wherever she was.

I flew over my neighborhood and looked down at the many different colored roofs of the old houses below, red, green, white, brown, all aglow with the light of the rising sun. I was making seriously limited progress, however, as though I was flying in slow motion. Suddenly, in front of me was a brick post, or a chimney, and I decided to fly through it, confident that there would be no impact, and passed through without a trace of resistance. I examined my hands; they appeared to be flesh and blood, identical to my physical hands, but too far away, as if my arms extended beyond their natural length. I looked down at my astral form to see what I was wearing and thought I could discern a sweatshirt. I concentrated harder to see the color, but it was too blurry.

I was languidly sailing across my neighborhood, only slightly higher than the rooftops, curiously inspecting the street level. I saw a man walk out of an indistinguishable building; it may have been a house, garage, or business. He appeared to be in his early forties, wore glasses, had a neatly trimmed beard, and hair that was a mixture of brown and gray, attractively styled so that it could be combed forward and to one side. To my recollection, I had never seen him before, astrally or physically. He smiled up at me and said something I was unable to hear clearly, as he motioned for me to come down to where he was. I flew on, however, intent on finding Judi.

Next, I found myself in a baking company two blocks from my house. Judi had been employed there many years ago, so I wondered if I had somehow ventured into the past. A young woman with short dark hair and wearing a red business suit hurried down a flight of stairs and entered the room I was in. I asked her if she knew Judi, who used to work there. Thoughtfully, the woman in red said she knew of someone by the same name who had worked there in the early eighties, but I reasoned that it must have been somebody else, because Judi had worked there before the eighties.

I attained awareness back in my body; a dog was barking outside, disturbing my concentration. I tried to ignore it by focusing on the morning glow around the window shade, wondering if I was perceiving astral or physical light, as the hypnopompic state broke and I became fully awake on the physical plane.

April 13, 1991, THE MIDDLE OF THE NIGHT

I had lain in bed for over an hour, concentrating on developing the ability, during sleep, to distinguish my dreams from physical reality, so I could change an ordinary dream into a lucid dream and enter the state of consciousness conducive to astral projection. I planned to leave my body, float straight up through the roof, and from there, see if I could contact a spirit guide.

I fell asleep and dreamed I was sleeping in my bed, but it was where my kitchen belonged, with the dream version of the room having been converted to a T.V. and reading room that opened onto the porch room at the back of the house. In the dream the porch room went all the way across the back of the house, but in physical reality, it is only eight feet wide.

I had a false awakening, dreaming that I got up from the bed where the kitchen was supposed to be, and walked into the porch room. Then I realized I was in astral form and flew through the east side of the house. I floated between my house and the house next door for a moment or two, but then I reentered my physical body, upstairs in my actual bedroom.

Immediately, I floated back out of my body, through the east wall, and hovered between the houses again. I clearly ascertained the white siding on my neighbors' house, the little wooden fence bordering the flower bed, and the corner of their front porch. Without willing it, I returned to my physical body.

I tried to exit again by willing my astral body to float straight up, through the ceiling, and onto the roof as planned, but I felt heavy and restrained by physical matter. Finally, using the simple strategy that had been successful for initiating previous OBEs, I threw the covers back and got out of bed, bumping the small bookcase beside my bed as I stood up.

I walked to the stairway and jogged down the stairs, with my feet bouncing lightly off each step. When I reached the last couple of stairs, I looked to my left and noticed dim light from outside shining in through the hexagonal panes of the window at the foot of the stairway. I clearly saw the details of the fluting along the edges of the narrow, rust colored strips of wood separating the geometric shapes of the glass panes.

I passed by the window, wondering if the living room furnishings were in place, and paused at the front door, where I was about to reach for the doorknob. The tapestry was on the wall behind the roll-top desk beside me, where it belonged, and the lace curtain was on the window of the door, as it should have been, so I decided against inspecting the rest of the room, believing it would be more interesting to explore somewhere else. (Physically, it is possible to see the whole living room from the stairway, but during this OBE, I could only see for a couple of feet. Everything else was cloudy.)

I still had to choose a destination. I decided to float through the door instead of opening it, and as my mind formed the thought, my astral body fused with the door. The world became a silver-gray blur, and I awoke physically, in my bed.

JUNE 2, 1991, VERY EARLY A.M.

I had lain awake for a long time, trying to go to sleep, when I started thinking about staying aware in the hypnagogic state and inducing an OBE. I relaxed, and after a while wondered if I was in the hypnagogic state. I tried to float out of my body, but was held in my material form. I considered just getting out of bed, hoping I would astrally get out of bed, although I felt I was too close to physical waking consciousness for that to succeed. Then I tried to go deeper into the hypnagogic state, but dozed off.

From sleep, I entered the hypnopompic state, and within a second or two slipped out of my physical body without conscious effort. I gently alighted on my hands and knees on the floor next to my bed. With the intention of standing up, I pushed against the floor with my hands, but they went through the rug and wood, followed by the rest of my astral body.

I emerged in the dining room, directly below my bedroom, and landed standing up. I observed the familiar rectangles of light on the walls from the streetlights shining in through the windows. I walked out of the dining room, through the living room, to the front door. I clearly saw the outdoor illumination defining the oval window in the door, its shape broken up by the intricate pattern of the lace curtain covering it.

I reached for the doorknob and was yanked directly back, through walls, ceiling, floor and furniture, to my physical body.

AUGUST 1, 1991, IN THE MIDDLE OF THE NIGHT

I "awoke" flying through a peaceful summer night. I was cruising at a speed of about thirty or forty miles per hour and an altitude of about one hundred feet, over a landscape I could vividly discern through the darkness. The soft, warm sky was charcoal gray, nearly black, and the lush, rolling grassland passing beneath me was a rich, deep, vibrant green. The grass was long, undulating in soft, wavy lines, with the blades curved in many different directions by the wind currents that swept the low hills.

I felt energized, free, and in complete control, until my mind registered the thought that I was out of my body. Then the exterior force pulled me backward so fast that I could only see a dark gray blur and experience the sensation of tremendous speed. I intuitively sensed that I was going back to my body. Soon I felt the realignment of my astral and physical bodies and awakened in bed, in physical reality.

SEPTEMBER 23, 1991, MORNING

The night before, I went to sleep concentrating on strengthening communication between my conscious mind and my higher self, with the resolution to remain receptive and pay attention to any messages that might emanate from my dreams.

I awakened to the clamor of a barking dog (one that lives nearby in physical reality and it actually was barking.) My dream memories swiftly vanished, but I kept my eyes closed and relaxed my mind and body. I was lying on my back. I drifted back into the hypnopompic (hypnagogic?) state and tried to concentrate on astral projection.

My astral double, at that time the location of my consciousness, ever so slowly and gently sat up, virtually operating by its own volition, because I expended little conscious effort to leave my body. I relaxed, allowed events to pursue their own course, and observed what would happen. As my double sat up, I felt steady, smooth vibrations resonating throughout my body. (I can imagine that this is how a cat must feel when it is purring loudly.) The barking dog distracted my attention, and I snapped back into my physical body.

I remained in the hypnopompic state with my eyes closed and my body still. My astral body sat up again, so I mentally expressed the wish to float above my bed. I started spinning around and around in my astral body, whirling faster and faster, until my concentration was broken again by the yapping dog, and I landed back in my physical body.

I held still, kept my eyes closed, and easily maintained the hypnopompic state. Astrally, I sat up again and thought about floating through the wall at the head of my bed, and then exiting out the front of my house.

Maintaining the sitting posture, I slowly moved backwards two or three feet, and sensed my astral vision beginning to function. My surroundings were dark, except for a small red light that appeared to be about half a centimeter in diameter. As I focused on the light, I lost control of my consciousness and entered a dream about a barking dog and its master, who lived next to an alley near my back yard. The dog's master was leading a huge lion into his house. There was much more to the dream, from which I finally awoke completely, to the sound of the barking dog.

I store a self-charging flashlight in the closet on the other side of the wall at the head of my bed. When it is charging, a red light comes on, the same size as the one I saw astrally.

OCTOBER 15, 1992, 8:00 A.M.

After waking at dawn, I had fallen back to sleep. As my awareness again emerged from slumber to the hypnopompic state, I felt warm, relaxed, and content, and remained at the balance point between sleep and wakefulness, fully conscious. I decided to leave my body.

I tried to impel my astral body to sit up, but I had the sensation of occupying only my physical body, lying in bed. I envisioned being in my astral body, floating up out of the physical, but remained in my dense form, subject to gravity. I recalled one of my early experiences with exteriorization, when I was living in my cabin—the time I moved my astral arm out of my physical arm. I decided to try that, and if it worked, to transfer the rest of my astral body out following my arm.

I immediately felt vibrations concentrated in my right shoulder. I slipped my left astral arm out of its physical confinement. The rest of my astral body flowed out after my arm, and I flew out the window on the left side of my bed.

I floated northeast and paused about fifteen feet above my next door neighbors' front yard. Their older, beautifully restored two story light green house was perfectly clear, surrounded by neatly fenced flower beds along the front and lining the walkways. The soft pinks, purples, golds, and greens of the carefully tended autumn foliage arranged artistically around the pastel green house gave a distinct impressionistic mood to the scene.

A strong astral force carried me southeastward; I decided to allow it to take me wherever it would. After a rapid, blurred transition to a different location, I was placed standing next to a chain-link fence, where a group of a dozen or so people were watching a prairie fire. (As I had known before going to bed, a prairie fire actually was burning southeast of town at this time.) Thick, dark smoke permeated the lower atmosphere, and a red fire engine was parked nearby, on the other side of the fence, amid a conglomeration of equipment and vehicles.

The astral force pulled me away from the scene, farther southward. I slowly floated through the inside of a large building full of machinery that seemed to be the workings of some type of production plant or operation. Metal catwalks, railings, pipes, and the metal casings covering gears and motors were painted bright enamel colors, some blue, some yellow, some red. A man in work clothes was on one of the platforms, surrounded by equipment. He politely told me Joe was up front in the operator's cage. I continued forward, wondering who Joe was. When I floated through an area that may have been the front part of the building, I saw a man on an upper level in a small room with metal mesh walls painted yellow. Although I did not recognize him, I waved and said, "Hi, Joe." He smiled and waved back as I passed through the front wall of the building.

I was outside the building, hovering above a graveled area which resembled a loading zone or a parking lot. I decided I wanted to do something more veridical, such as going to Ben's office at Black Hills State University in Spearfish, about fifty miles away, to see if he was there. I reasoned that if he was, it would be interesting to determine if he could perceive my presence, and if he was out, perhaps I could observe something in his office and confirm it later, in physical reality.

I was about to head northwest to Spearfish, when an overpowering current pulled me away. With no conscious control, I felt as though I was moving at an extremely high rate of speed and could hear the faint barking of a dog, becoming louder and louder. I opened my physical eyes and looked at the clock. It was 9:00. A dog was barking across the alley from my back yard.

* * * * * * *

As the events of my physical life develop, progress, and transform, my astral odyssey continues to take me to invisible worlds, where the unexplained and unexpected are always waiting. These strange adventures in mysterious realms have radically altered my perception of reality and raised countless questions to which, over the years, I have devoted much thought and research. By exploring OBEs, we can more fully understand and appreciate all the parts of our total being, with which we are only beginning to become familiar. The merging worlds of physical and astral reality provide clues to the true nature of existence.

Chapter 10

Merging Worlds

Late one clear and moonless night, on a rugged high plateau somewhere north of the Black Hills of South Dakota, far from civilization's lights, I paused beside a stream where it formed a deep, quiet pool of water. I looked up. In the black sky above shined a vast, brilliant multitude of stars, radiant in the distinct three-dimensional effect seen only at high altitudes in isolated areas. Some near, some far, all were majestically suspended in the deep darkness. I gazed outward, into positive infinity.

I looked down into the pool. The very same vastness penetrated the black water below. The stars glittered in the dark watery depths, down, down, down as far as I could imagine. I saw a universe within a world, an outer world merging with an inner world. I felt I was looking into reverse, or negative infinity.

Does our physical, emotional, mental, and spiritual structure exist in a similar arrangement? Is a human being a macrocosm reflected in a microcosm, as suggested by philosophies passed on and recorded since antiquity? Are the invisible worlds a reflection of external reality within our consciousness? Or are the invisible worlds external reflections of our consciousness? Perhaps, with ESP, we can project our consciousness both externally into objective reality, and internally into subjective reality, wherein external reality is reflected. If so, toward which infinity, positive or negative, does our consciousness project during OBEs? External? Internal? Both?

If hypnagogic imagery is successfully monitored with waking consciousness, it is observed that the visions become more complex until they precipitate a dreamlike world of objects, scenes, and events. At one moment the image is contained in the mind within the self, and an instant later the mind and the self are inside the image. Consciousness may briefly vacillate between the physical world and the hypnagogic dream before it becomes one with what appears to be a mentally constructed world.

Sometimes when consciousness suddenly bursts out of a dream, into waking reality, a persistent dream image may linger, superimposed upon the physical environment. The vision appears actually to change from an internal locus to an external locus before it vanishes. We believe that dreams take place internally, but at certain times we see dream images as we see external objects.

When mental projection is experienced, does an internal image of the external object form within the mind, or does a part of the mind actually relocate in the external object?

During transition state ESP, initially consciousness appears to focus on an internal image, which it can then briefly enter into, and then experience the sensation of focusing on an external environment. Suppose material perceived during transition state ESP is later verified by corresponding external events in physical reality. Did a reflection of the external event appear in consciousness, or did consciousness appear at the location of the external event?

In cases of dual consciousness, the mind appears to be in two places at once, an internal location and an external location. Is the external consciousness perceiving an internal or external reality? What about the internal one? Is it perceiving an internally generated image of a projected astral body?

Has anyone proven that consciousness exists in the cranium? Perhaps the cranium exists in consciousness. It could be that consciousness becomes a part of its own creation, entering the worlds manifested by its power, and then becoming convinced of their separate reality. If so, we can conceive of consciousness existing both inside and outside material reality, and material reality existing both inside and outside consciousness. We can imagine a similar situation for nonmaterial reality.

Then reality would consist of the merging of internal and external, material and nonmaterial worlds.

Where does personal reality end and consensus reality begin? Where does reality become illusion?

Opposing Opinions

Is the astral world inside or outside the boundary each of us imagines enclosing the self? Nobody knows. Different researchers have opposing opinions concerning the "reality" of the OBE world. Some offer psychological theories, believing the OBE environment exists in the imagination as internal subjective reality, and others offer ecsomatic theories, believing a nonphysical substance literally separates from the physical body and forms a part of external objective reality.[1] Neither type of theory sufficiently accounts for all OBE phenomena.

Attempts can be made to classify all cognitive phenomena as either external objective or internal subjective, whether it is of the physical world and physical body, thoughts, hypnagogic and hypnopompic visions or sensations, dreams, ESP, or OBEs. However, some types of phenomena require additional catagories. For example, persistent dream images appear to be in external reality, so they could be classified as subjective external. Clairvoyant images or transition state ESP visions, such as the cargo plane crash, could be classified as internal objective. When we consider dual consciousness, in which a projector views the astral form from a physical vantage point, we have a dilemma, either a subjective or objective vision of the subject which could be either external or internal. An even more enigmatic dilemma results when a projector views the physical body from an astral point of view. Here classification requires knowledge of whether an astral form actually leaves the physical body.

---

[1] H. J. Irwin, *Flight of Mind: A Psychological Study of the Out-of-Body Experience* (Metuchen, NJ: Scarecrow Press, 1985), pp. 219–259.

If the astral world exists internally, it may be a state of consciousness sensitive to ESP, with the additional feature of vivid mental imagery of occupying a second body in a world-like vision. OBEs would comprise an alternative state of consciousness, ESP, and an imaginary dimension similar to dream worlds, containing some distortions, but generally more accurately patterned after physical reality. The sensation of being awake combined with the convincing realism of the imagery causes the projector to accept the experience as external objective reality. If the subconscious contains memories of everything in exact detail and has the ability to construct dream worlds as convincing, at the time they are presented, as physical reality, it is plausible that the OBE world exists only in the mind as an elaborate vision. This vision is then coupled with the psychological faculties of waking consciousness. The astral plane may be a convincing hallucination created by the subconscious in which powers of ESP present veridical images of the past, present, and future physical world. If so, OBEs would consist of a combination of three factors: a fairly realistic mental construction, waking consciousness, and psychic abilities.

Susan Blackmore, who has written extensively about OBEs, contends that they are internal and that the mental constructions are based upon memory.[2] According to Blackmore, the distortions, omissions, and additions to the astral world reported by so many projectors result from faulty memory, with gaps filled by imagination.

From my experience, I believe that during my OBEs, when aberrations appear in the astral world, my memory is working about as well as in physical waking. When I saw the framed print of the old woman on my fireplace mantel, I knew, from memory, that it was not there physically. When I glided down my stairway and saw that all my living room furniture was miss-

---

[2]Sue Blackmore, "A Theory of Lucid Dreams and OBEs," in *Conscious Mind, Sleeping Brain: Perspectives on Lucid Dreaming*, eds. Jayne Gackenbach and Stephen LaBerge (New York: Plenum Press, 1988), pp. 373–382.

ing, I remembered exactly where each piece should have been. When I saw venetian blinds on my bedroom window, I knew they were fake and a shade actually covered the glass. If the astral world is actually constructed from memory, the mistakes are due to something other than memory lapses.

Alternatively, the astral plane could exist as a part of external, objective reality that can only be perceived from specific states of consciousness. It could be as esoteric doctrine presumes, an invisible world interspersed with physical matter. If this is the situation, something—either a purely mental aspect or a spiritual constituent made of "astral matter"—must actually leave the physical body and function in the astral world.

There are a few reported cases of mutual projections, in which more than one person shared an OBE with correlating times, places, and events.[3] Mutual projections could imply an external, objective astral world, but they could also be the product of some form of telepathy in which two or more people participate in the same mental construction. But then, esoteric teachings claim that the astral world is created from thought forms anyway.

There are also reports of physically awake witnesses perceiving the astral forms of projectors.[4] Such OBEs indicate that it is plausible that something does leave the body and function in the external, objective world. Reports provide differing types of evidence, with some apparitions appearing solid and life-like and others translucent and ghost-like. Perhaps anyone using physical vision can see the apparition, but it may be that clairvoyant vision is necessary. Whether the astral double of a projector is seen by any type of vision at all may depend upon the density of the projected form.

---

[3]Some cases are related in the following books: Oliver Fox, *Astral Projection: A Record of Out-of-the-Body Experiences*; Yram, *Practical Astral Projection*; and D. Scott Rogo, *Mind Beyond the Body*.

[4]Herbert B. Greenhouse, *The Astral Journey* (Garden City, NY: Doubleday, 1975), pp. 88–95.

Similar evidence that something actually leaves the physical body and exists in external objective reality is provided by numerous cases of deathbed experiences, when individuals in physical waking consciousness witness the astral form exit the corpse and depart in ghostly fashion.

If the astral world actually does exist externally, it could consist of an astral replica of everything in the physical world and extend to other dimensions. If this is the case, when an individual is projected in astral form, perhaps it is the astral counterparts of physical objects that are being perceived. One problem with this is that often projectors report viewing their physical bodies, indicating the possibilty that the projector is viewing the actual physical world from an astral point of view. It is also common to see the personal astral form while projected, just as when, in physical reality, we look down at ourselves and see parts of the physical form. Maybe the worlds do overlap.

Whether OBEs are external objective phenomena or internal subjective phenomena, veridical cases provide strong evidence that they consist of some type of paranormal activity. On a Christmas Eve in the late 1960s, my friend, Judi, had an OBE and observed events hundreds of miles away which she later verified.

Judi's other friend Carol has a sister who lived in Chicago at that time. Judi had met this sister only once, but for some reason astrally visited her in Chicago on Christmas Eve.

That night, at her home in Rapid City, Judi fell asleep without any conscious thought of Chicago, astral projection, or Carol's sister. She awakened, however, to find herself floating near the ceiling of a strange apartment. She had no memory of how she had gotten there, and, because she was so surprised, she did not think to look at her astral body and see how it appeared.

Instead, she peered down through a thin, cloudy mist and saw two people sitting on the floor, surrounded by tools, trying to put large boxes together. Although she could not see them clearly, Judi recognized Carol's sister and she assumed that the man was her husband. The next thing Judi knew, she was sitting up in her own bed, wondering why anybody would be putting cardboard boxes together. Again, she had no sensation of having traveled from Chicago to Rapid City when she returned to her physical body. She looked at the clock—the time was 2:30 A.M.

The next day Judi related the experience to Carol, who telephoned her sister and asked how she and her husband had spent Christmas Eve. Her sister replied that they had stayed up most of the night trying to put together a bookcase and entertainment center they had bought themselves for Christmas. After much aggravation, they had finally finished their project and had gotten to bed shortly before dawn.

Some believe OBEs are internal phenomena, and others believe they are external phenomena. Another possibility is that both ideas are correct, with an objective universe reflected in a subjective world, and subjective thought constructions projected into objective reality. Perhaps the OBE world and physical world merge inwardly and outwardly, each a separate reality perceived by a mind with specialized states of consciousness for each.

Are the invisible worlds truly separate realms? When we see the "astral world," are we actually looking at the physical world? Or are the invisible worlds all imaginary? We have much to learn about the invisible worlds, such as whether they are external, internal, or both. Much research remains to be done if we are to know whether OBEs are nothing but hallucinations, if they are ESP intermingled with vivid mental images, or if something actually leaves the physical body. If nonmaterial essence actually does leave the body, we have the problem of detecting and measuring a nonphysical phenomenon with physical instruments.

To understand the invisible worlds, we must determine and define the mental states that create them or observe them, and the thoughts or the material and energy which compose them, how many there are, where one ends and another begins, and more reliable methods to visit them. We also have much to learn about ourselves, our states of consciousness, and the nature and abilities of our nonmaterial bodies and how they influence our mental capabilities and physical bodies. Finally, through discovery of fundamental principles, natural laws, and relationships of cause and effect, we must learn how the invisible worlds and our functioning in them affect our physical world and the role we play in it.

Benefits of OBEs

The most obvious direct benefit of OBEs is the ability to operate in new dimensions, transcending the limitations of the physical world and attaining the prospect of freedom only imagined previously. The astral plane provides opportunities to journey to ordinary and extraordinary places, at many rates of speed, whether it is gliding across the room, visiting another country, or instantaneously projecting to a higher realm.

In any astral location, near or far, the possibility of encountering strange entities always exists. Many case studies suggest that we can meet with them and converse with them, lend assistance to those in need, exchange information with physical or nonphysical friends and loved ones, or obtain wisdom and guidance from those more advanced than we are. We can learn about astral entities of all forms, whether good or evil, simple or highly evolved.

Besides these direct benefits, the experience of astral projection has profound effects on ourselves, including our concept of reality, outlook on life, and feelings concerning death. Consciously leaving the body increases our understanding of ourselves, the universe, and our relationship with the universe, but it also raises countless questions and disrupts forever previously held beliefs, either by turning them into knowledge with evidence in their favor or obliterating them with evidence against them. All of these effects cause permanent changes in one's personal philosophy of life.

During my lifetime, nothing has been more revealing of the true nature of reality than the several minutes when I first voluntarily experienced consciousness outside my body. Those brief moments changed forever a lifetime search for answers about what and where we are. I no longer simply ponder the plausibility of various doctrines, because I know, rather than believe, there is more to life than physical waking reality. As with the attainment of any knowledge, however, this new enlightenment presents more questions than answers.

Whether the invisible worlds exist outwardly as dimensions of external reality, or inwardly within vailed layers of consciousness, or both, their exploration provides an expanded perception of the universe. Awareness of extended horizons that reach past mundane daily existence fulfills an ever present longing for a sense of significance in life. The attitude that life truly is significant enriches all endeavors, whether they are material, emotional, intellectual, or spiritual.

By pushing the limits of human experience outward, the exploration of dreams, the hypnagogic and hypnopompic states, and the astral world gives us opportunities to discover new means to acquire knowledge and attain a greater understanding of higher mental processes. Insights attained through personal contact with the invisible worlds broaden our understanding of the nature of reality and our capabilities as human beings, resulting in increased optimism as we face our daily concerns.

The increased development of psychic abilities, which naturally occurs during journeys through invisible worlds, gives us additional tools to use in coping with physical existence. Dream studies, inspiration, mental projection, transition state ESP, and OBEs demonstrate more of our true mental potential than realized from exclusive physical awareness. An awareness of these capabilities automatically reenforces their use, which increases their effectiveness, which in turn stimulates more awareness. The ever increasing span of awareness on the interrelated consciousness continuums brings us into contact with our higher selves and reveals our true nature as cosmic beings capable of infinite knowledge and self-awareness. Feelings of self-worth, personal potential, growth, and creativity are enhanced. Personal existence, which includes being, perceiving, experiencing, and knowing, takes on universal dimensions, giving life more meaning than ever before imagined.

Existence outside the body indicates that we are more than just a biological organism with emotions and an intellect; it demonstrates that we also have a nonmaterial part, or spiritual aspect. By experiencing astral projection, we know the spiritual part can function separately from the body either in an external reality, in an internal reality, or in a merged reality. Although we can only speculate whether the spiritual constituent survives physical death, it is encouraging to at least know we have one, because a nonmaterial aspect is a necessary condition for life after death. Knowledge of its existence is an important step in the proof of survival after physical death.

Near-death experiences (NDEs), which are so similar to OBEs, provide strong evidence that an astral form does survive physical death. Whether or not this astral form is indicative of a spiritual form that survives long after the death of the physical body, it does give good reason for hope.

According to esoteric teachings, the astral form only has a temporary postmortem existence; then it disintegrates while an even finer body consisting of the mental and causal bodies goes on to a higher plane. Ater experiencing life out of the physical body, this possibility seems entirely feasible.

As shown by several studies,[5] most persons who have undergone either an NDE or an OBE have virtually overcome their fear of death, making life more pleasant by eliminating or reducing one major worry. The feeling of invulnerability enhances the sense of significance acquired by a new concept of the universe and the optimism resulting from the insights attained through expanded awareness. The evidence of continued existence makes what we do now seem more important!

I believe that we are immortal and that our lives in the invisible worlds are far richer than we realize from the veiwpoint of physical, waking consciousness. I believe that the nonphysi-

---

[5]Irwin, *Flight of Mind*, p. 216.

cal part of us is experiencing life in the invisible worlds long before physical death, and long before physical life. I do know, however, that there definitely is more to our nature and the nature of the universe than life in a physical body on a physical plane. I expect that anyone else who has experienced a conscious OBE knows this, too.

The hypnagogic and hypnopompic states appear to be states of consciousness in which the invisible worlds collide, creating windows and doorways from one to another. By developing continuity of consciousness from waking life, through transition states, into the dream continuum, superconsciousness, and the OBE continuum, it is possible to subjectively explore these alternative realities.

As the invisible worlds become more familiar, it appears as though each one fits in its particular "space" as a type of awareness. This sense of space supports the esoteric theory of different planes of reality coexisting and interpenetrating each other. These alternative realities could represent different systems made up of different types of energy and matter, with each one becoming a finer, more diffuse, and more intensely energized form of creation than the one "below" it.

Entering the invisible worlds, then, appears to be a matter of focusing consciousness upon the correct pathway in the hypnagogic or hypnopompic state, and energizing the correct inner body, astral, mental, or causal, to act as a vehicle for cognition.

The challenges facing future astral travelers include mastering techniques of entering and functioning in the invisible worlds, determining the properties of the astral body and the astral world, incorporating their discoveries and understanding into the complex processes of human behavior, and using interdimensional experiences to improve physical life. Hopefully, the knowledge attained through exploring invisible worlds will reduce the polarities of life and death, knowledge and ignorance, potential and actualization. As with any academic discipline, study of the invisible worlds involves development of theoretical formulations, reliable techniques, and practical applications.

Through experiencing the invisible worlds, we can glimpse hidden dimensions of reality and explore vast uncharted regions of existence. By joining our conscious selves with our higher selves, we can overcome many of the limitations of the physical world. Embarking on an astral odyssey exploring invisible dimensions may lead us to master true knowledge, joy, and freedom.

* * * * * * *

On that dark night north of the Black Hills, as I paused by the quiet pool, if my astral double could have traveled to a planet revolving around a distant star, and stopped to gaze with infinite telescopic vision into the dark starry depths of a pool on that world, would she have seen a reflection of herself on earth, gazing into an illusion?

The human mind, reflecting upon starry heights and starry depths, is compelled to contemplate the infinite external worlds surrounding it, the intelligence behind their orderly progression, and the nature of its role in them. In questioning its own nature, the human mind is led on an inward search, into inner worlds just as infinite and mysterious.

It could be that positive and negative infinity converge at a point we refer to as self, like the surface of a pool full of stars.

BIBLIOGRAPHY

Arms, Karen, and Pamela S. Camp. *Biology: A Journey into Life.* Philadelphia: Saunders College Publishing, 1991.

Baker, Douglas M. *Practical Techniques of Astral Projection.* Wellingborough, England: Aquarian Press and York Beach, ME: Samuel Weiser, 1977.

Battersby, H. F. Prevost. *Man Outside Himself: The Methods of Astral Projection.* New Hyde Park, NY: University Books, 1969.

Bishay, N. "Therapeutic Manipulation of Nightmares and the Management of Neuroses." *British Journal of Psychiatry* 147 (1985): 67–70.

Blackmore, Susan J. *Beyond the Body: An Investigation of Out-of-the-Body Experiences.* London: Heinemann, 1982.

———. "A Theory of Lucid Dreams and OBEs." In *Conscious Mind, Sleeping Brain: Perspectives on Lucid Dreaming.* Eds. Jayne Gackenbach and Stephen LaBerge. New York: Plenum Press, 1988.

Bord, Janet. *Astral Projection: Understanding Your Psychic Double.* New York: Samuel Weiser, 1973.

Brennan, J. H. *Astral Doorways.* London: Aquarian Press, 1971.

Budzynski, Thomas. "Tuning in on the Twilight Zone." *Psychology Today*, August 1977.

Cartwright, Rosalind Dymond. *Night Life: Explorations in Dreaming.* Upper Saddle River, NJ: Prentice Hall, 1977.

———. "Affect and Dream Work from an Information Processing Point of View." In *Cognition and Dream Research.* Ed. Robert E. Haskell. *The Journal of Mind and Behavior*, Special Issue, Vol. 7, Nos. 2 and 3, 1986.

Cartwright, Rosalind D., Stephen Lloyd, Sara Knight, and Irene Trenholme. "Broken Dreams: A Study of the Effects of Divorce and Depression on Dream Content." *Psychiatry*, Aug. 1984, pp. 251–9.

Cohen, David B., and Charles Cox. "Neuroticism in the Sleep Laboratory: Implications for Representational and Adaptive Properties of Dreaming." *Journal of Abnormal Psychology* 84 (1975): 91–108.

Crookall, Robert. *Out-of-the-Body Experiences: A Fourth Analysis*. Secaucus, NJ: Citadel Press, 1970.

———. *More Astral Projections*. Secaucus, NJ: University Books, 1972.

Dane, Leila. "Astral Travel: A Psychological Overview." *Journal of Altered States of Consciousness* 2(3) (1975–6): 249–58.

Delaney, Gayle. *Living Your Dreams*. New York: HarperCollins, 1981.

DeLong, George. *Awakening to Your Dreams*. Castro Valley, CA: New World Press, 1991.

Dement, William C. *Some Must Watch While Some Must Sleep*. San Francisco: San Francisco Book Company, 1976.

Denning, Melita, and Osborne Phillips. *The Llewellyn Practical Guide to Astral Projection*. St. Paul, MN: Llewellyn Publications, 1979.

Eadie, Betty J. and Curtis Taylor. *Embraced by the Light*. Placerville, CA: Gold Leaf Press, 1992.

Faraday, Ann. *The Dream Game*. New York: Perennial Library, 1974.

Fiss, Harry. "An Empirical Foundation for a Self Psychology of Dreaming." In *Cognition and Dream Research*. Ed. Robert E. Haskell. *The Journal of Mind and Behavior*, Special Issue, Vol. 7, Nos. 2 and 3, 1986.

Fosshage, James L. "The Psychological Function of Dreams: A revised Psychoanalytic Perspective." *Psychoanlysis and Contemporary Thought* 6 (1983): 641–69.

Fox, Oliver. *Astral Projection: A Record of Out-of-the-Body Experiences*. Secaucus, NJ: Citadel Press, 1976.

Gabbard, Glen O., and Stuart W. Twemlow. *With the Eyes of the Mind: An Empirical Analysis of Out-of-Body States*. New York: Praeger Scientific, 1984.

Gackenbach, Jayne, and Jane Bosveld. *Control Your Dreams*. New York: HarperCollins, 1989.

Gackenbach, Jayne, and Stephen LaBerge, eds. *Conscious Mind, Sleeping Brain: Perspectives on Lucid Dreaming*. New York: Plenum Press, 1988.

Garfield, Patricia. *Creative Dreaming*. New York: Simon & Schuster, 1974.

Garrett, Eileen. *My Life as a Search for the Meaning of Mediumship*. London: Rider, 1937.

Giesler, Patric V. "Lucid OBEs: A Case Report." *Parapsychology Review*, Sept./Oct. 1986, pp. 5–7.

Gillespie, George. "Without a Guru." In *Conscious Mind, Sleeping Brain: Perspectives on Lucid Dreaming.* Eds. Jayne Gackenbach and Stephen LaBerge. New York: Plenum Press, 1988.

Green, Celia. *Out of the Body Experiences.* London: Hamish Hamilton, 1968.

Greenhouse, Herbert B. *The Astral Journey.* Garden City, NY: Doubleday, 1975.

Harary, Keith, and Pamela Weintraub. *Have an Out-of-Body Experience in 30 Days: The Free Flight Program.* New York: St. Martin's Press, 1989.

———. *Lucid Dreams in 30 Days: The Creative Sleep Program.* New York: St. Martin's Press, 1989.

Hearne, Keith M. T. "An Automated Technique for Studying PSI in Home 'Lucid' Dreams." *Journal of the Society for Psychical Research* 51 (1982): 303–4.

Hobson, J. Allan. *The Dreaming Brain.* New York: Basic Books, 1988.

Holzer, Hans. *The Psychic Side of Dreams.* St. Paul, MN: Llewellyn Publications, 1992.

Irwin, H. J. "The Psychological Function of Out-of-Body Experiences: So Who Needs the Out-of-Body Experience?" *The Journal of Nervous and Mental Disease* 169 (1981): 244–8.

———. *Flight of Mind: A Psychological Study of the Out-of-Body Experience.* Metuchen, NJ: Scarecrow Press, 1985.

———. "Out-of-the-Body Experiences and Dream Lucidity: Empirical Perspectives." In *Conscious Mind, Sleeping Brain: Perspectives on Lucid Dreaming.* Eds. Jayne Gackenbach and Stephen LaBerge. New York: Plenum Press, 1988.

Kaplan-Williams, Strephon. *The Jungian-Senoi Dreamwork Manual.* Berkeley, CA: Journey Press, 1987.

Krakow, Barry, and Joseph Neidhardt. *Conquering Bad Dreams and Nightmares.* New York: Berkley Books, 1992.

LaBerge, Stephen. *Lucid Dreaming: The Power of Being Awake and Aware in Your Dreams.* New York: Ballantine Books, 1985.

LaBerge, Stephen and Howard Rheingold. *Exploring the World of Lucid Dreaming.* New York: Ballantine Books, 1990.

Langs, Robert. *Decoding Your Dreams.* New York: Henry Holt, 1988.

Leadbeater, C. W. *The Devachanic Plane.* London: Theosophical Publishing Society, 1896.

———. *The Astral Plane.* Wheaton, IL: The Theosophical Publishing House, 1977.

Leveton, Alan F. "The Night Residue." *International Journal of Psycho-Analysis* 42 (1961): 506–16.

Levi, Eliphas. *The History of Magic*. York Beach, ME: Samuel Weiser, 1970.

Levine, Joseph S., and Kenneth R. Miller. *Biology: Discovering Life*. Lexington, MA: D. C. Heath, 1991.

Liddon, Sim C. "Sleep Paralysis and Hypnagogic Hallucinations." *Archives of General Psychiatry* 17 (1967): 88–96.

Mavromatis, Andreas. *Hypnagogia: The Unique State of Consciousness Between Wakefulness and Sleep*. London: Routledge & Kegan Paul, 1987.

Maybruck, Patricia. *Romantic Dreams*. New York: Pocket Books, 1991.

Mitchell, Janet Lee. *Out-of-Body Experiences: A Handbook*. New York: Ballantine Books, 1990.

Monroe, Robert A. *Far Journeys*. New York: Doubleday, 1985.

———. *Journeys Out of the Body*. 2nd ed. New York: Anchor Press/Doubleday, 1973.

Moss, Scott C. "Treatment of a Recurrent Nightmare by Hypnosymbolism." *The American Journal of Clinical Hypnosis* 16 (1973): 23–30.

Muldoon, Sylvan, and Hereward Carrington. *The Phenomena of Astral Projection*. London: Rider, 1951; York Beach, ME: Samuel Weiser, 1970.

———. *The Projection of the Astral Body*. York Beach, ME: Samuel Weiser, 1977.

Ophiel. *The Art and Practice of Astral Projection*. York Beach, ME: Samuel Weiser, 1977.

Powell, Arthur E. *The Etheric Double*. Wheaton, IL: Theosophical Publishing House, 1969.

———. *The Astral Body*. Wheaton, IL: Theosophical Publishing House, 1973.

Reed, Graham. *The Psychology of Anomalous Experience*. Boston: Houghton-Mifflin, 1974.

Rickman, John and Charles Brenner, eds. *A General Selection from the Works of Sigmund Freud*. New York: Doubleday Anchor Books, 1957.

Rogo, D. Scott. *Mind Beyond the Body*. New York: Penguin Books, 1978.

———. "Traveling Light." *Human Behavior*, Oct. 1978, p. 37.

———. "Psychological Models of the Out-of-Body Experience: A Review and Critical Evaluation." *Journal of Parapsychology* 46 (1982): 29–45.

———. *Leaving the Body: A Complete Guide to Astral Projection.* Upper Saddle River, NJ: Prentice Hall, 1986.

———. "Researching the Out-of-Body Experience: The State of the Art." *Anabiosis—The Journal for Near-Death Studies* 4 (1984): 21–49.

Salley, Roy D. "REM Sleep Phenomena During Out-of-Body Experiences." *The Journal of the American Society for Psychical Research* 76 (1982): 157–65.

Schacter, Daniel L., and Edward F. Kelly. "ESP in the Twilight Zone." *The Journal of Parapsychology* 39 (1975): 27–28.

Schacter, Daniel L. "The Hypnagogic State: A Critical Review of the Literature." *Psychological Bulletin* 83 (1976): 452 81.

Schapiro, S. A. "A Classification Scheme for Out-of-Body Phenomena." *Journal of Altered States of Consciousness* 2(3) (1975–6): 259–65.

Sheils, Dean. "A Cross-cultural Study of Beliefs in Out-of- the-Body Experiences, Waking and Sleeping." *Journal of the Society for Psychical Research* 49 (1978): 691–741.

Slap, Joseph W. "On Dreaming at Sleep Onset." *The Psychoanalytic Quarterly* 46 (1977): 71–81.

Slate, Joe H. *Psychic Phenomena.* Jefferson, NC: McFarland, 1988.

Sue, David, Derald Sue, and Stanley Sue. *Understanding Abnormal Behavior.* Boston: Houghton Mifflin, 1990.

Smith, Susy. *The Enigma of Out-of-Body Travel.* New York: New American Library, 1965.

Swann, Ingo. *To Kiss the Earth Good-bye.* New York: Hawthorne Books, 1975.

Swedenborg, Emanuel. *The Spiritual Diary*, vols. I–V. G. Bush and J. H. Smithson, eds. London: Speirs, 1883–1902.

Tanous, Alex, and Timothy Gray. *Dreams, Symbols, and Psychic Power.* New York: Bantam Books, 1990.

Tart, Charles T. "The Control of Nocturnal Dreaming by Means of Posthypnotic Suggestion." *Parapsychology*, September 1967, 184–9.

———. "A Second Psychophysiological Study of Out-of-the-Body Experiences in a Gifted Subject." *International Journal of Parapsychology* 9 (1967): 251–8.

———. "A Psychophysiological Study of Out-of-the-Body Experiences in a Selected Subject." *Journal of the American Society for Psychical Research* 62 (1968), 3–27.

———, ed. *Altered States of Consciousness*. Garden City, New York: Anchor Books/Doubleday, 1972.

Taylor, Jeremy. *Dream Work*. Ramsey, NJ: Paulist Press, 1983.

Tholey, Paul. "A Model for Lucidity Training as a Means of Self-Healing and Psychological Growth." In *Conscious Mind, Sleeping Brain*. Eds. Jayne Gackenbach and Stephen LaBerge. New York: Plenum Press, 1988.

Todd, John, and Kenneth Dewhurst. "The Double: Its Psycho-Pathology and Psycho-Physiology." *Journal of Nervous and Mental Disease* 122 (1955): 47–55.

Twitchell, Paul. *Eckankar: The Key to Secret Worlds*. San Diego, CA: Illuminated Way Press, 1969.

Ullman, Montague, Stanley Krippner, and Allen Vaughan. *Dream Telepathy*. New York: Macmillan, 1973.

Van de Castle, Robert L. *Our Dreaming Mind*. New York: Ballantine Books, 1994.

Walker, Benjamin. *Beyond the Body: The Human Double and the Astral Planes*. London: Routledge & Kegan Paul, 1974.

White, Stewart Edward. *The Betty Book*. New York: E. P. Dutton, 1937.

Yram. *Practical Astral Projection*. York Beach, ME: Samuel Weiser, 1977.

Index